Mental Retardation and Its Social Dimensions

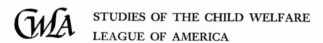 STUDIES OF THE CHILD WELFARE
LEAGUE OF AMERICA

MARGARET ADAMS

MENTAL RETARDATION AND ITS SOCIAL DIMENSIONS

COLUMBIA UNIVERSITY PRESS

New York and London / 1971

Margaret Adams is consultant in social work at the Eunice Kennedy Shriver Center, Walter E. Fernald State School, Waverley, Massachusetts.

Copyright © 1971 Margaret Adams
ISBN: 0–231–03456–3
Library of Congress Catalog Card Number: 72–138294
Printed in the United States of America

FOREWORD

This book by Margaret Adams points the way to another much to be desired advance in the evolution of thought and action in mental health—an evolution that in these recent times has been steadily upward in the fuller understanding and acceptance of the mentally retarded as fellow human beings to whom every opportunity for self-realization is owed.

This work is especially welcome for its comprehensive and specific exposition of the vital role that social work plays in a total modern program for the prevention of mental retardation and for positive, imaginative service to those who face this handicap. That this role has been much more potential than actual in social work performance generally and that as a consequence an essential ingredient has been largely wanting in a broad generic and multidisciplinary approach give heightened value and timeliness to Miss Adams' well-documented presentation.

Miss Adams' credentials give validity and cogency to the text and the ring of conviction to this, her testament of faith in the retarded. The book brings the mentally retarded before us for what they are —members of the human family who share the struggle of all of us to make a life—a good life. The social task is to mobilize the positive forces and resources that will enable them to rise above handicaps and to reach up to their highest capacity and greatest personal fulfillment.

Keenly aware of the wide-ranging manifestations and needs and of the differing backgrounds and personalities of all ages of those who are considered to be mentally retarded, the author fully recog-

nizes the imperative of the multidisciplinary approach. Noting that "the disciplines of clinical medicine, psychology and education have in previous phases successively provided the dominating skills," she observes that today a fourth "diagnostic dimension has illumined the character of mental retardation further by identifying the social factors operating in the heritage, background and current life experiences of retarded individuals."

From this identification of the social factors in diagnosis and evaluation, succeeding chapters contain thoroughgoing and concrete descriptions of the ways in which time-tested social work methods can and should be related to all phases of direct service with the mentally retarded and their families and to the prosecution of broad measures in their behalf: social casework, social group work and community organization, reinforced by social action and social research. The book's chief emphasis is that to combat the complex and multiple problems of mental retardation, all these social work methods must be integrated.

From skilled counseling, guidance, and supportive services to the family upon the impact of the shock and grief that comes with the first knowledge that a child is mentally retarded to the tremendous challenge of prevention that must be directed primarily to the elimination of poverty and deprivation, social work and social workers have indeed a very special opportunity and responsibility throughout the entire field of mental retardation.

Although it is primarily directed toward social work, particularly students or those practitioners who encounter the retarded in their day-to-day practice, this volume also has relevance to the other disciplines involved in dealing with this disability; for example, medicine, nursing, psychology, education.

One encouraging evidence of progress in the cause of mental retardation in this modern period has been the growth of sound professional and scientific literature that already includes some meritorious social work contributions. In this context Miss Adams' book takes its own place as an important and significant addition.

Miss Adams' book, however, should be much more than a library addition. It should be read and reread as a guide to maximizing the unique place of social work generally and specifically in mental retardation.

Stanley P. Davies

PREFACE

With a few notable exceptions, most child care agencies have given mentally retarded children only limited care, as for example in the case of illegitimate babies surrendered in infancy who are subsequently found to be retarded. There are several reasons for this situation. One is the historical trend underlying services for the retarded which has tended to conceptualize their problems in medical and educational terms, with the result that their care has been primarily under the auspices of these disciplines. Another reason is that other deprived and troubled children so have absorbed the limited resources of the child welfare field that a need that was served elsewhere received a lower priority. A third, more dynamic, reason is that neither the complex social dimensions of mental retardation nor its close relationship with many other contingent problems of child welfare have been fully understood until recently.

This situation is changing rapidly with the discovery that retardation of the mild (and also most prevalent) variety is closely linked with the nonstimulating and depriving environment of poverty, and that the poor health status of mothers and babies is often responsible for the more severe types of retardation arising from biological damage. Furthermore, a more sophisticated understanding of the family problems contingent upon the presence of a retarded member has enabled social work to use its philosophy and skills constructively.

The publication of this book on the methods of social work intervention into the problems of the mentally retarded is an indication of this change in thinking. It was prepared by a member of the staff of the Child Welfare League of America, with funding from the Children's Bureau, thus signifying the simultaneous concern of both the private and public sectors of child welfare about the plight of the retarded child in all its aspects—his vulnerable childhood, the burden his hardship imposes upon his family, and in some situations, his permanent dependency. The inclusion of a publication on this topic in the Child Welfare League of America Studies Series implicitly demonstrates the progress that has been achieved in bringing the mentally retarded child within the scope of child welfare practice.

Joseph H. Reid, Executive Director
Child Welfare League of America, Inc.

INTRODUCTION

In writing this book the intention has been to demonstrate the complexity of social issues that surround mental retardation in today's world and to highlight their relevance to social work intervention. Because the condition covers such a broad range of impaired social functioning, it is not easy to pinpoint either a uniform client group or a consistent pattern of intervention. Therefore, instead of dealing with specific aspects of the problem, I have attempted to project a climate of thinking about retardation and its victims in the hope that this will develop a compassionate understanding of their difficulties and trigger off imaginative ways of dealing with them. The fresh imaginative approach is very necessary for social work because of the long history of stereotyping that this client group has been subject to and the resultant rigidly defined problems and services.

In lieu of the clinical model which has focused on the deficits inherent in retardation and its social consequences, I have centered my thinking on the concepts of social role and interaction. This approach shifts the perspectives on retardation by placing equal responsibility for retarded functioning upon the society to which the individual belongs instead of burdening him with it exclusively. This diagnostic approach, which derives from sociological rather than clinical theory, presupposes a mode of social work intervention based on public health principles rather than those of clinical medicine, with greater attention paid to developing a healthy functional milieu for the handicapped instead of concentrating on the maladaptive responses that the disabled individual makes to environmental demands.

This frame of reference is formulated in the first three chapters. Chapter 1 describes the socioclinical basis of retardation, that is the biological organism with impaired developmental and adaptive functioning. Chapter 2 explores the history of services in America for the retarded in order to reflect over time how this society has perceived the problem and mobilized its resources to deal with it. Chapter 3 discusses the concept of the restitutive milieu in which the combined forces of professional knowledge and social welfare systems and informal social supports create the spectrum of services that provide a permanent compensation for the equally permanent deficit. The succeeding seven chapters relate traditional social work practice to the needs of the retarded and their families, with suggestions on how existing techniques and methods may be modified if necessary.

In addition the book has tried to show the close relationship existing between retardation and many other social problem areas, in the hope that an understanding of these common factors will help social workers in practice to feel more competent to deal with the *seemingly* unusual problems of the retarded, as well as being able to borrow insights that will increase their competence for dealing with the social maladjustment experienced by other client groups.

All these ideas represent the distilled experience of three widely separate practice settings which have coalesced to produce the amalgam of this volume. These are a community mental health setting in a working-class London borough under the National Health Service of Great Britain; a specialized evaluation clinic in a voluntary hospital in Brooklyn, N.Y.; and lastly, the oldest state institution for the retarded in the United States located near Boston. During these professional odysseys I have been assiduously assimilating the ideas, opinions, support, and stimulation of innumerable colleagues from a wide range of professional disciplines, most of which cannot be acknowledged except in the form of a sort of block debt of which I am very gratefully cognizant. Beyond this nameless number, I would like to acknowledge the more specific help given by the undermentioned colleagues and friends who have provided advice on topics outside of my ken; read portions of the manuscript in its indigestible first draft stages; transfered indecipherable handwriting into trim manuscripts; and offered the sustaining encouragement and support that are absolutely essential to the production of a book:

A. For chapter review and expert guidance

Chapter 1: Dr. Carl Drayer, Jewish Hospital of Brooklyn; Dr. Lewis Holmes, Massachusetts General Hospital; Miss Cornelia Mack, Massachusetts Department of Public Health; Dr. Zena Stein, Columbia University Department of Public Health (also Chapter 3).

Chapter 2: Stanley Powell Davies, New York State Department of Mental Hygiene (also Chapter 3); Miss Lucille Grow, Child Welfare League of America; Stewart Perry, Cambridge Institute, Cambridge, Massachusetts.

Chapter 4: Mrs. Stephanie Barnhardt, Adelphi University School of Social Work (also Chapter 5); Mrs. Zitha Turitz, Child Welfare League of America; Howard Wolf, Jewish Family and Childrens Services, Boston.

Chapter 6: Gerard O'Regan, Director of Social Service, Willowbrook State School, N. Y.

Chapter 10: Dr. Robert Perlman, Florence Heller School of Advanced Graduate Studies in Social Welfare; Robert Porter, University of West Virginia School of Social Work

B. For secretarial assistance

Mrs. Eleanor Berman, formerly of the Child Welfare League of America; Mrs. Sylvia Goldstein and Mrs. Mildred Leavitt of the Eunice Kennedy Shriver Center, Walter E. Fernald State School.

C. For research assistance

Mrs. Edith Frankel, Librarian, National Association for Retarded Children.

D. For grant support

U.S. Department of Health, Education and Welfare, Children's Bureau, Grant PR 500 (1966–68); National Institute for Mental Health, Grant 5 T1 MH–5331–17 (1968–70)

E. For legal advice

John Pate Esq.

My special thanks are due to Mrs. Lydia Hylton, formerly of the Child Welfare League of America, and Mrs. Helen Perry who have read almost every chapter and kept faltering footsteps on the hard path by constant encouragement, and to Dr. Gunnar Dybwad and Mrs. Rosemary Dybwad who have given me unfailing moral support in this and every other venture in retardation that I have embarked upon since coming to America.

Margaret Adams

Eunice Kennedy Shriver Center
Walter E. Fernald State School
Waverley, Massachusetts
September, 1970

CONTENTS

Mental Retardation and Its Social Dimensions

1 *THE SOCIOCLINICAL NATURE OF MENTAL RETARDATION*

MENTAL RETARDATION is a diverse condition which stems from an assortment of etiological sources, covers a wide range of functional impairment, and is attended by extremely varied social problems and issues. Because it is not a discrete entity but rather the end product of a series of separate factors interacting with each other, many lay and professional people unfamiliar with the condition are justifiably puzzled by its protean manifestations. The use of the term "retardation" to cover such apparently unrelated phenomena as the gross physical and mental handicap of a profoundly retarded child at one end of the spectrum, and the less obvious but more complex adjustment problems of a mildly retarded adult at the other compounds this confusion. For social workers it poses the question of how to provide appropriate help for such a divergent client group.

Therefore, even at the risk of repeating what may already be known to many readers, it is vital that a book on social work in this field should start with a fairly specific account of the nature and characteristics of mental retardation as it is understood in our society today so that there is no ambiguity in the subsequent chapters about what sort of individual is being discussed and what his special needs are.

Since the latter part of the nineteenth century, when physicians and other workers in the field began trying to identify the specific characteristics of mental retardation, the condition has been subject to many different descriptions, depending on the professional bias of the person writing on the subject and whether he saw the problem primarily in medical, educational, psychological, or social terms. All of these disciplines exert some influence on most of the manifestations of the handicap. From the medical angle, retardation appears as a multiplicity of symptoms that may derive from organic pathology and result in physical and mental malfunctioning in varying degrees of severity. To the psychologist it presents itself as defective intellectual equipment revealed specifically in areas of performance that require cognitive ability plus fine and gross motor behavior. The teacher sees poor capacity for learning. From the socio-legal standpoint retardation is perceived as a condition that is responsible for overall failure to meet generally accepted social demands (including infringement of the social code) and requires special provision to cope with its associated deviance.

These four interpretations are all valid in their own way and represent separate facets of a single phenomenon, but because of its complex origins and manifestations, there is frequent overlap in the activities of the different disciplines involved in retardation and in planning for its special needs. To illustrate: the discipline of psychology now covers a broad range of cognitive adaptive behavior, from abstract thinking processes at the top of the scale down to the most primitive responses of the autonomic nervous system. Since these responses are expressed in physiological terms, they have traditionally belonged to the discipline of medicine. Similarly, education now includes in its repertoire operant conditioning,[1] which derives from the psychology of Pavlov and Skinner, and the behavior modification resulting from these techniques is an integral ingredient in the socializing process. Education, therefore, has major significance for social work and its goals.

In this book social malfunctioning will be emphasized as the primary criterion of retardation, and social work will be presented as the profession which has major responsibility for intervention. Because we recognize the equally important contribution that other disciplines make to the understanding and treatment of the handicap, however, there will be many allusions to factors derived from other spheres of knowledge. For example, when dealing with an individual with Down's syndrome (mongolism) the social worker is concerned with his capacity for being contained within the family as a child, with his future as a semidependent adult engaged in occupation, and with plans for a lifetime of semidependent care. Related to these social work concerns, however, are the basic clinical anomalies associated with the syndrome, the potential for education in childhood, and the scope for vocational rehabilitation in the postschool phase. Within this broad frame of reference—that is, the retarded individual's adjustment in all spheres of social functioning—the responsibility of social work is to take an overview of the entire situation, seeing how the separate manifestations of deficit dovetail, assessing the relative weight that failure in each area contributes to the total dysfunctioning, and identifying the social components that are involved. To encompass these diverse features it is necessary to establish a workable definition of retardation which will prescribe its essential characteristics within manageable limits and yet provide scope for its wider implications.

The most concise definition, and one which finds common acceptance in the United States, has been propounded by the American Association on Mental Deficiency.[2] Retardation is described as "subaverage general intellectual functioning which originates during the developmental period and is associated with impaired adaptive behavior." *Subaverage* means more than one standard deviation below the normal average level of intelligence commonly accepted (in the United States this average lies between 90 and 110); *developmental period* extends from birth to approximately age sixteen; and *impaired adaptive behavior* may be reflected in (1) maturation, (2) learning, and (3) social adjustment, each area representing a phase or facet of the social maturational process. This definition, which embraces developmental and learning deficits, intelligence, and behavior, and relates them to social adjustment, covers retardation admirably insofar as it applies to retarded individuals and their deviant functioning. It is, however, less adequate in the sociological sphere and does not highlight the relationship that has been postulated over the past fifteen or twenty years between retardation as an individual disability and the sociological factors that are closely tied to its occurrence.[3]

Since this book is primarily concerned with those aspects of retardation in which social work can be the major mediating discipline, the sociological facets of the condition will be emphasized. Before describing in detail some of the more frequent types of retardation, we shall outline the sociological framework within which these will be viewed. The sociological significance of retardation lies in the fact that the existence of this disability on a large scale is essentially a phenomenon of societies which have evolved to a high level of complex social functioning and organization. This is true for the following reasons. First, societies with a more complex pattern of organization call for a higher level of adaptive ability than what passed as average in earlier stages, so more people fall below the norm of behavior and functioning which is expected and needed for survival. As with the Darwinian process of *natural* selection, the people of above-average intelligence by previous standards become the norm in the next evolutionary phase, and the slow ones drop back to become the social casualties of the new order. The operation of this principle of Social Darwinism helps to explain the emergence of a vast number of socially malfunctioning, intellectually subnormal individuals during the period of industrial expansion in Western Europe and North America. Further, the unplanned shift to a technological economy, with its resultant urbanization and displacement of unskilled workers from agrarian jobs, created an environment that was for many inimical to physical, emotional, and social growth. High population density, poor housing, recurrent unemployment, the disruption of family life, and pervasive poverty all add up to a context of deprivation which not only stultifies potential intellectual development in biologically normal children but also contains health hazards that produce biologically deficient children.

Intertwined with these societal explanations of mental retardation are two important clinical issues. One is the fact that in more highly developed societies medical and allied sciences have been developed which promote the survival of the biologically defective: abortions and miscarriages are averted, premature babies are kept alive in oxygen tents, surgery and antibiotics take care of the cardiac and respiratory problems that previously used to carry off children with Down's syndrome in early childhood. In consequence, many children who would have perished naturally in a more primitive social milieu now survive to become chronically handicapped adults. Allied to this is the fact that a highly technological culture sharpens up instruments of diagnosis so that a greater number of retarded individuals become identified and eventually more services are developed to meet their overt needs.

This capacity for more precise and subtle diagnosis, whether in clinical or social terms, has an important bearing on social work because the complexity of needs that are identified as a result of better diagnostic skills points up the necessity of providing a wide range of preventive and rehabilitative services. When these increased needs are recognized, they help to identify the number of individuals in the community who require help to neutralize this handicap. In consequence, the social problems emerge as both quantitatively and qualitatively greater and social services have to be stretched to new dimensions. This leads into another important social issue which is inherently related to mental retardation: its prevalence as a social problem which severely penalizes both retarded individuals and their families is intimately bound up with society's level of tolerance toward deviance and its degree of willingness to invest or withhold its resources in measures to mitigate the difficulties that the handicap brings in its train. For all levels of retardation the disabling effects of the impairment are in *inverse* proportion to the help that is available to counter its stresses. The conviction that the disability of retardation is determined as much by environmental factors, in the broadest sense, as by the innate deficits of individuals, has crucial implications for social work. This fundamental premise will be explored further in subsequent chapters dealing with social services and social work practices.

To identify the retarded in current society, it is perhaps logical to start with a description of them in administrative terms because, in the main, services for them are related to these criteria. For administrative purposes the overall definition of subaverage intellectual functioning and impaired adaptive behavior quoted above is further broken down into the two categories of medical and behavioral characteristics. The medical category will be discussed further on in this chapter. Within the behavioral classification there are five subgroups based on intelligence test scores and associated functioning capacity: (1) *borderline* intelligence* (I.Q. ranging between 83 and 68, which represents one standard deviation from the mean), (2) *mild* retardation (I.Q. 67 to 52, representing two SDs), (3) *moderate* retardation (I.Q. 51 to 36 and three SDs), (4) *severe* retardation (I.Q. 35 to 20 and four SDs), and (5) *profound* retardation (I.Q. below 20 and five SDs).†

In terms of functioning capacity, the *mildly* retarded may show some developmental lag in early childhood, which becomes more pronounced in the school phase when the demands of normal education impose standards that are too high. The mildly retarded can benefit from special education and, if performing optimally, can achieve academic skills to the sixth grade by their late teens. If they are given special education and helped to find suitable work, most of the mildly retarded make a satisfactory adjustment to adult life unless they are exposed to an undue degree of stress, either in their personal life or through some more generalized social hazard such as chronic and widespread unemployment. This assertion is supported by follow-up studies in both the United States and Great Britain on the adult careers of pupils who had been referred for a special class or school.[4]

The *moderately* retarded usually show conspicuous developmental lag as babies, and have very limited capacity for academic learning, but they are capable of being trained in concrete tasks and of achieving some level of independence in self-care, though this depends on the sustained support of concerned adults. As adults themselves, most of them—if they do not have marked physical handicaps —can be trained to be quite productive in routine industrial tasks in a sheltered workshop setting and to participate in a limited range of social activities under supervision.[5] Individuals in the top range of *severe* retardation have been shown to be capable of achieving some of the training and social skills of the moderately retarded group, but they are likely to require closer supervision and direction in most

---

* The Expert Committee of WHO is currently considering the exclusion of this category from its definition and classification of mental retardation.
† I.Q. ranges vary for different tests. Figures quoted here are based on revised Stanford-Binet Tests of Intelligence.

aspects of their life; those at the lower end have a more restricted existence resembling that of a preschool child in dependency needs and achievement of self-help skills. The *profoundly* retarded are dependent on other people for their care and survival, and since most of them have gross central nervous system pathology with severe physical handicaps, their capacity for any level of social interaction is extremely limited.

The varying levels of dysfunction depend on the degree of impairment of the individual's total adaptive mechanism, which in turn is largely determined by residual neurological damage. With the mildly retarded, only the higher levels of adaptive behavior tend to be affected—that is, their perceptual capacity, attention span, impulse control, judgment, memory, thought, and language processes. By contrast, individuals in the three lower grades of retardation show a progressive involvement of the total nervous system in their malfunctioning patterns, until with the profoundly retarded the primitive involuntary mechanisms are affected, and the child or adult does not develop even basic *physical* adaptive behavior such as motor skills, sphincter control, and so forth. Between these two polarities are differing levels of adaptive competence, with a corresponding need for an increasing complexity of medical, educational, and social services.

Under the prevailing system of services for the retarded, the mild and borderline grades have been catered to by special education within the public school system; this, together with the provision of residential facilities in the state-run institutions, was until recently considered adequate social help to meet their needs. The retarded of all ages within the three lower grades are much less well served, and while the public schools in most states have established classes for *trainable* children (who usually fall within the moderate or severe ranges), there are still some areas in which these facilities have to be maintained privately. Very few services, public or private, exist for the more seriously disabled categories. This limited provision for the lower ranges reflects the social status they have occupied in society, which has tended to view them as quasi-invalids who could neither benefit from social rehabilitation nor be expected to become part of normal society.

We have been discussing the administrative categories into which the mentally retarded are divided and the behavioral and social characteristics of each of these. Now it is necessary to look at the major factors that have been identified as causal agents of this disability. We shall approach this etiological area along two lines— one dealing with the biological or organic causation and the other with the sociocultural factors that have a close correlation with the condition's incidence.

The biological causes of mental retardation are complex and numerous, and it is neither appropriate nor feasible to treat them in any detail in a book that is primarily concerned with the social aspects of retardation. Since, however, medical or organic aspects have serious and far-reaching social implications, it is essential that social workers be aware of the types of clinical problems they may encounter and what their social consequences may be. The breadth and complexity of this aspect of retardation is illustrated by the fact that a new comprehensive work on diseases associated with retardation describes over 150 conditions.[6] Furthermore, knowledge in this area is extremely fluid at present because, with greater sophistication in research methods, new categories keep on emerging, new facets of an existing condition become highlighted, and incidence rates change (for example, the current figure for chromosome anomalies is 1:250 live births). In addition, other conditions assume a greater significance than formerly—for example, intrauterine infections.

This chapter therefore cannot do more than briefly sketch the principal biological causes identified at present. For the reader who has a specific interest in this side of retardation, the medical writings included in the references are recommended.[7] For a more circumscribed orientation we shall list the categories formulated by the American Association on Mental Deficiency[8] and the American Psychiatric Association[9] and discuss the social implications of the more frequently recurring or seriously disabling conditions. Since several of these appear in both listings, they will be combined, with the source indicated by the initials AAMD and APA for those conditions not listed by both organizations.

1. Diseases and conditions due to infection
2. Diseases and conditions due to intoxication

3. Diseases and conditions due to trauma or physical agent
4. Diseases and conditions due to disorder of metabolism, growth, and nutrition
5. Diseases and conditions due to new growth (AAMD)
6. Conditions associated with gross brain disease (postnatal) (APA)
7. Diseases and conditions due to (unknown) prenatal influence
8. Conditions associated with chromosome abnormality (APA)
9. Conditions associated with prematurity (APA)
10. Diseases and conditions due to unknown or uncertain causes with structural reaction alone manifest (AAMD)

If we look at this list from another angle than that of biological etiology, we can regroup most of these conditions according to a different frame of reference. This would see them in terms of whether their biological origins were related to extrinsic factors within the social environment or to intrinsic factors within the individual organism—that is, the child or adult. This approach probably has more relevance to social work, in that it carries the causal factors underlying a substantial number of biological conditions beyond the limited sphere of medicine into the wider arena of social issues, which is social work's primary bailiwick. To put this more specifically, infection (as in meningitis), intoxication (as in lead encephalopathy), trauma or physical agent (as in a difficult birth or head injury), and premature delivery constitute biological insults that occur to the child from without—they are *extrinsic*. By contrast, disorders of metabolism and chromosome abnormalities occur independently of environmental influences and are *intrinsic*. Between these polarized areas is a twilight zone which contains more shadowy entities that do not fall so clearly into either grouping. Is *congenital* syphilis which is transmitted to the child in utero from the mother intrinsic or extrinsic? It is an inseparable part of the child's congenital makeup but was originally acquired by the mother from an environmental source. In categorizing environmental influences we have to include the prenatal environment provided by the mother and the hazards that she is susceptible to and which can have a severely adverse impact on the unborn child. Such hazards may be clearly identified, as in the case of rubella (German measles), or surmised, as in the case of poor maternal health and its association with prematurity and the potential sequela of impaired development and functioning.[10]

The extrinsic causative factors may operate to cause retardation at any phase of an individual's developmental continuum. In the prenatal period, infection from rubella occurring at a critical stage of embryonic development is liable to affect the child *in utero*. During the birth process, anoxia due to delayed or difficult delivery can cause cerebral damage. In the neonatal period, high fever due to infection, or convulsions, may injure the newborn child's nervous system. In subsequent phases of childhood and adolescence, the individual is liable to infectious, intoxicating, or traumatizing hazards. For example, infection can cause meningitis or encephalitis, which could result in severe neurological damage; lead encephalopathy (due to eating lead paint in rundown housing), if frequent enough or severe enough, can cause retardation; and any sort of cranial injury due to an accident can result in permanent mental disability. The social implications that these extrinsic conditions raise are both preventive and remedial in focus. That is, effort must be directed toward identifying and eliminating the environmental factors that may have contributed to the condition in order to ensure that other children in the family or the community are not similarly affected. Along with this must also be an investment of time and services in the retarded child himself to ensure that his handicap does not impose too great a burden upon the rest of the family.

The intrinsic factors of causality are represented by a functional aberration within the child's anatomical or physiological makeup which is not directly affected by external environmental influences. There are two major categories that illustrate this intrinsic component. One includes the metabolic disorders, in which inborn errors of metabolism interfere with the physiological processes necessary for normal growth and development. The best known of these is *phenylketonuria* (PKU), in which failure to metabolize the amino acid phenylalanine creates a toxic condition that affects the brain and produces severe retardation unless the condition is detected within the first three months of life and treated with a special phenylalanine-free diet for a prolonged period. The occurrence of this disorder is one in every 10,000 births. The second major category of intrinsic factors includes the chromosome abnormalities, which cover a wide assortment of clinical conditions, not all of them associated directly with retardation. The one that is, and is most widely known, is Down's syndrome (or mongolism). Within our intrinsic group must also be included many syndromes which are known to be genetically determined but for which the etiology is still unknown.

In many of these intrinsic conditions where a genetic factor is either known or suspected, the serious social consequence is the impact that this hereditary factor has upon the family in which it crops up. In most of these conditions the genetic mechanism is recessive rather than dominant, but insofar as this means that subsequent pregnancies carry the likelihood of being damaged (for example, in one family two children were born with PKU within three years of each other) and that normal relatives (siblings, uncles, aunts) may be carriers, the immediate and long-term social implications are crucial. A secondary social factor is that the child's manifestation of his faulty biological inheritance may be a severe degree of impairment or, in a few conditions, a degenerative process which will eventuate in the child's death after a progressive deterioration in mental and physical functioning. Tay-Sachs disease and Duchenne's muscular dystrophy illustrate this.

From even this brief account it is clear that the biological factors associated with mental retardation carry many important social implications. Information on the medical aspects should always be imparted to the family by the physician in the first instance in order to give the weight of medical authority to this anxiety-laden topic and also to allow the parents an opportunity for exploring the more abstruse clinical aspects. However, the topic will inevitably be raised by the family in their contact with other professional workers, particularly the social worker when she is helping them to plan for social contingencies that they are facing. It therefore behooves her to be well versed in the rudiments of the condition, its functional manifestations and the anticipated outcome so that she can gauge the effect that all these factors are likely to have on the family's functioning and plan intervention stratagems accordingly.

While organicity in differing degrees of severity can be identified as the basis for the retarded development and functioning of individuals in the moderate, severe, and profound ranges of handicap, it has not yet been possible to identify a similarly circumscribed cause for the much larger category of mildly retarded. The specific social and intellectual deficits which have been traditionally associated with this numerically superior group—that is, problems in learning, short attention span, poor judgment, lack of impulse control—cannot be attributed to one single cause or even a particular cluster. Instead, other explanations for their disability are being advanced, the most cogent of which relate to the fact that the bulk of children and adults identified as mildly retarded are found in significantly large proportions in the lowest socioeconomic strata of society, with high representation in ethnic minority groups. These findings have led to the assumption that retarded development and functioning are closely associated with environmental influences, particularly those correlated with poverty. Both the AAMD and APA Manuals cited on page 8 make provision for this possibility; section VIII of the AAMD classifications refers to "Mental Retardation Due to Uncertain (or Presumed Psychologic) Cause with Functional Reaction Alone Manifest," and the APA specifies "psycho-social (environmental) deprivation" as a causative factor under this heading. The APA Manual lists the same definition. The absence of a more conclusively established biological etiology, taken in conjunction with the overwhelming evidence of the connection with retardation and poverty, supports the notion that adverse social conditions in their many different aspects play a large part in inhibiting social and intellectual development.[11] Further, a relationship has been established between these depriving social conditions, serious health hazards in pregnancy, and organically damaged babies with attendant psychological anomalies.[12] Thus, environmental deprivation is frequently a contributory factor to retardation of both the more severe and mild varieties, and the question yet unanswered is whether these pervasively negative health conditions in mother and child may not also produce an organic impairment of a diffuse kind which appears in learning and behavior disorders without any hard clinical manifestation. Whether this argument is accepted or not, the more obvious factors of inherited poverty remain, with the easily identified concomitants of malnutrition, a low status of health which affects sensory development related to learning (i.e., vision, hearing, speech), and inadequate housing which does not provide enough space for developing motor skills. These threats to biological survival may be further compounded by inadequate parental care, and a lack of play material to stimulate imaginative play and conceptual thinking. Together these deficiencies conspire to produce a material and psychological environment which blunts the developing intellectual capacity of a growing child. The climate of hopelessness and alienation that pervades the total subculture to which the poor belong reinforces this negation by reducing interest and motivation for learning.

The distinction made between the characteristics, problems, and origins of mild retardation and those associated with the small minority of retarded whose handicap is due to clearly identified biological damage makes it difficult to treat these two groups as an entity and also raises questions as to which sphere of professional knowledge can be most effective in dealing with the adjustment difficulties each presents. The organically impaired fall initially within the purview of medicine, since their condition is predominantly clinical in origin and often has associated medical components that require ongoing medical supervision. Diagnosing and dealing with the biological defects must be a preliminary to subsequent rehabilitation by other disciplines such as education and vocational training.

In contrast, the mildly retarded group does not have a primary need for clinical diagnosis and treatment (although it may present many general health problems that are not intrinsic to the retarded condition) and the hard core of their difficulties lies in the area of social welfare, in that term's broadest sense of encompassing the total spectrum of remedial measures that derive from other professions than social work. This multidisciplinary concept and its relationship to mild retardation have been cogently described by Jane Mercer who writes of "the interstices between disciplines" and the fact that the mildly retarded with their marginal impairment "fall into the interstitial region between medicine, psychology and sociology" in terms of how their disability is to be conceptualized.[13]

This ambiguity concerning the mildly retarded raises the question as to which of the professions should carry major responsibility for care for this group and for the other more defective categories. The answer depends on clarifying the characteristics that are peculiar to each of the different categories of the retarded, the nature of the problems they present, and the type of service each requires. But because mental retardation has origins in pathological social conditions in many instances, and its disabling effects are expressed in social dysfunction and maladjustment, social work has a special mandate to be involved in its many aspects. Sometimes this may take the form of a primary function, as, for example, counseling parents around their feelings toward, and plans for, a severely retarded child; or it may serve a secondary role of initiating or amplifying treatment that belongs primarily to another discipline, such as finding a facility to carry out a special medical regimen or seeking an appropriate educational or vocational rehabilitation program.

The emphasis on the social nature of retardation is an extremely important concept, because it is an implicit challenge to the earlier idea of retardation as a static and fundamentally irreversible condition not amenable to the therapeutic efforts of physicians, educators, or social workers. Advances in psychology and sociology have done much to counter the concept of irreversibility, so that now retardation is considered as having various etiologies and an equal number of different outcomes. In the area of psychology and social adaptation an incalculable potential for growth and change has been revealed from a variety of sources. In 1950 the idea of training low-functioning severely retarded adults to master quite complex industrial tasks would have been inconceivable, but the research projects of the Clarkes[14] in Great Britain and programs in the United States and elsewhere have demonstrated that it is an entirely feasible rehabilitative practice. From another angle, the discipline of sociology has taught us to view the retarded as a hapless by-product of our social history who were rendered obsolete and ineffectual by the accelerated development of a technological economy and the social displacement to which this led. The rejection by society, the alienation from the main sociocultural stream, and the regressive modes of functioning which are associated with alienation created the social phenomenon of mild mental retardation with which we are confronted today; and subsequent societal trends related to the differential position of groups of people in the dominant value system have perpetuated this situation.[15]

By adopting the sociological approach to the individual disabilities of the subgroup of the retarded and recognizing their condition as a social artifact instead of the result of heredity, we underwrite the implication of its being reversed. More explicitly, the evolutionary machinery of social change, which in the nineteenth century contributed heavily to the increased incidence of retardation through the resultant social pressures, can today be given a further twist by social action. This will create new elements in the social system that will provide an environment more favorable to the maximum development of the capacities of the retarded, and will offer special services to compensate for the residual handicaps which interfere with adequate functioning.

In order to gain this change in perspective and goals, mental retardation has to be scrutinized carefully through the prism of many different scientific approaches, so that the separate causative factors in the overall malfunctioning can be identified precisely and treated with appropriate rehabilitative measures. Further, the genesis of the entire condition in all its complexity must be perceived not in vacuo but as part of a dynamic process that is as much determined by social values and systems as by the personal flaw in the individual's biological makeup or functioning capacity. If health, training, education, and social services can be devised to compensate for the adaptive impairment of society's retarded members, they will disappear as a social liability and be perceived instead as individuals who, because of their decreased potential for normal social development and adjustment, have a greater claim on social resources for their maintenance and support. Within the conceptual framework of a welfare state the retarded represent that segment of society which will be its first and also permanent wards, since those individuals with less competent intellectual functioning and adaptive capacity will always be marginal in their adjustment to the complicated norms of modern society.

2 THE HISTORICAL BACKGROUND TO SERVICES FOR THE MENTALLY RETARDED

THE QUALITY and degree of concern that any society demonstrates toward a handicap, whether it is due to an individual's disability or to a more generalized social hazard such as mass unemployment or endemic disease, seem to be determined by two major factors. They are (1) the level of specialized knowledge which makes it possible to identify the nature of the handicap or social problem; and (2) the level of social development achieved by that society, particularly as this is reflected in the climate of opinion regrading the vulnerable and weak. Depending on the predominant social values, the attitude toward a handicap may be one of compassionate concern for its adverse impact upon the lives of the afflicted and a desire to avert or assuage these ill effects; or it may be an overwhelming fear that the socially adverse by-products of the handicap constitute a threat to the rest of society. Both of these reasons bring the handicap into social prominence, and measures may be initiated to deal with either of them. It is probably a combination of the two that forms the viable basis of social welfare.

At various phases of their evolution, services for the retarded in the western world have exemplified each of these points of view. A study of the successive patterns of care for this particular group delineates the general development of social services in the United States. It also illuminates the different social philosophies underlying philanthropic endeavors, the social welfare programs these have given rise to, and the trends now emerging that will dominate the future scene. Since social service cannot be divorced from social philosophy, which gives it its existence and impetus, and since social philosophy derives from the broad sphere of political thought and action, the development of services for the mentally handicapped has to be viewed in this wider context.

The first significant indication in modern times of informed concern for the mentally retarded—or idiots, as they were generically designated—occurred toward the middle of the nineteenth century, revealing itself almost simultaneously in most of the leading countries of Europe and in the United States. This unexpected and unprecedented flowering of philanthropic and scientific endeavor in behalf of the mentally retarded was an offshoot of the new movement in psychological medicine which was developing in Europe at the end of the eighteenth century.[1] Positive rehabilitative and humane treatment for the mentally ill began to replace the deterrent management hitherto in vogue; and this gentler, therapeutic climate of thought aroused a general interest in all aberrations of the human mind. Establishment psychiatry of this era formulated a diagnostic distinction between mental illness and mental deficiency (idiocy in the current vernacular) and pronounced the latter irreversible.[2] At this time idiocy probably denoted a condition in which mental capacity and functional behavior were noticeably impaired and where the biological manifestations suggested neurological lesions. In both Europe and the United States special care for the retarded originated in a treatment regimen for specific sensory defects. In France where the movement started, the physician Itard was connected with the Institute for the Deaf and Dumb; and in the United States the first specialized center set up for educating the mentally defective was located in the Institute for the Blind in Boston because its director had become interested in this secondary handicap when working with blind defective children.[3]

Itard started the movement to care for the mentally retarded somewhat inadvertently when in 1799 he became involved in the intimate care and training of a "wild boy" of about eleven who was picked up in the woods of Aveyron—a remote rural area in provincial France.[4] The boy manifested the traits of a completely unsocialized being—walking on all fours, using smell as the principal means of exploring his environment, responding to most human overtures with biting and scratching, and displaying habits of eating, drinking, and elimination like those of an animal. Itard attributed this uncivilized behavior to the effects of extreme sensory and social deprivation, and intended to foster these absent faculties by training in the hope of eventually restoring the boy to the appropriate level of intelligence and socialization. Although his therapeutic principles were sound (they included sustained individualized attention, plus a regimen of sensory, social, and physiological stimulation and some limited education in formal subjects), his diagnostic and prognostic criteria were less so. After five years of sustained effort the boy (Victor) had made only limited progress. In the areas of social responsiveness and recognition, there was improvement, but his impluse control and judgment were still at a very primitive stage. In adolescence he became unmanageable, and the project had to be stopped because the institution where Itard was conducting his experiment could no longer contain him. It is difficult to see how Itard could have made a more reliable evaluation because he had no social data about the degree and length of deprivation Victor had been exposed to, and could therefore only conjecture on flimsy circumstantial evidence the extent to which the retarded development derived from this cause and how much was due to innate defect aggravated by unpropitious social circumstances. Itard thought Victor had been abandoned at the age of two, and from various scars on his body, including a deep one on his throat, concluded that there may have been an attempt to kill him. What is certain is that when the boy returned to civilized living, his level of functioning and capacity for adapting to social norms placed him well within the category of retardation according to present-day behavioral criteria.

The outcome with Victor frustrated Itard's hypothesis of restoring normalcy to a deprived child through therapeutic educational methods, but paradoxically it was of much greater significance in the field of mental deficiency since it demonstrated that such special techniques could be effective in modifying the behavior of rather low-functioning individuals even if they did not alter fundamentally the underlying defective condition. Whatever its original focus and goal, this venture of Itard's into a hitherto neglected area of psychological malfunctioning blazed a trail of interest in the mentally subnormal which sparked the next beacon phase of scientific endeavor.

Some thirty years after the termination of Itard's project a young physician who had once been his pupil—Edouard Onesymous Seguin—embarked upon a similar task of attempting the social education of an idiot boy.[5] This venture was undertaken in the face of considerable pessimistic skepticism by the medical establishment, which included Seguin's mentor, Esquirol. He seriously questioned the validity of Seguin's theories and the efficacy of his practical efforts very much as Pinel had poured professional cold water on Itard's experiment at its start. Both august gentlemen eventually came round to acknowledging the value of their disciples' efforts though they continued to question whether real improvement could be made in a so-called idiotic individual. After a year's work Seguin reported his results to a Commission from the Academy of Sciences in Paris, and the outcome of his apparent success in this new and allegedly hopeless field was an official appointment permitting him to continue his educational methods on a wider scale, using children who were in the idiots' sections of the two pauper hospitals in Paris—Bicêtre and the Hospice des Incurables.

Seguin probably had fewer illusions about the prognosis for his patients since, as Esquirol's former pupil, he would have been exposed to his teacher's pessimistic views on idiocy. He was less interested in trying to restore a temporarily retarded individual to normal functioning than in raising limited capacity to its full potential by specially devised methods. He seems to have been the first person to accept the defects of the retarded realistically and at the same time maintain an optimistic belief in their capacity for improvement if given appropriate help. The extensive material published by Itard and Seguin on their educational experiments with the intellectually handicapped became the basis of scientific literature on the psychological characteristics and educational potential for this category of persons.

Concurrent with this exciting activity in France, Guggenbuhl in Switzerland[6] was tackling the problem of retardation from another clinical facet, cretinism, which was widespread in some areas of the country because of iodine deficiency in the water. He founded a residential center at Abendberg in 1840 for the treatment of this condition and its attendant symptom of retardation, and provided a well-organized regime of medical, social, and educational care, generously laced with idealism and the conviction that the whole syndrome could be cured by appropriate treatment. Unfortunately, the hysteria surrounding the project, the fame it attracted, and Guggenbuhl's zealous belief in total cure led to a serious neglect of professional standards, amounting at times to malpractice. The result was an international scandal, which led to the removal of the institution's main source of support and its eventual closure. It is an ironic reflection that today we know cretinism to be one of the clinical conditions causing retardation which can be both prevented and reversed, its physiological basis in thyroid deficiency having been located.

Efforts to care for the mentally deficient were under way in England at this time;[7] and in America increasing interest in the rehabilitation of children with sensory handicaps, such as blindness and deaf-mutism, was leading physicians to consider the related condition of mental defect. The Asylum for the Deaf and Dumb in Hartford had included a few retarded among its pupils in 1818, and various medical pioneers were in contact with their European colleagues on this subject. Dr. Hervey Wilbur, who opened the first private school for defective boys in Barre, Massachusetts, in 1848 and later became the first superintendent of the Syracuse State Asylum for Idiots, N.Y., was inspired to enter this field after reading accounts of Seguin's work in Paris by a correspondent of *Chambers Journal* and by Dr. Edward Connolly in an English medical journal.[8] As chairman of the Massachusetts Commission to inquire into the condition of idiots in the Commonwealth, set up in 1846, Dr. Samuel Gridley Howe visited Guggenbuhl at Abendberg. Seguin's decision to emigrate to America for political reasons in 1850 added another enthusiastic and well-informed protagonist of the cause, forging a link of scientific and philanthropic continuity between the old world and the new.

The establishment with *state* funds of the experimental school for idiots within the Perkins Institution for the Blind in Boston in 1848, and its subsequent transformation into the Massachusetts School for

Idiotic and Feebleminded Youth, was the first sign of *public* concern in the United States. This was followed up by the action of three other states in the next decade: schools were set up in Albany, N.Y. (1851); in Germantown, Pa. (1853)—later the Elwyn School; in Columbus, Ohio (1857); and in Connecticut (1858), though initially this school was under private auspices and did not receive state support until 1864.[9]

The movement gathered steam, and by the turn of the century nineteen states had set up twenty-four institutions for children of school age who exhibited some potential for training and eventual rehabilitation in the community. The original criteria for admission laid down by Samuel Gridley Howe in 1851 were geared to special education and training for those who could not meet the standards in schools for normal children but who might be expected to show improvement with special help. He described them as "scholars of the lowest grade of intellect . . . lower even than the youngest children. They cannot go about alone, they cannot go to common schools, they cannot talk, they can hardly think. There must be a school expressly for them, else they be neglected." Howe also observed that "children who are epileptic, hydrocephalic, insane or paralytic should not be retained to the exclusion of others about whose capacity for improvement there is little doubt," [10] By modern standards he sought to provide for the educable child with good training potential; and these criteria for admission prevailed, with few exceptions, for the next thirty years until radically different social circumstances dictated new types of care.

Within the first quarter century of their founding, all the institutions had flourishing and forward-looking programs which embraced the clinical, educational, and social aspects of retardation at a high level of professional expertise and commitment. The formation of the Association of Medical Officers of American Institutions for Idiotic and Feebleminded Persons in 1876 provided a forum for the exchange of ideas and knowledge at its annual meetings, and lively communication also took place with colleagues in other countries. Workers from both sides of the Atlantic visited each other's facilities, comparing different approaches to the care of the mentally deficient and pooling information on newly emerging clinical conditions and their causes. A paper by G. E. Shuttleworth[11] from England on In-temperance as a Cause of Idiocy was read at Syracuse in 1878. At the 1881, 1890, and 1891 meetings reports were made on work done in institutions in Great Britain, Norway, Denmark, and Germany, while honorary membership in the Association included representatives from these countries and from Tokyo.

These reports presented at the Association's annual meetings suggest that the standards of care in the institutions were of very high quality, with careful attention given to details of physical surroundings. The 1888 report from California refers to "the wonderful physical and very pleasing mental improvement of most of the inmates which is accounted for very largely by the care we have bestowed upon their meals, bathing and beds. In the midst of the greatest fruit garden in the world we are enabled to give our children a variety of fruit—ripe, delicious and healthy the whole year round." A description of the grounds mentions "palms, roses, pepper trees and other subtropical plants which ornament the grounds and tend to gladden the eyes of children and quicken their sluggish brains to thought." [12] This observation reflects a genuinely compassionate and imaginative approach to the retarded as well as optimism in their capacity to react favorably to good surroundings and material care. It is also in line with modern theory of making the physical environment an integral part of the therapeutic process for both disturbed and retarded individuals.[13]

The older established institutions almost vied with each other in making innovations, as a result of which a varied repertoire of care developed. The Columbus school, for example, had social gatherings in the music room, with dancing and calisthenics four nights a week and singing and marching in the mornings; there was also an orchestra comprising two cornets, a bass horn, bass viol, violoncello, two first and three second violins, one flageolet, one flute, and one triangle. It was observed that while the children could not read words, they seemed to be able to follow music.[14] Media, Pa. (later called Elwyn) started a kindergarten section because it was felt that early training was very important. "From the early hand-training to which these little juniors are submitted we shall have finer capacities in the future for our industrial classes and our work will be much superior to the past." [15] Frankfort, Kentucky, introduced industrial training between 1878 and 1879 in order to prepare the residents for economic independence after their ten-year period of institutional care; boys were employed in carpentry, shoemaking, mattress-, broom-, and mop-making, and the girls in sewing, cooking, laundry, and kitchen work. The unit was self-supporting by virtue of the maintenance services it rendered to the institution (fencing, building, laundry work, mending and supply of shoes, mops, etc.) and after four years Dr. Stewart, the Director, estimated that "from results already attained, 80% of all we receive can be made self-supporting." [16] In 1888, 80 out of a total of 150 residents were receiving this training and in ten years 39 had been placed satisfactorily. The attention given to this training and subsequent placement can be deduced from the Director's statement: "One boy (in the carpentry department) will leave next spring with his kit which he has earned with his labour here." [16]

The psychological needs of the children were also recognized, Dr. Stewart asserting that "the object of industrial pursuits in this institution takes the higher ground of increasing the mental and physical development of the child, elevating him in his own opinion by giving him a feeling of independence in the knowledge of his own ability to earn his own support," a concept which, in slightly more dressed-up language, is today accepted as fundamental to the social rehabilitation of the mildly retarded child or adult. Industrial training was quickly incorporated into most of the institutions' programs and by 1885 at least nine reported on their progress in this direction. The original objective of educating those who were potentially independent for return to normal life within the community had emerged as a new facet of industrial rehabilitation, and on the whole a very good job seems to have been done.

At this point it may be relevant to reflect on the rather unusual phenomenon of why there should have been such compassionate and well-informed concern for the mentally handicapped, which was translated into practical measures of good care supported by substantial public funds at a time when social services for the general public were still rudimentary and mainly supported by private philanthropy.[17] The answer probably stems from two different factors, one manifest and the other latent. The manifest reason for this humane and sensible form of social welfare is to be found in the fact that education was always highly prized in America. The early programs of care for the retarded were strictly educational in focus and aimed at preparing the obviously handicapped group of retarded to take their place in adult life more efficiently, and they were in line with similar welfare schemes for the deaf, started in Hartford in 1817, and for the blind, in Boston in 1832.[18] These handicapped groups benefited from the Jeffersonian theory that universal education was an inherent feature of a democracy, and also from the less well articulated idea that in a new country dependent on flexibility and innovation for success the youth must be equipped to maintain themselves adequately, both for personal reasons and for their contribution to national productivity. The changing pattern of institutional care from formal education to vocational training chimes in with this view.

The other interpretation of the mid-nineteenth century's concern for the plight of the mentally handicapped is to regard it as a rare demonstration of humanitarian thinking, and of commitment and responsibility, reflecting certain features of the social history of the time. As Kanner has pointed out, both the old and the new worlds were imbued with a strong element of idealistic thinking which embraced deep concern for the suffering and welfare of the downtrodden and socially disadvantaged.[19] In France and in America there was a pervasive freedom in social and personal affairs, emanating from the great upheavals of the French Revolution and the War of Independence, both of which represented a breakaway from older, static, inequitable regimes. The humanistic values liberated by these events informed many areas of thought: Jefferson's view of democratic political institutions, Rousseau's educational theories, Pinel's principles of positive psychiatric care, and the European Romantic Movement in the arts.

It is easy to see how this new freedom and the belief in the untapped potential of liberated man could spill over to the mentally retarded, fostering the idea that they too could be delivered from the fettering effects of their innate deficiencies if they were exposed to positive social and educational conditions—in today's idiom, a therapeutic regime or community. Freedom in its various aspects was a recurring motif of the time, whether expressed in the storming of the Bastille, in Pinel's removal of chains from his patients at the Bicêtre or, fifty years later, in Karl Marx's famous utterance that the workers have nothing to lose but their chains. It was not accidental that Howe was involved in the Greek War of Independence, that he and his family were ardent champions of Negro emancipation (his wife, Julia Ward Howe, wrote the "Battle Hymn of the Republic"),[20] that Seguin came to America because of disillusionment with the political regime in France after the restoration of Louis Philippe; and that in Massachusetts, where the movement for the care of the retarded began, the cultured, humanitarian group formed by Thoreau, Emerson, and Alcott, and their extensive following was spreading in influence.[21] The climate of hope generated by these exciting trends embraced even the retarded, so that in the twenty-five years from 1848 to 1873, thirty-four European countries and eight states in America had set up rehabilitation programs for a handicap that had hitherto been recognized only as a life sentence of hopelessness.

Unfortunately, these dedicated and progressive efforts were doomed to fall short of their aspirations, not because of the inadequacy of the training or the irreversible condition of the retarded, but because of the drastic change in social conditions since the initiation of care in the 1850s. As the industrial revolution took hold in America, accompanied by the complexities of urbanization, a vast array of social pathology resulted from the rapid and severe dislocations in patterns of living. It soon became clear from the unsuccessful experience of former residents who were discharged from institutions to fend for themselves in the community that, however well trained in industrial, domestic, or other work, the young retarded adult or adolescent would be unlikely to remain intact for long in the harsh and chaotic social conditions prevailing outside, unless he was able to return to an exceptionally stable and sympathetic environment. Moreover, because of the devastating social forces that were dislocating so many people's lives, most of the children admitted to institutions came from very poor backgrounds and either were orphans with no home to which they could be discharged or had families whose poverty or social dysfunctioning made them unable or unsuited to assume their supervision or care.[22]

By the last quarter of the nineteenth century it became obvious that rehabilitation into the community was not a feasible plan for many. Therefore, a new type of custodial care providing for adult defectives who could not manage in the community had to be devised, with different objectives, different organization, and inevitably some change in the type of care. This trend, which first became obvious to the institutions themselves, received impetus from the community when in 1876 the State Board of Charities of New York became concerned about the number of women with illegitimate babies in the county poorhouses who seemed to be of imbecile or idiot level.[23] This discovery lent a new perspective to the problem of retardation. The result was a committee set up by the Board to meet with a similar body to be appointed by the trustees of the State Asylum for Idiots in order to discuss how this serious problem could be handled on a cooperative basis. A proposal was made to the New York State legislature for an appropriation to set up a custodial asylum on an experimental basis to test the need for such a facility and the expenditure involved in its maintenance. It was explicitly stated by Dr. Wilbur that because of the facility's long-term nature it would have to be run on different economic lines from the short-term educational establishment at Syracuse, and would be so organized that inmates who were competent to work would be largely responsible for the upkeep of their institution and would also contribute where possible to that of the parent body.[24]

The proposal was approved and in 1878 a separate establishment was opened in Newark, N.Y., to which forty residents from Syracuse were transferred as founding members. There was also vigorous contact with the Poor Law administration within the state, most of the poorhouses being informed of the new venture with a request for suitable referrals, and Dr. Wilbur visited several personally to explain the program. By 1882 there were 130 inmates. Two years later a similar proposal was approved for a custodial establishment for male adults who were to be housed on a farm which would provide milk, produce, and other maintenance services for the parent and two satellite institutions. This example again was followed up quickly, and six institutions (in Pennsylvania, Illinois, Massachusetts, Iowa, Ontario, and Minnesota) had branched out into this new form of care within the next three or four years.

The unmet needs of the retarded were a constant source of concern to the institution personnel who frequently found themselves wondering in which direction their professional and social obligations lay, and how to assume responsibility for the increasingly large mass of retarded without so reducing the quality of their original programs as to render them valueless. The Columbus institution in 1878 expressed concern about whether a new appropriation should be used to extend the efficient training program for 400 inmates then in existence or to take care of "the immense class of defectives in the state that are being painfully cared for in county infirmaries" [25] (the former plan won). In 1888 the director of Elwyn —Dr. Isaac Kerlin—formulated his new policy in the following statement: "With the appalling numbers of applicants for admission and from a conviction that the State will not burden taxpayers with the support of more than a fraction of those needing it, it becomes imperative for us to devise economical methods by which a moderate good shall be done for the greatest number." [26] A sector still lacking the specialized care that their condition was deemed to warrant were the doubly handicapped who suffered from mental defect and physical disability. In 1891 and 1892 the directors of the New York and Kentucky institutions both referred to this unmet area of need. These findings, linked with another comment from New York in 1885 that the majority of children born illegitimately to idiotic and imbecile females in the county poorhouses were either idiotic or deformed or in some way destined to become dependents or paupers, complete the cycle of recurrent social pathology and neglect.[27]

At this time Elwyn had started a unit for epileptics and paralytics in their custodial asylum section, and legislation was expected in New York, so some attempt was being made to cope with this additional aspect of social care. It also meant that the character of the institutions was changing from a single to a multipurpose one in which education, industrial training of children on a rehabilitation basis, and long-term custodial care for socially incompetent adults and for medically handicapped of all ages were being organized under one roof—except in New York where separate establishments had been set up. As problems arose and were identified in the community, the institutions were looked to as the inevitable solution; little attempt was made at this time to find an alternative answer within the community, probably because the chaotic state of society was not propitious for handling social problems and the most severe social deviations were felt to need a segregated setting.

For the retarded this development of long-term custodial care was both a realistic and perceptive step in providing them with a protective environment which utilized their skills and offered them some sort of social role. As institutions were still relatively small (rarely over 500 residents), it was possible to have a personal atmosphere and to preserve both human dignity and individuality in the programs. The Superintendent of Fort Wayne, Indiana, in discussing adult trainable imbeciles, asserted that they must not be regarded as patients or pupils or prisoners but as laborers, and he went on to describe the useful working activities in which they were competent and by which they contributed to their own upkeep and that of their social group, the institution. At a meeting in 1891 there was a lively discussion between the heads of six institutions on the thorny topic of how to remunerate workers without their becoming corrupted by handling money whose worth they did not fully appreciate.[28] Various solutions were propounded, and the examples of inherent pitfalls in the system are the sort familiar to workers in the field at the present time.

Although the institutional regimes at the turn of the century had a paternalistic ring not in tune with modern concepts of self-determination, they embodied a humane plan. While it involved deprivation of individual liberty, the socially vulnerable were protected from the excessive price in social dysfunctioning that would be paid for their freedom outside. The degrading life to which destitute girls of low mentality were exposed in the Poor Law institutions can be glimpsed from the allegation of one such girl admitted to the Newark Custodial Asylum for Feebleminded Women from the Dutchess County poorhouse that the keeper of the house fathered her second illegitimate child.[29] The squalor in which women of limited intelligence struggled with the exigencies of raising their children—as described in the studies of the home visitor on members of the Kallikak family[30] and in reports from the Special Schools social worker in Cleveland [31]—suggests that for their own sake and their unborn offspring they were probably better off inside a well-run institution even if it meant celibacy and a regimented life. The superiority of special institutional care over the alternative food-and-shelter level offered in the almshouses is indicated by an Indiana officer's statement: "One of our boys who came from one of our county poor farms, the superintendent of which informed me that the boy was of no account, would never improve, has advanced so much and promises to be self-sustaining, so that we have concluded to place him in the bakery and teach him to bake. He will be of service to us there." [32] The frequent references by superintendents to the inmates as "our family" suggest an environment in which individual needs and capacities received personal attention. The Victorian prints of these institutions—published in the Proceedings of the early meetings of the Association of Medical Officers of American Institutions for Idiotic and Feebleminded Persons—showing cosy villas and impressive Gothic structures flanked by imposing trees, give the impression of a well-ordered life and evoke nostalgia for a time when paternalistic care offered a haven from the stresses of life in the outside world.

The concept of custodial care, which succeeded the earlier objective of social rehabilitation and originated in the wish to protect the socially vulnerable from the insuperable difficulties they would encounter in the outside world, covered all kinds and degrees of social maladaptation, whether due to physical afflictions such as epilepsy or paralysis, to poor judgment and low impulse control (dubbed *moral weakness*), or to adverse social experiences. A private institution at Barre, for example, broadened its original policy of training children to one of accepting on a long-term basis adult defectives from "good families who fail to stand intellectually with their brothers and sisters." Among the case histories of many of the public institutions were several examples of children and young adults suffering from severe emotional disturbance or reactive behavior disorder undoubtedly contributed to by the adverse social experiences they had undergone. The type of care was well organized and, by applying the training principles which had originated in the short-term rehabilitation programs, the long-term residents were helped to develop their abilities and put them to some social use, thereby also insuring the continued maintenance of the institution.

However, within the next twenty-five years a new note was introduced which shifted attention from the aim of protecting the mentally handicapped from the ravages of a cruel and exploitative society to protecting society from the feared contamination of inferior mental stock and its perpetuation in increasingly large numbers. This phase, known as the "eugenic scare," was probably the result of several interrelated factors, some of them general in character and not exclusively associated with mental defect. First, the alarming increase in pauperism, vagrancy, alcoholism, delinquency, and the many other manifestations of the severe social pathology and dislocation that were lumped together under the general unscientific and pejorative heading of "moral degeneracy" drew attention to the many individuals in society who were functioning at a *socially* subnormal level. Second, the recurrence of certain patterns of sociopathic behavior within identified families and kinship groups suggested that these undesirable tendencies were of an inherited nature. Third, the association of low mentality with many of these other traits among these families (the Jukes, the Kallikaks, Dwellers in the Vale of Sidem, the Pinneys) gave rise to the idea that low intelligence was genetically determined and was the constant factor underlying, and responsible for, all the other symptoms of social failure. Furthermore, since one of the outstanding characteristics of this socially displaced subculture—whether of normal or defective intelligence—was sexual promiscuity and fertility, it was feared that this class of inferior persons, unless rigidly controlled, would become numerically dominant and eventually reduce the national level of intelligence. The coincidence of Binet's evolving a standardized test that claimed to make objective measurements of intelligence offered at the same time an instrument by which the mentally defective could be identified in large numbers through the measurement of this single psychological factor; and since there was no similar technique for identifying—let alone measuring—other indices of social pathology, this calculable factor was naturally singled out for attention. Goddard translated Binet's first edition of *Le Mesure du dé-*

veloppement de l'intelligence chez les jeunes enfants (1905) in 1909, a year before the publication of Goddard's classic study of the Kallikak family, which was to prove, by complex genealogical tracing and history, the validity of the theory of genetic mental defect. Lastly, the existence of facilities for the long-term care of the retarded strengthened both the reasons and the rationalization for the movement for custodial segregation.

Social control of the feebleminded, who were feared to be waiting in untold numbers to prey on society with their destructive patterns of life, became the dominant theme; and attempts to implement control were expressed in legislation for sterilization and in the proposal to extend custodial care to cover all the retarded in the country during their child-bearing period, if not for life.[33] The first sterilization law was passed in Indiana in 1907, followed by seven other states (Washington, California, Connecticut, New Jersey, Iowa, New York, and Nevada) over the next seven years; and community social agencies, schools, law courts, and the institutions for the feebleminded were concentrating on the problem of providing enough institutional places to cope with this growing mass of retarded children and adults. In 1915 the number of feebleminded in the United States was estimated at 275,000 (3 per 1,000 of the population) of whom only 28,000 (roughly 10 percent) were in institutions.[34] As Davies has pointed out, the extravagant concept of total social control of the mentally retarded was never much more than an idea, and in fact neither sterilization nor wholesale commitment for custodial care was implemented, although a great many speeches advocating these measures on humane and eugenic grounds appear in the literature of the time, all invested with strong emotional content and good scientific arguments. The professional workers in the field were primarily motivated by genuine concern for the retarded whose plight they were familiar with firsthand, but they got carried away by the abstract concepts involved in the eugenic scare and temporarily lost sight of the enormous practical difficulties of incarcerating a substantial segment of society for life at public expense. The agitation was relatively shortlived; and by 1919 Dr. Walter Fernald, Director of the Massachusetts Institution, who had been a strong proponent of the idea, admitted that because of the magnitude of the problem and its cost, and the reluctance of families to cooperate in sending their relatives away for life, it had proved very difficult to carry out the measure.[35]

The eugenic scare, however shortlived and ineffectual in its social measures, was more significant for the attitudes it embodied toward the retarded and the underlying social outlook. Whereas the mid-nineteenth century saw the emergence of a compassionate approach expressed in remedial plans for care of the retarded based on sound scientific principles, the twentieth century witnessed a very different concept of their needs and social role. The realities of the situation were also very different in that the character of this population had now changed from the vulnerable and relatively helpless—mainly children—who needed and deserved society's support in the shape of education for a fuller social life (to become "more of a man and less of a brute")[36] to incompetent adults whose involvement in society and manner of relating to existing social institutions was fraught with problems and in a self-perpetuating way tended to create more. For such a population it was not a matter of rehabilitation or preparation for later life, but of long-term control to prevent the ill effects of their behavior from spreading.

The new trends in social care were not in themselves harmful; their harm lay in the philosophical rationale underlying the pattern of services and its acceptance by society as a whole. It contributed to the social devaluation of the retarded as human beings, and to their psychological and physical alienation from society, and singled them out on a fundamentally negative basis in a way that no other group had experienced since the quarantining of lepers in the middle ages.[37] The location of poor intellect and subsequent social malfunctioning in a genetic origin stigmatized them as hopeless, in spite of the concepts of improvements through education and training that had been formulated by the early pioneers and later confirmed by the experience of the institutions. The extremely negative social values this led to were expressed in a paper by the Reverend Karl Schwarz at Syracuse in 1908 [38] on the justification for the social segregation of the mentally defective. He voiced concepts so socially destructive—embodying what today we should unhesitatingly call a Fascist philosophy—that the professional workers in the field (including Goddard, who was one of the foremost champions of eugenic control) responded unanimously with more cautious and humane counsel. That anyone could advocate such sentiments at a public meeting, however, is a sobering reflection of the thinking of the times.

The reason for this strong emphasis on the genetic basis of mental defect is open to various interpretations. One is that a prognosis of hopelessness and irreversibility absolved the social conscience from attempting any really challenging and constructive remedial measures on a large scale and permitted the ambiguous situation whereby the need for social control was loudly proclaimed but not in fact implemented. This double value exemplifies the laissez-faire policy which dominated social and economic affairs in this period since it appeared to be tackling an avowed problem without having to invest any significant time or money in it. A corollary to this attitude is that, by anchoring mental defects firmly to genetic morbidity, attention was distracted from the social forces that were causing pathological conditions and patterns of functioning among the poor, unskilled working classes as a whole (which in this country included a host of destitute immigrants as well as displaced native Americans) and became focused on a small, easily identifiable example of social dysfunctioning. This forestalled the necessity for analyzing the possible economic causes behind so much of the social maladjustment, which, if scrutinized closely, would have logically led to a fundamental questioning of the entire socioeconomic structure of the country—an examination which, at that stage, could not have been tolerated.

In England such questions were being raised by the Minority Report on the Poor Law Commission published in 1909,[39] in the postulated theory that poverty and social ills are often the result of economic forces over which individuals have no control rather than of personal failure, but these ideas were voices in the wilderness of complacency and skepticism and found little acceptance in theory or practice. In America, whose pioneering ethic cherished the ideal that individual competence and talent are the determinants of one's fate, this concept of social forces creating individual incapacities was quite untenable. The philosophy and sociopolitical demands of the time were much more in tune with the idea of inherent and irredeemable individual deficiency.

Two other factors entered into this viewpoint. One was the Puritan ethic that equates competence and success in this world with spiritual grace (and vice versa), an attitude which—as Max Weber has demonstrated—was a concomitant to the growth of the capitalist economic system.[40] The other is the fact that exploitative and fundamentally inequitable social regimes invariably try to maintain their precarious status quo in the face of their obvious failure to meet the needs of the majority by the alienation and derogation of their most socially victimized members. This device has been applied to other socially devalued subgroups besides the retarded, as recent history in Europe and current trends in the southern states of this country demonstrate. When Goddard stated, "if the Jukes family were of normal intelligence a change of environment would have worked wonders. But if they were so feebleminded then no amount of good environment could have made them anything else but feebleminded," he was echoing not only the conscious scientific conviction of most of his informed colleagues, but also the unconscious wish of society to find an explanation for the social maladjustment prevalent around them. By hitting on a circumscribed cause to account for what must have been a very widespread social pathology and locating it in a relatively small segment of society whose social vulnerability and failure could be objectively measured, the psychologists and society unwittingly found a very useful scapegoat.

The special character of the Binet test procedures, based on mass-scale identification, also contributed to this approach. With their quantifiable results, their supposed infallibility, and the mechanical character of their diagnostic method, they reflected perfectly the Gestalt of a technological society geared to large-scale mass production in which the precision of mechanical equipment dominated individual skills. The biological and social evaluative approach originally propounded by the French physicians, which had developed to greater levels of clinical refinement by their successors in Europe and America, had been succeeded by the more predictable standardized measurement which focused almost exclusively on the psychological component involved in educational and social failure. For this circumscribed aim, the newly devised intelligence scale was very valuable; but as a diagnostic tool for the total condition of retardation, it was exceedingly limited, too heavily biased in the direction of intellect, and did not take into account the role of social factors in contributing to the condition.

This extra social perspective, which today we take for granted, was missing because the constituents and dynamics of social life were only half understood, and while it was conceded that the individual might have an effect on the society to which he belonged, there was no awareness of the reverse situation that society might shape the behavior of individuals. A paper published in 1916 by Helen Mac-Murchy, Inspector of the Feebleminded in Ontario, on the relationship of feeblemindedness to other social problems is entirely a one-way presentation in which social pathology in three areas (public health, public safety, and public morality) is described in terms of causation by feebleminded individuals. These social problems included the spread of infectious diseases (T.B. and V.D.), alcoholism, infant mortality due to maternal neglect, prostitution, and a long list of dangerous crimes (including fraud!).[41] Earlier, the Superintendent of Elwyn analyzed the family histories of 100 feebleminded patients in the institution and compiled a list of gross social symptoms to support the argument of inherited familial degeneracy,[42] but what forcibly strikes the reader today is that the conditions he cites so frequently—consumption, alcoholism, mental illness or severe emotional disturbance, violent behavior, disrupted marriages—are what we should consider reactive symptoms to excessive social strain and not primarily its cause. This excellent compilation of depressing social ills gives only very sparse information on the external social circumstances of these families and the environmental pressures which might have been considered contributory to social breakdown.

Half a century later and armed with the knowledge of complex social forces provided by the discipline of sociology, we are shifting from exclusive preoccupation with the individual components involved in the social maladaptation called retardation to those factors within the environment that breed, foster, and perpetuate the condition; and a new biosocial concept has emerged. This is because social theory and sociological practice have provided tools for evaluating these elements which enable us to identify and assess factors in the external social environment that exercise a positive or negative influence on development and functioning, whether they relate to urban growth, housing, educational and medical services, work prospects, health hazards, or to the more intimate environmental sphere of interpersonal relationships. In the evolutionary phase of identifying the condition of retardation and its societal origins and manifestations, this sociological thrust is as vital for obtaining a comprehensive picture as the previous diagnostic instruments of clinical evaluation and psychological testing.

Ironically—but also perhaps typical of the American habit of *implementing* quietly limited useful activities while *discussing* grandiosely conceived but impractical proposals—during all this verbal furor there had been a steady progress in the development of services for the identified retarded in the direction of social support within the community. The establishment of special educational facilities within the public school system laid the foundation for community rehabilitation. Special classes were set up in Providence, R.I., in 1896; and later in Springfield, Mass.; Chicago; Boston; New York; Philadelphia; Los Angeles; Detroit; Elgin, Ill.; Trenton, N.J.; Washington, D.C.; Bridgeport, Conn.; Newton, Mass.; and Rochester.[43] These were for children of subnormal intelligence who could not be educated in ordinary schools but had satisfactory homes and so did not need residential care.

Gradually other programs of medical-social care evolved which provided alternative forms of help to retarded children and adults and to their families within the community. In 1891 a weekly diagnostic outpatient clinic was established at Waverley (Massachusetts State Training School)[44] to cope with the numerous requests for advice on problems of retardation that the institution was receiving, and to determine whether all patients for whom institutional admission was requested needed this form of care. By 1920 the clinic had handled over 6,000 inquiries, either through letter or telephone or by direct diagnostic examination, and its valuable preventive function was demonstrated by the fact that during this twenty-nine-year period the majority of clinic patients who had been diagnosed as feebleminded had not subsequently applied for admission to the institution or been in obvious trouble in the community outside. This innovation was the start of effective community care because in addition to offering a diagnostic evaluation it also provided follow-up examinations at yearly or half-yearly intervals, long-term contact with families who understook the care of their retarded members themselves, and practical counseling on appropriate management within the home—the latter service supplemented, where necessary, by visits of parents and relatives to the institution to observe training and nursing methods used there. As a result, a greater number of mentally defective children and adults were being cared for extramurally in 1920 through advisory help given to their families than were looked after directly in the institution. This care was reserved for cases too disabled to be handled at home or who had such serious social adjustment problems that they required a structured institutional setting. In 1915, at the request of the public school authorities, the scope of this clinical service was extended to include monthly diagnostic examinations for schools in the four leading cities within the institution's orbit. The types of problems dealt with were essentially educational in character—either learning difficulties or persistent truancy—and the schools carried responsibility for making referrals and for implementing the recommendations of the clinic team within the community; only the cases presenting severe behavioral maladjustment or very adverse social conditions were put on the waiting list for Waverley.

This informal cooperative effort preceded a state-supported program of community care drawn up by the institute's Director (Dr. Fernald) in 1919 [45] and translated, in slightly modified form, into legislation in 1921.[46] By this law all school children who were more than three years behind in scholastic performance had to have a psychological examination to determine whether they were feebleminded and what sort of special education they needed. To meet these statutory obligations the state set up diagnostic clinics in twelve different regions, staffed by the personnel of the state mental hospitals or training schools for the feebleminded.[47] Since the two state schools (Waverley and Wrentham) were responsible for areas containing large urban constellations set at considerable distance from each other, they developed traveling clinic teams which visited each community within their region once a year, stayed a week and examined between 50 and 60 children. In addition, all feebleminded persons who appeared in the courts on delinquency charges had to be committed by the judge to the care of the State Department of Mental Diseases instead of receiving the normal sentence. This department (which had a Division of Feeblemindedness) would then decide whether the individual required segregated care in one of the institutions or would be able to readjust to life in the community if given appropriate social help and supervision. Associated with this was the establishment of a social service within the Division which employed three trained psychiatric social workers, to review the waiting lists for institutional admission, visit the homes of feebleminded applicants and their families, and where the social diagnosis did not indicate the need for residential care, try to offer some alternative form of help. By this effort the waiting list was reduced within fourteen months (between March 1923 and May 1924) from 1,467 to 731. Supervision within the community was beginning to supplant custodial care as a means of controlling the social inadequacies of the mentally defective. It was oriented to fostering their positive capacities for self-support instead of focusing on a deterrent to their negative features.

By this time surveys of patients who had been paroled (or had escaped) from the institutions[48] and follow-up studies of children leaving special classes in several of the states with more advanced programs (Massachusetts and New York)[49] had indicated that not all the mentally defective were so unredeemedly bad as had been feared, and that many showed a considerable potential for leading stable adult lives if given appropriate help. Although Massachusetts took the lead in community care at this juncture, other states were beginning to develop schemes for identification and supervision of their retarded within the community. To provide this type of support New York[50] and Pennsylvania[51] set up diagnostic clinics, while as early as 1911 and 1912 two physicians in Rochester[52] and Pittsburgh[53] were independently making an attempt to do preventive and early detection work with young children who might later show retardation.

Paralleling this move to provide sustained and comprehensive care within the community were the endeavors by institutions to shift some of their patients back to society, to make room for the types of cases that really needed institutional care, and to give the more competent and well-trained residents a chance to try their adaptive capacity in the outside community. This thrust had two directions, one of which was the return of patients to live in the community on a *parole* basis (usually with their relatives) and the other, being the *colony plan.* Parole was the earlier development, which started informally at Waverley in 1890 and formalized in the 1921 legislation as part of the community care scheme. In New York parole was made legal in 1912 so that from the beginning of the century—despite the eugenic scare—there was a consistent movement toward getting the higher-grade, more stable adults out of their custodial setting.[54]

The colony plan represented another means of providing the social protection the feebleminded were thought to require while utilizing their considerable manpower for productivity.[55] It started with the acquisition of a series of abandoned farms in Massachusetts, New Jersey, and New York, each of which was organized as a separate unit managed by a farmer and his wife who trained and supervised groups of between 10 and 20 boys and young men. The first Massachusetts farm colony at Templeton comprised 7 farmsteads scattered over 1,920 acres and was begun with two groups of youths, 50 in all. Rome Custodial Asylum, New York, started with one farm of 187 acres and 8 boys in 1908, gradually expanding till five such establishments were producing 25 percent of the maintenance costs of 1,570 patients and 230 employees in the parent institution and the five colonies. By 1919 this institution, which had developed this type of care in a most imaginative way, had nine farms employing 240 men, one forestry and one industrial colony. In 1914 it branched into a similar venture for girls, renting or buying large houses in well-populated communities and placing groups of girls in their late teens or early adulthood under the care of a matron who was employed by the institution. The girls, who had already been trained in the institution, were placed from the colony in daily work, returning to the colony at night. Four of these houses specialized in domestic workers who were employed in private homes—looking after children, house cleaning, doing laundry, sewing, and the like; one housed girls working in a local mill; and the other, girls employed at a factory. They received approximately normal rates of remuneration (the domestic workers received 15¢ an hour and the industrial workers between $5 and $10 a week). Wages were appropriated by the matron for the colony's running expenses, with each girl receiving 25¢ pocket money, 50¢ banked for savings, and a share of the common pool maintained for clothing and other heavy expenditure items.

The colonies, particularly those located in urban settings where there were greater demands on social adjustment, not only provided a protective environment and productive pattern of life for the residents but had the equally strong purpose of training them in appropriate social behavior so that eventually they could be discharged from the institution's care. The social worker played an important part in teaching the girls the amenities and certain patterns of social intercourse not encountered in the institution (e.g., selecting clothes in a store, going to magic lantern shows, attending church in the community). And the matrons also appear to have been a very forceful factor in fostering their social adjustment. A 1921 report[56] gives an illuminating picture of the therapeutic role these women played in helping these deprived and often unstable girls adjust to the world at large. Their approach to individual problems and to the society which had to assimilate the girls was remarkably progressive. One matron, for example, who had 22 Negro girls under her care, made a special point of involving the whole community in the project, interpreting her protegees' needs to the local people and enlisting community help in making them feel accepted. She was particularly emphatic that her girls should not be perceived or treated differently from normal people and strongly denounced such indignities to her girls as wolf whistles from the town's libertine youth.

The success of this scheme (in this one year 42 out of 67 made a success of their trial and remained at the colony while 25 had to return to the institution for unsuitable behavior such as *flirting*) was almost certainly due to the initiative and outlook of Rome State Colony's superintendent, Charles Bernstein, who had a fundamentally sympathetic understanding of his charges, was optimistic about their potential, and had a realistic grasp of how society should use its resources to meet the needs of this segment of its population. His philosophy, expressed in 1921 after thirteen years of experience in colony management, contains all the psychological components necessary for successful rehabilitation.

There are at least two very good arguments in support of colony care for those who are subject to or in need of assistance during the period of their incapacity or enforced limited freedom and action, namely: First, the great need of making the limited funds available reach the largest number possible; Second, rendering the enforced restriction of freedom and economic and social limitations as humane and as little humiliating as possible. . . . Rather than handing out alms we are supervising self-earned support and instructing our patients not only in hygiene and animal inhibition but also in habits of industry, and thrift and honorable self-support, the sheet anchors of moral prophylaxis.

The colonies of New York State were in effect prototypes of the halfway houses (since residents had to have a preliminary period at the institution) which are in operation in most of the advanced European countries and are being gradually introduced into America. Great Britain, for example, set up agricultural hostels during the war to house high-grade institutional patients in the rural food-producing areas and now has hostels in most of the large industrial cities for high- and medium-grade subnormal adults. Holland has a network of group foster homes in the cities which closely resemble the girls' homes in New York in the twenties. What is discouraging is that this excellently organized type of care which flourished forty years ago was allowed to fall into desuetude so that it is now appearing in all the new state plans for retardation services as a novel and revolutionary idea. Again, the reason is to be found in the political and economic situation: the depression, which crippled productivity and rendered millions of normal people unemployed, halted this attempt to reinstate the socially less competent into the country's productive system.

After the colony system, designed for the high-grade, relatively competent young adult, the next phase of community-directed care was *family* care for children or older patients who needed a protective setting and were unlikely to graduate to the eventual independence that was the goal for the colony resident. New York State appears to have led the way. In 1935 and 1936 there were reports from Newark Custodial Asylum of an experiment to place adults and children in families living in several villages or small towns around the institution.[57] The plan was well conceived; in addition to the usual arrangements for foster care placement (which the scheme essentially was), it developed the unusual feature of a community center which was relatively accessible to most of the foster homes and served several valuable community functions. It provided a social center for the older patients in family care when they had free time and allowed them to keep in touch with their peers from the institution who were also living in the neighborhood. If a foster parent had to be away from the home for more than a few hours or overnight, it provided temporary accommodation so that the patient would not be left alone in the house. In case of illness which could not be handled in the foster home the patient could be taken into the colony center pending transfer to the institution. The center was staffed by an institution nurse who acted as unofficial adviser to the foster parents and confidante to the patients when they had personal problems they needed to ventilate to an outsider. This arrangement seems to be the prototype of a well-contrived therapeutic community, with the normal resources of private families being tapped to provide care for the vulnerable retarded and the supportive specialist facilities of the institution available in the background.

Family care spread quite rapidly to most of the states and the literature of the thirties and forties is full of reports on its different manifestations, characteristics, and problems. An interesting fact about the colony and the family care programs is that they were both skillfully articulated with certain significant economic factors. In the farm colonies the propitious linking of large tracts of abandoned agricultural land with a reservoir of able-bodied workers consigned to long-term social segregation in protective custody provided a productive role for both and retrieved the potential of two hitherto discarded sources of productivity. In family care, which started in the early thirties, the placement of residents in rural areas where home-grown food was plentiful but money short endowed the boarding allowances of family care patients with financial value and made such care a desirable economic activity. And the rural setting, with its less complex economy and more direct personal lines of communication, made these village communities a benign environment for children and adults whose social mobility was permanently limited and who were hindered rather than helped by the supposedly uncircumscribed opportunities that industrial urban environments were thought to offer. A similar program was successfully built up in the highlands of Scotland where comparable conditions of rural isolation and limited objectives prevailed.

A review of the separate aspects of care for the mentally retarded that were being independently developed in various parts of the country in this period suggests that most of the components of a comprehensive and coordinated service had been conceived and attempted in some place at some time.[58] If these isolated individual efforts could have been pooled and welded into one universally accepted program, there would have been established twenty-five or more years ago the *continuum of care* which the President's Panel of 1962 projected as the prototype of care for today's retarded population.[59] Furthermore, interest in the problems of the retarded, traced from its beginnings in 1848, shows a consistent pattern of active concern, throughout its shifts in emphasis, focus, and values. The original institutional training for return to the community developed the secondary type of help through long-term custodial care, which in its turn began to be modified from its initial unwieldy proportions by the development of the alternatives of parole, colony, and family care. Simultaneously, the problem, which had swelled enormously and sprouted sociological facets not hitherto envisaged, began to be tackled from the angle of preventive and supportive care within the community. The liveliness and creativity of the ideas behind the emerging developments (Wilbur's custodial asylum in 1876, Fernald's clinic in 1891, Bernstein's colonies in 1919, the Massachusetts plan for community supervision in 1921, and Vaux' family care project in 1933) and the degree of intelligent concern with which they were executed are impressive. The pace and variety of developments in the 90-odd years after Massachusetts set up the first specialized facility for the retarded is a testimonial to the professional people in the field who were committed to struggling for these necessary changes.

In retrospect one must also ask what forces intruded into the picture in the succeeding decades to slow down this progressive trend so that the United States, which had started on an equal footing with Europe in 1848, was by 1960 at a standstill and noticeably behind most of the leading countries of northern Europe in its ideas and programs. The enthusiasm with which earlier endeavors were applied to studying the needs of the mentally handicapped and the devoted sense of responsibility for meeting their plight had drained away, and by the mid-twentieth century the impression prevailed that retardation was a specialized, isolated area which received little attention from society at large. Although the professional workers in the field were applying themselves conscientiously and with imagination to the necessary job of providing assistance to the retarded who came their way, they seemed immured in the strong walls of their institutions and society's indifference, and their efforts lacked the necessary reinforcement from the professional mainstream. This was particularly true of the social work profession, as we shall see in the following chapter.

Again, the explanation for these atrophied services seems to lie in external events, particularly in sociopolitical factors. The Great Depression, which ravaged the economy with singular destructiveness (particularly since the United States had built no ark of safety against the cataclysmic event) plunged almost the entire wage-earning population into economic dependency. The most competent and intelligent were reduced to the level of social ineffectiveness of the mentally retarded. Inevitably attention was drawn away from the problems of the relatively small and most vulnerable segment of society that the retarded constituted, and focused instead on the survival of the normal working class. Because the successful assimilation of the retarded depends basically on the existence of a viable society, attempts to rehabilitate them were doomed. A report in 1934 on the effects of the depression on the feebleminded mentions the reduction of parole because of inability to find work, an increased number of low-functioning individuals on relief, and a higher admission rate of children who could not be looked after at home because their mothers needed to be available for work if any turned up.[60] In these circumstances it is easy to understand how the institutions, through the best of motives and under pressure to admit patients who could not be maintained in the community, increased their numbers and reduced the quality of care. Instead of caring for a manageable group, these overcrowded institutions became custodial in fact as well as in name. The advent of the Second World War, while it revived the economy, focused the nation's psychological and material resources on successful prosecution of the war and further obscured the needs, if not the very existence, of the mentally handicapped except for such worrisome revelations as the unusually high number of rejections for the armed forces because of subnormal intelligence. The combined effects of these two national upheavals seem to have relegated the problems of the retarded to limbo. After approximately twenty-five years of this earlier unintentional neglect, services in the United States today still lag behind those of European countries, including even some that suffered Nazi occupation, such as Denmark, Holland, and Norway.

However, the intervening "lost years" were not entirely barren— they could perhaps be more charitably described as lying fallow— because a fresh demonstration of social concern for the retarded emerged in two entirely new areas of activity, both of which added another facet to the evolving pattern of social services for the retarded and contributed significantly to the changes in social welfare and social action in the latter half of the century that we are now witnessing. This pattern, which has a different origin from the earlier one based primarily on the involvement of the institutions, comprises the demonstration projects, coordinated plans, and new legislation which have come into being over the past two decades. These are unquestionably moves in the direction of nationwide comprehensive care embracing alleviative, rehabilitative, and preventive programs.

The first such move was the participation by the federal government through the creation of the former Children's Bureau (formed in 1912), which in its broad mandate to "investigate and report upon all matters pertaining to the welfare of children and child life among all classes of people" included mental retardation.[61] Its first gesture in this direction was to sponsor a study on the mentally defective in the District of Columbia, and in 1917 this category was included in a wider study that was being done on the educational and social needs of children in Delaware. The results showed that 82.5 percent of the retarded lacked appropriate care and also stressed the high correlation between poverty, abnormal home conditions, neglect, and dependency and mental defect. This was followed up by a study in 1919 of a circumscribed area of the same state entitled *Mental Defect in a Rural County,* and in 1923 a study of the employment of mentally deficient boys and girls indicated concern in another dimension of social care. A general study of dependent children and state provisions for them also included the retarded since many of the dependent children were of this category as findings from other sources had already indicated. For example, in an investigation of the psychological status of 1,246 children in homes for dependent children, 9.9 percent were found to be feebleminded and 6.1 percent of borderline intelligence.

Toward the end of the thirties the Bureau kept an eye on developments in the care of retarded children taking place in the various states and thereby became an invaluable reservoir of information on available services and the different forms they were assuming throughout the country. The Social Security Act of 1935 also played a part in shaping services for the retarded when the Bureau became the responsible agent for administering federal grants for maternal and child health services, crippled children, and child welfare. As a result, and following a survey of the medical services available to cope with the problem of retardation, the Bureau took the initiative in establishing demonstration projects on the medical care required to meet this disability. Diagnostic and treatment clinics were set up: by 1956 there were 26, and at present there are over 200 supported by federal funds. The interest of the Bureau in retardation was also signified by the appointment of two well-qualified social workers to act as consultants on mental retardation in the areas of medical care and child welfare.

The second significant step in the evolution of services for the retarded was the formation in 1950 of a national parents' organization. While sporadic groups of families with retarded members had been forming in such widely separated states as Ohio, Washington, and New York since 1933, they had remained isolated until 1947 when a paper presented at the annual convention of the American Association on Mental Deficiency focused attention on this newly emerging phenomenon.[62] In 1949 three speakers dealt with this topic; two were representatives of parent groups, and one a social worker who had experience with the organization through her professional work with the retarded. The subject came up again at the 1950 meeting, and in the fall of that year 40 individuals from thirteen States met in Minneapolis to form the National Association of Parents and Friends of the Mentally Retarded. A charter was filed in 1953 under the name of the National Association for Retarded Children. In 1970 this body had expanded its membership to over 100,000 individuals and nearly 1,500 constituent associations.[63]

In the twenty years since its inception this organization has wielded great pressure on both local and national levels and has been one of the prime forces in formulating and promoting new measures for comprehensive services for the retarded of all ages (despite its misleading title).[64] As noted previously, services for the retarded initially comprised special education within the public schools for educable children over seven and institutional care for the more seriously retarded if their families did not feel able to handle their care and training at home without any professional help. This limited provision was undoubtedly a legacy from the earlier nineteenth century view that for those who could not be expected to be independent or self-supporting custodial care was the best remedy. It illustrates the static thinking surrounding mental retardation as a social disability and its failure to take account of the vastly changed social factors operating in the 1950s, which rendered *wholesale, indiscriminate* institutional placement inappropriate and psychologically open to question. These factors were the advances in medical science which aided the survival of babies with biologically determined defects and created a sizable population of children whose retardation was independent of social origin; in fact, many belonged to prosperous middle-class families who had a sophisticated attitude toward their rights to public services for their disabled children, and skill and knowledge in arguing their case. The prevalent psychological theory that maternal separation had a negative influence on children's development affected both parents and professional workers' attitudes toward consigning a small, helpless baby to an impersonal institution for life; and the extremely low standards—with few exceptions—of publicly supported residential care enhanced this reluctance. As a result, local groups became very active in setting up pilot projects to fill the gap in services and to demonstrate the need on a community-wide public scale. Such facilities as industrial training centers, preschool programs, group activities, and smaller rehabilitative residential centers, which had not previously been included in the canon of facilities for the retarded, were initiated in this fashion.

On the national scale there was campaigning for more services; educational drives to convey a better understanding of the problems and needs of the retarded and their families to the general public; and a move for local and federal legislation to provide the funds to build better programs. Thus a cause that earlier had had to depend on the philanthropic and socially conscious efforts of dedicated professionals in the field found itself harnessed to the tremendous energy stemming from the frustrations of a desperate and articulate consumer group.[65] This ground swell of interest symbolized by the parents group moved into official circles, and in October 1961 President Kennedy appointed a panel of 27 experts from the various disciplinary fields related to retardation to review the situation and recommend the extension or development of services to meet the neglected needs of this group. The report of this body was published in 1962 under the title *A Proposed Program for National Action to Combat Mental Retardation.*[66] Its 194 pages contained a depressing account of the status of the retarded (for example, that there were only 500 full-time doctors to care for 160,000 patients in institutions) and that the national average cost per day per patient was $4.55), and proposed new services in eight different sectors of care. A year afterwards, and one month before his tragic and untimely death, the President signed legislation which was to be the start of many government-sponsored efforts to implement the Panel's Report. The bill (H.R. 3386) was designed to amend the Social Security Act "with the objective of assisting States and communities in preventing and combatting mental retardation through expansion and improvement of the maternal and child health and crippled children's programs, through provision of prenatal, maternity and infant care for individuals with conditions associated with childbearing which may lead to mental retardation, and for other purposes." It was ratified on October 24 as the Maternal and Child Health and Mental Retardation Planning Amendments Act of 1963 (PL 88–156) on the third day of the annual convention of the NARC being held in Washington, and after the official signing, the President joined the Association at luncheon and talked briefly about the new program. It was an occasion of great rejoicing; and the presence of several other members of the Kennedy family provided a reminder of their own intimate involvement in the problem and pointed up the organization's basic function of helping their own and other retarded children through personal efforts geared to public action.

The legislation was characterized by two important features. One was the emphasis placed on preventive measures through an extension of health services to mothers and children at risk (as they have been subsequently designated), which carried the admission that retardation was closely connected with poverty and adverse social circumstances. The other was the provision of means for stimulating services at a local level but on a nationwide scale through federal grants to enable each state to review its current facilities and draw up plans for their coordination and extension in the future. By doing this the legislation gave mental retardation a national context, implying that such a prevalent and seriously handicapping condition could not be properly dealt with by local resources alone but needed federal backing. It also ensured a certain minimum level in services regardless of where they were established. This new law put mental retardation into the center of a general welfare nexus since the preventive measures inherent in the extended maternal and child health plans would inevitably benefit all children as well as protecting the most vulnerable ones from harmful social and health hazards. Thus the condition which is the largest single handicapping disability among children today would paradoxically become a source of protection to all children through the comprehensive services that the disability evoked. Further, the philosophical implications of this act are also of great social import: in providing care for the most disabled and least socially productive members of the nation, it implicitly laid down a concept of social welfare that has not so far found unqualified acceptance in this country—namely, that the deficiencies of the weak and less well endowed should be the responsibility of the total society in which they live and should be subsidized by the more fortunate whose productive capacity is unimpaired by personal or social handicap. The second important piece of legislation, Construction of Research Centers and Facilities for the Mentally Retarded (PL88–164), was signed, shortly afterward, indicating a thrust for services in the other and equally vital direction of training professionals in the field.

Since then there have been four other legislative changes affecting the retarded in a direct or indirect fashion. These are the Social Security Amendments of 1965 (PL89–97), Mental Retardation Facilities and Community Mental Health Centers Construction Act Amendments of 1965 (PL89–105), Elementary and Secondary Education Act of 1965 (PL89–10), and Vocational Rehabilitation Amendments of 1965 (PL89–333). And finally, the Economic Opportunity Act of 1964 (Title 11 Urban and Rural Community Action) includes comprehensive measures for combating poverty and social deprivation through which it is hoped to provide a means for the early detection of possible retardation in children from adverse environments and educational measures to counteract the pernicious influences of poverty. The extension of day care and preschool facilities, help in the home, remedial reading programs, and other programs focusing on cultural and social stimulation should play a large part in combating cultural retardation on the one hand, as well as making it possible to identify at an early stage children with retardation of organic origin and to orient them to specialized remedial services.

This impressive array of legislation to deal with the far-reaching and complex problems of mental retardation on a national scale represents the explicit acknowledgment of society that individuals and families who come under the shadow of this handicap need and merit nationwide and permanent assistance. When the services embodied in these laws have been implemented, together with those already in existence, they should eventually translate into reality the ideal postulate of the continuum of care.* Like the peak development of previous eras, this somewhat rapid and dramatic expansion of care in this field of handicap must be related to certain dominant social features of the times, particularly the humane values contained in the current social philosophy, the sociopolitical situation of the country, and the contemporary state of knowledge in the medical and the social sciences.

In regard to the contemporary state of knowledge there are two particular features to be noted. Whereas the disciplines of clinical medicine, psychology, and education have in previous phases successively provided the dominating skills for the study and treatment of mental defect, in more recent decades a fourth diagnostic tool —sociology—has been introduced into the field. This added diagnostic dimension has illuminated the character of mental retardation in two ways. First, it has helped to throw into relief the easily identifiable factors that operate in the heritage, background, and current life experiences of retarded individuals to contribute in varying measures to the genesis of their handicap.[67] Second, it has demonstrated that ascription of the term "retarded" to sections of the population is not dependent solely on their characteristics but also on the characteristics, goals and value system of the society of which they are a part.[68] These insights have created a demand for new styles in the sort of social endeavor that this group requires, and the proliferation of broader and deeper knowledge among all disciplines about retardation adds a technological reinforcement to this changed philosophical stance. In the development of professional social work, emphases and thrusts in service have shifted as social philosophy and relevant expert knowledge have pointed up new directions. The problems of the mentally retarded and their families and the communities to which they belong present a challenge to this developmental flexibility. Subsequent chapters of this book will attempt to explore these new ways of thinking about retardation and show how the profession's reservoir of traditional skills can be exploited to translate these attitudes into appropriate service patterns.

* At the time of going to press, fresh legislation expressly geared to meeting gaps in existing services has been enacted, in the Developmental Disabilities Act signed into law by President Nixon, October 30, 1970.

3 SOCIAL WORK PERSPECTIVES ON MENTAL RETARDATION

THE MASSIVE social implications of mental retardation delineated in the preceding chapter point up the great need for social work intervention on behalf of this disability, and in the following chapters we shall examine the various ways of providing effective professional help. As a preliminary it is necessary to clarify the essential nature of the social problems associated with retardation and to show the overall remedial goals that social work must set in order to deal with them.

Broadly speaking, the social problems of the mentally retarded fall into the two basic areas of *being* and *doing*. The retarded suffer from a chronically impaired ability to meet the accepted norms of functioning within their social milieu, and in times of rapid social change such as the present this basic impairment is subject to constant cumulative aggravation. The pressures of contemporary life impose an increasing burden of social demands upon the mentally retarded who possess only a limited capacity to perceive the nature of these demands and the changes in behavioral response they imply. This adaptive impairment represents a serious social deviance in a culture that sets great store by conformity and in an area of functioning that is highly prized—namely, intellectual endowment and achievement. Innate personal shortcomings and their expression in subaverage social adjustment (which in itself produces many practical difficulties) subject the mentally retarded to an unprecedented degree of social rejection as *persons*—aside from their performance—and frequently cut them off from participation in the normal activities of their social setting. This double penance of personal nonacceptance and social exclusion was clearly reflected in the earlier services traditionally provided for the retarded; these were based in part on the belief that individuals with this disability were a social subgroup with different characteristics and needs from those of the population at large and therefore warranted a qualitatively different mode of care. This was provided in specialized settings that were isolated both geographically and psychologically from the main body of society.

This extreme manifestation of stereotyped thinking about mental retardation is disappearing gradually, but a residual lingers in the reluctance in some quarters of the social work profession to invest resources in the care of the retarded—or, where there is willingness, in the recognized lack of expertise in how to provide this care. Because of its high investment in informed social thinking and action, social work is inevitably a potent force for promoting new trends in social development; and it now has an unequivocal responsibility for trying to reverse the two overriding social disadvantages that the mentally retarded have been saddled with. The broad dual function of overcoming the alienation of the retarded from society, on the one hand, and of compensating for their social malfunctioning by provision of services, on the other, is a taxing challenge to the profession's resources. Therefore, before examining the sort of services to be encompassed in this comprehensive goal, we must first look at traditional and current patterns of social work to see how well its dominant philosophy, methods, and techniques equip it for meeting these demands, and what modifications may be required.

In general the mainstream of social work in America has not demonstrated a concern for retardation and its social implications commensurate with that given to other problem areas or with the needs of this client group. Therefore, responsibility for social service to this category of handicapped has been borne by a small number of social workers operating in the specialized retardation facilities—mainly the state institutions and more recently the community evaluation clinics. Although a tradition of conscientious and imaginative service has been maintained, the isolation of their professional settings has prevented these workers from making a significant impact upon the main body of social work. However, there have been some notable exceptions, particularly between the 1920s and 1940s and even earlier. Mary Richmond has several perceptive references to the problems of the feebleminded in her 1917 study *Social Diagnosis;*[1] the late Gordon Hamilton gave a paper based on her experience as secretary of the Committee for the Feebleminded of the New York City Charity Organization Society;[2] and Stanley Powell Davies, who was Executive of the State Committee on Mental Hygiene of the State Charities Aid Association of New York, described the problems and needs of the retarded in his classic, *Social Control of the Mentally Deficient.*[*][3]

In the late thirties the National Conference on Social Welfare included a symposium by workers from a variety of agencies on the relative merits of specialized versus generic care for the retarded,[4] but in the two succeeding decades interest in this disability dwindled—or at least was not highly visible. During the ten-year period 1956–1965 the two leading social work journals, *Social Work* and *Social Casework*, included, respectively, 7 out of 515 and 10 out of 456 articles or reviews of literature on the subject, while hardly any of the classical textbooks on social work mention the handicap except in passing or discuss its special features and utilize case material to illustrate generic concepts. Conversely, the specialized literature in the retardation field reveals a number of contributions from other disciplines than social work, notably clinical medicine, psychology, and education.

Mental retardation was rated the fifth most seriously handicapping condition in the United States by the President's Panel in 1962, and both its etiology and manifestations include social components of the greatest importance. The paradox of this relative neglect by social work, therefore, demands a searching explanation. The reasons undoubtedly go beyond the scope of this profession's responsibility, but here we shall narrow our focus to one factor which seems central to this enigma—the developing trends in social work in this country and the varying emphases in service they

---

* Reprinted in 1959 as *The Mentally Retarded in Society* by Columbia University Press.

have dictated. We are emphasizing this historical perspective because only by understanding the circumstances that have been responsible for excluding the retarded from many sources of social work help can we envisage future developments that will be more favorable to this client category. To appreciate the influence of past trends on current practice, as it relates to the profession generally and to the retarded specifically, a brief analysis is needed of the evolution of social work, particularly its long-standing relationship with the older sister discipline of medicine.

Social work, as we understand it today, has developed as a hybrid compounded of charitable intentions for relieving the glaring social distress and injustices experienced by individuals and groups of individuals, and the application to these pervasive problems of poverty and social maladjustment of a scientific analysis which extends beyond immediate relief to a comprehension of causation and to the prevention of recurrence. It was brought into being by the serious social dislocations that resulted from urbanization, mass immigration, cyclical unemployment, and the failure of existing methods for relieving social distress (embodied in the Poor Law and in the sporadic efforts of private charity) to meet these exigencies. The philosophy of deterrence under which the Poor Law operated, the bureaucratic rigidities that this negative attitude created, and the minimal support it received from public funds rendered this system completely ineffectual for dealing with the large and complex problems of poverty and destitution created by uncontrolled economic activity. Furthermore, its essential structure embodied elements that were bound to both perpetuate and even increase certain patterns of social dysfunction. The minimal subsistence level of outdoor relief was psychologically demoralizing and lacked any rehabilitative purpose, while the conditions within the county poor houses invariably bred more problems than they solved. The unsupervised accommodations in which destitute individuals of both sexes, all ages and all conditions (from physical illness to extreme mental disorder) were indiscriminately herded together, produced a subculture existing at the lowest possible material level in a setting that lacked even minimal social mores. As a result these individuals invariably declined into a condition of physical degradation and moral defeat that was virtually irredeemable.

The new system of social welfare that emerged to deal with the escalating social problems of the times developed along two different lines although its goals were related to a unified social philosophy.[5] One was the Settlement House movement, which concentrated on providing assistance to people living within a given geographical location in the hope of solving, or at least mitigating, the more serious problems which interfered with social functioning in the community. In today's parlance it was a multipurpose service facility, and one important feature of its varied repertoire was to organize the working people within the community into a force for ameliorating some of the inequitable and exploitatory practices of industry. This concern with the economic basis of social distress demonstrated the scientific bias that the new social work movement was developing, in that attention was going beyond the immediate relief of individual instances of social maladjustment to the broader causes underlying them.

This social action thrust was accompanied by the recognition that for some problems an individualized approach was required, particularly where the factors leading to the social breakdown affected specific individuals as well as being part of the wider social context within which they functioned. For this more circumscribed type of need a different social work operation evolved, the prototype of which was the Charity Organization Society. Originating in London in 1869, it was introduced into the United States in 1877; the first office was opened in Buffalo, N.Y.[6] The organization's explicit aims were to replace the mass-oriented relief concept of the Poor Law, and its bureaucratic inflexibility, with an approach that would tackle the problems of poverty in a rational fashion, and also demonstrate the importance of a scientific understanding of causes and effects. The first objective was to be achieved by coordinating the work of the myriad private charitable bodies into a single effort, while the latter was embodied in a thorough evaluation of all the circumstances relating to an individual and his request for help. This method was borrowed from the practice of clinical medicine, and the techniques that physicians applied to physiological dysfunction—the identification of significant symptoms and the diagnosis of causation—were applied to the apparently similar situation of social dysfunctioning.

Given historical circumstances which produced social breakdown on the same massive scale as epidemic disease, and the recognition that these problems must be attacked on a rational basis deriving from scientific analysis, it was logical that the emerging profession of social work should adopt as its model the well-established profession of medicine, with which it shared many problems. The subsequent history of social work in America is intimately bound up with this identification. If we examine the developing entity of social work during the half century between 1875 and 1925 for resemblances to the medical field, we can see two trends working themselves out in these professional fields during this period but with slightly different emphases in each.

In the sphere of medicine these two trends were, first, the long-established practice of clinical medicine, which dealt with the effects of disease on individuals, and second, the newer field of public health, which was concerned with the environment as a source of disease. These two facets of health care are simulated in social work by the sociodiagnostic approach,[7] primarily related to the individual and his personal problems of adjustment to the environment to which he belonged, and by the community social action orientation,[8] directed toward the environment and its adverse effects on individuals and their social functioning. In both professional fields the two aspects of care in the clinical and public health patterns are fundamentally concerned with the same problem, or problem-complex; their differences lie in where the major emphasis is placed. In the clinical frame of reference this is placed on the individual—how he reacts, for example, to the disease entity of the tubercule bacillus or to the social trauma of unexpected income loss by prolonged unemployment, and what medical or social remedies will best restore him to normal functioning, in health or in social terms. From the public health viewpoint the focus shifts from the affected individual (or group of individuals) to the physical and social environment to which he belongs, and the factors within it that have been responsible for his physical and social disease. In the medical situation just cited these may be insanitary conditions of living and working which foster the growth of the disease-producing pathogen and facilitate its spreading; in the social situation it is likely to be a complex of economic factors that have dislocated the machinery of industrial production and distribution.

Despite their differing foci of operation, there was a close fundamental relationship between the two forms of social work at the beginning, and the techniques each developed for discharging their special function had many common factors and fed into each other. *Social Diagnosis,* for example, while it represented the most explicit expression of the scientifically based principles applied to the *individually focused* casework approach, also had implications for the wider social action approach in that the practice of applying scientifically formulated diagnostic criteria to problems of social maladjustment contributed significantly to an objective understanding of the complexity of the social phenomena that were involved in an individual's social dysfunctioning. This was a healthy and essential counteraction to the Victorian conviction that poverty and social degradation were the results of moral weakness and/or bad genetic inheritance. This more objective attitude was equally necessary for dealing with problems of social malfunction in separate individuals or in the aggregate, since it alone could form the foundation of a social work program on a rationally planned basis. Viewed in retrospect over half a century the two aspects of social work just described constituted an effective and well-balanced program which distributed attention and resources equally between the specific instances of distress that required an immediate remedy and the general environmental phenomena that required a long-term, fundamental solution. For example, the widowed mothers with young children whom Mrs. Shaw Lowell cites in her COS papers in 1898 [9] needed the individualized help of a regular financial subsidy, and support and guidance in managing their family affairs which the Charity Organization Society of New York could provide, just as their working counterparts in Chicago needed the day care center that was started in Hull House in 1889.[10] Both women and their hard-pressed families indirectly needed the social action thrust that eventually resulted in federal legislation for the public maintenance of income for fatherless families.

Unfortunately this well-balanced beginning was not sustained, and the next phase introduced a serious bias which tipped the bulk of the profession's well-developed resources (in terms of intellectual commitment, manpower, money, and philosophical values) toward the individual clinical approach, while the more socially oriented methods declined in importance. This lopsided trend was a consequence of the profession's close adherence to clinical medicine as its disciplinary mentor, and particularly of the reinforcement that this model received when social work extended allegiance beyond the scope of general medicine to the specialized branch of psychiatry and espoused with singular devotion the psychodynamic theories of behavior derived from Freud. This psychiatric orientation, based on a functional rather than an organic frame of reference, was the perfect medium for cementing this alliance of skills and concepts between the two professions of medicine and social work, because while its origins were in the physiological sphere of neurology, its major preoccupations were with problems of social adjustment, particularly as expressed in interpersonal relationships. This added a social dimension to the clinical therapeutic regime, and the almost symbiotic union that developed with the older and more prestigious discipline of psychiatry deflected social work from its original purpose of helping to solve problems of social origin and functioning. Instead it developed an intense preoccupation with the intrapsychic forces operating in the lives of individuals which, when carried to extremes, distorted the identity, functions, and goals of the profession and fostered practices that have had several unfortunate results.

The first disadvantage to treatment based principally on psychoanalytical techniques is that the time-consuming process of long-term therapy can by its very nature serve only a limited number of clients. There is also qualitative exclusion in that a treatment requiring regular and frequent visits, and the use of verbal and intellectual skill, is impractical for a large sector of clients who have neither the material nor cultural resources for involving themselves in such a regimen. Second, because of the choice of depth psychology as its therapeutic terrain, this trend in social work has encouraged an abnormal preoccupation with pathology to the detriment of more positive approaches which concentrate on modifying adaptive behavior patterns even when underlying pathological processes are not accessible. Third, it has distracted attention from noxious factors in the environment, which may be the more fundamental cause of the individual's problem, and dwelt on the personal disabilities of clients, which are often only symptomatic of deeper and more general social malaise.

As a result of this psychological orientation, social work until very recently was placed in the situation of withholding help from many client groups because their pattern of disability or source of maladjustment did not fit into the psychodynamic frame of reference. This is the clue to why the profession has not given dynamic attention to the problems of the retarded. Neither of the two causes postulated for their condition—biological impairment within the individual organism or sociocultural deprivation within the environment—lend themselves to the diagnostic approach based on psychoanalytical thinking, nor has the maladaptive social behavior that characterizes the disability been regarded as a suitable target for this form of treatment. Furthermore, since the sociological components are often of greater significance in this condition than intrapsychic ones, an approach that focuses primarily on the individual's malfunctioning and ignores the weight of environmental influences cannot be either appropriate or adequate. In general the totality of problems associated with retardation are not amenable to the interpersonal treatment modality alone and effective service must also draw on the two other methods of social work; namely, group work and community organization. In addition the profession must also reconceptualize the sort of remedial and rehabilitative goals that are most suitable for this client group. For this broader approach some of the profession's existing patterns of operation must be refashioned and fresh ones devised to encompass the more recently identified areas of need.

To revert to the analogy between medical and social work practice, it would appear that the latter has now reached a stage in its evolutionary development when it should revive its earlier tentative

identification with the public health model and refocus its concern
beyond the scope of individual inadequacy to environmental forces
and their contribution to the particular manifestations of social maladjustment that recur so frequently. This trend has already become
evident in the general field of social work and social welfare,[11] and
because of its greater preventive implications, it will have more
relevance to mental retardation than did the earlier problem-solving
model. To state this seeming paradox more explicitly, the extremely
wide and varied repertoire of social issues associated with retardation
invites preventive intervention at a series of levels, depending on the
type, degree, and source of the *social* disability involved. *Primary*
prevention of both mild and more serious types of retardation may
be feasible if a concerted attack is made upon the environmental
pressures that have been postulated (and to some extent confirmed)
as active contributory factors in the genesis of this handicap among
the poor.[12] Here can be seen a close resemblance between the social
control of certain environmental conditions associated with tuber-
culosis (i.e., bad housing, overcrowding, poor ventilation, and inadequate nutrition owing to low income), which has drastically
reduced the incidence of this disease over the past fifty years.[13]
This public health approach lends itself with equal cogency to the
social factors which can lead to retarded development or functioning—that is, low standards of health among pregnant mothers in
the poverty group, physiological trauma during birth and the neonatal period due to inadequate medical care, physical and psychological neglect in early childhood because of poor parental care and
disorganized family life.

From another angle psychological stress and dysfunctioning in
families may be prevented if the right sort of social intervention
(and in this context the word "social" embraces medical, educational, and other techniques besides those of social work) can be
offered at certain crisis points in the life cycle of a family with a
retarded member, the first and most crucial being the point of discovery that the child is retarded. This is a form of *secondary*
prevention in that the potentially crippling effects of having a
mentally defective child are mitigated by appropriate help; this
fits in with the concepts of prevention in social work postulated

by Rapoport and Wittman.[14] According to their theory, prevention of social breakdown may be averted if help is provided for the *healthy* members of society at junctures of potential crisis. In the field of retardation there is less difficulty in identifying the socially healthy members and offering them this prophylactic crisis intervention than in other vulnerable groups because the crisis-producing agent—the child's handicap—is visible, often comes early to health or social welfare agencies for treatment, and in most cases the bewildered or overwrought family is only too anxious for help.

For the residue of social problems that are inseparable from retardation of organic origin, a more conventional rehabilitative approach is necessary. In such cases permanent damage has occurred, with lasting impairment to social functioning, and social therapy consists in making available a range of complex services that will minimize the disabling effects of chronic defect, whether these impinge most upon the affected individual or his family. This pattern of intervention represents *tertiary* prevention in that it diminishes social disability and dependence.

There is also a fourth preventive component which has great pertinence to retardation; this is concerned with identifying, establishing, and sustaining factors within the total environment that *promote* healthy social functioning. This aspect of the public health model, which we are trying to translate into the realm of social work and social welfare, is of special value to the retarded because their survival as human beings and their social development depend ultimately on creating a social milieu tailored to their specific needs. The concept of a therapeutic or restitutory milieu has wider application than to the special client group of the mentally retarded and contains significant implications for social work in general in that it may provide a model for similar therapeutic situations for other client groups whose rehabilitation depends primarily on a deliberate manipulation of their environment.

Moreover, a construct geared to meeting the atypical exceptional needs of a category of individuals who share a wide and diversified range of social handicaps may produce data on the factors that appear to be significant in aiding social functioning, which in turn will throw light on the essential components of the health-promoting social system. For example, a careful retrospective scrutiny of the environmental conditions to which large and easily identified groups of retarded children have been exposed (e.g., state institutions or special classes in the community) might point up the factors in their background that seem highly correlated with this condition. The original work on deprivation by Skeels[15] and his colleagues is a prototype of this which has led to more recent discoveries about the effects of this particular environmental hazard (institutional deprivation) on a wider group of children.[16]

The idea of being able to identify positive health factors by studying the specialized needs of a conspicuously disabled subgroup may strike a paradoxical note, but it is just because the mentally retarded have a clearly identified deficiency which renders them highly susceptible to both positive and negative factors in their environment that this particular handicap provides such a good index for measuring the environment's deficits and assets. The social dysfunctioning of this group represents a discrepancy between the environmental demands and the individual's capacity to meet them, and on the analogy that good health is usually identified by comparison with its opposite, it should be possible to calculate what would convert the normal environment into a therapeutic one by plotting the areas of their malfunctioning and then introducing special measures to offset this behavioral lag. The exploitation of these specially devised social facilities is based on the principle of compensation and, like the prosthetic appliance to replace a limb or insulin therapy for diabetes, they are geared to correcting the imbalance between the retarded individual's innate subnormal capacity and the adjustive pattern of behavior he must achieve to survive. It is in the process of trying to compensate *deliberately* for what the retarded lack *inherently* that the socially healthy milieu is both conceptualized and created.

This idea of structuring a total therapeutic milieu for the socially inadequate and vulnerable retarded individual and his family has relevance to an important concept that has emerged in social work and social welfare philosophy in the past decade. This is the institutionalization (in the sociological meaning of the word) of social welfare which is more explicitly contained in the concepts of *social utilities* and *developmental provision*.[17] Both these ideas originated in regard to the legitimate needs of normal people which have been created by certain elements arising out of the social phenomena of modern industrial life. Although the utilization of social services provided within this conceptual framework is intended to be free of eligibility criteria and unrelated to *personal* inadequacy, they may be made available on the basis of *status*. By this token the mentally retarded, who have a clearly defined long-term functional incapacity, share a common status which qualifies them for the sort of sustained social services (taken in their broadest sense) that their poor functioning requires. In addition there is a category of help, therapy, and rehabilitation as case services by right which is provided as need dictates and on the basis of professional diagnostic judgment. This type of service provision also applies to the retarded in that not every individual requires identical treatment; in fact with such a widely varied client group this would be impossible as well as undesirable. However certain services—both generic and specialized—are essential for the mentally retarded, irrespective of functioning levels. Early case-finding procedures— for example, diagnosis and evaluation—are basic to the provision of other services such as education, training, family support, and vocational rehabilitation, just as financial support and living provision are necessary at the other end of the life span when the original natural family environment has disappeared. *Institutional provision* is also relevant to retardation because some of its problems stem from societal conditions which either impose too high a demand upon adaptive capacity or create environmental pressures that produce or foster retarded development.

In order to embody this principle of social utilities, institutional provision, or the therapeutic milieu, in a practical reality, we must examine what is needed to produce such a benign setting and try to conceptualize an ideal environment. To illustrate, we shall look at the patterns of services to the young retarded adult within the moderate to severe range of retardation because this individual demonstrates most clearly the discrepancy between his social capacity and the role he is expected to perform by normal adult standards. It is to fill this gap that the therapeutic network of services must be devised. To demonstrate the vital need for such help, we shall close the chapter with two case studies which illustrate the difference in social adjustment that the retarded individual and his family achieve when services are available and utilized and when they are not.

Such a client requires a well-articulated battery of social services to meet his own complex needs and those of his family. Successful social adjustment as an adult depends on good health care from birth, recognition of the defect and its social implications as soon as it becomes apparent, appropriate training or education, and a stable family or substitute family situation, with all the scope for informal socializing that this implies. In adulthood the primary need is for industrial training which will lead either to productive economic employment or to work in a sheltered industrial facility. Accompanying this primary prerequisite should be provision for social activities with peers. Support and guidance must also be available for the family to help them provide a materially and emotionally stable home, and if this is not available, foster or group home care should be provided which will permit the retarded client to live and function in the community.

Underpinning these specific services should also be a social welfare resource readily available to offer consultation and intervention at critical points in the individual's life and to ensure continuity of planning when crucial changes occur—such as the breakup of the nuclear family and transfer to a substitute home. The overall therapeutic orientation of this sustained continuum of social services is not directed primarily at meeting *specific acute* problems in personal adjustment (though that inevitably is included in the therapeutic endeavor) but at *sustaining* the retarded individual and the responsible adults who support him in the *chronic problem situation* which results from the handicap. This is achieved by creating a social setting which will foster the development of resources for positive response and action within the client, whether this happens to be the retarded individual or his family or both. The case histories of Michael Rogers and Sylvia Leavett will show what may or may not happen with such intervention.

Michael Rogers is twenty-three and moderately retarded owing to organic brain impairment. He lives in an urban community that has fairly advanced services for the retarded. He therefore attended a special class for trainable children in the local public school system from the age of seven. Here he made such good progress that he was reevaluated and transferred to the class for educable children at the age of twelve. In high school, he received some simple prevocational training and after graduating at eighteen he entered an industrial training center; here over a three-year period he learnt simple industrial routine tasks and good work habits, together with such social skills as traveling by public transport, essential to the normal working situation. From the training center he was placed in a sheltered workshop where he is engaged in contract work for a small light industry firm in the neighborhood. This is paid on a piece basis, and his present weekly output earns about one-third of a normal wage. This is expected to improve as his speed quickens.

Michael comes from a stable lower-middle-class family (the father is a longshoreman and is in regular well-paid employment). The family consists of both parents, two older and one younger sibling, plus a large circle of interested and supportive relatives. His parents were alerted to his condition shortly after birth, and throughout his early childhood they received a good deal of guidance from their local pediatrician and from the staff of the special diagnostic center to which Michael was referred for evaluation at the age of four. As a result of this early intervention and the help it provided in understanding the implications of the handicap and their reactions to it, the parents have achieved a fair degree of philosophical acceptance, which is reflected in the way Michael's deviances have been presented to the normal siblings and other family members. As soon as the other children became aware of Michael's special characteristics, they were given a factual explanation and encouraged to regard him as a regular member of the family in spite of his differences. His brothers and sisters and their friends have, therefore, accepted him as an individual, even though his limited abilities frequently preclude his joining their activities. To counteract any feelings of exclusion, his parents enrolled him in a recreational group for retarded children, and from this early contact he has moved on to join an adult group run by the same organization, which has various social and sports activities during the week and the weekends and a summer camp where he spends his vacation.

Because of these special facilities available to him, Michael's pattern of life is not essentially different from that of his peers. He travels to work on his own, puts in a full working day, earns a regular if small wage, and has a circle of friends and companions among those he works with and meets at the recreational center. Through the self-reliance that his family has fostered, he has a life of his own (which is minimally supervised by his parents) and is therefore not totally dependent on the rest of his family for emotional support or social intercourse. This leaves his parents and siblings free to pursue their separate activities and interests, though they also have many joint family affairs which automatically include Michael. Moreover, as his parents are active members of the local parent organization and closely involved in enlisting the sympathetic understanding of the community in the problems of the mentally handicapped, he has always been exposed to a wide variety of people who have an understanding of his disability and accept him as an individual. In an emergency there are many people who would temporarily assume his care, if his family were unable to do so. In such an environment as this, even his quite seriously handicapping disability and the stress that might have resulted have been mitigated for both the retarded individual and for his family. The social adjustment of the total family unit and of the individual members has not been significantly affected by the initially traumatizing event of a chronically handicapped child. Furthermore, the community, through a firsthand contact with a retarded individual, is developing a new perspective and greater tolerance toward individual disability and deviances.

A contrasting picture is presented by Sylvia Leavitt, who is the same age and has the same degree of mental impairment but in a less obvious form since her physical appearance is normal and even pleasing. Her parents have always found it hard to accept her obvious limitations, refused special clinical help in her preschool years, and bitterly opposed her entering the special trainable class in school. When she reached graduation age, her parents did not permit her to go on to the industrial training center so that she remains at home helping about the house in a desultory way and exasperating her rather volatile mother by her extremely slow ways. A good deal of chronic tension is thereby generated between the two, into which the father is drawn when he comes home from work. The one younger brother, who has always been very jealous of, and antagonistic toward, Sylvia, spends most of his spare time outside of the house, rarely brings his friends home, and is only perfunctorily involved with his sister, who feels slighted by this lack of attention. In this situation the girl occupies the ambiguous social status of a dependent child and is so regarded by people in her locality. She is very much frustrated by not being able to join in the activities of the normal girls around her, realizes she is different from them without knowing why, and as a result is chronically discontented, the boredom of which state she occasionally varies with a bout of hysterics or temper tantrums.

Sylvia's emotional life is entirely centered on her parents whose own life has been attenuated in having to meet her level of needs and interests, and all social activities are shared by the three, with the brother always opting out. This "permanent trio" pattern has tended to cut down social contacts except with very close and accepting friends who are prepared to include Sylvia in all their invitations. The family unit of two parents and two children has been eroded, with the younger child having prematurely severed his attachment to the family in late adolescence and the remaining members having coalesced into a tight-knit group geared exclusively to meeting the specialized needs of the one disabled member. There is considerable marital disharmony. The father, who is a railroad worker, puts in a good deal of overtime to curtail the time that he spends in the house; the mother has developed a recurrent skin condition of psychological origin; and both parents are riddled with unconscious resentment about the impasse and a nagging anxiety about what will happen to their daughter when they are no longer available to provide this overprotective setting for her. In this instance there is a double irony in the situation, in that a special environment has been created for the retarded child by the parents;

but because it does not contain the necessary ingredients to compensate for Sylvia's functional deficiencies and widen her scope of social interaction, it is *not* a therapeutic milieu. Further, the emotional and social lives of the whole family have been stunted and diminished because of its narrowed scope. The exact opposite situation prevailed in Michael's case, where the social resources of the community were harnessed to neutralize the specific handicap of the one individual, in turn assuring the normal and healthy development of the family group as a whole.

The creation of this special benign environment lies very much at the heart of social work, and for this innovatory concept to develop into a viable reality it must have the support of all the accumulated skills and expertise of the profession. The acceptance of the retarded subgroup by the broader social group depends on much more than the simple fact of setting up a specialized facility; it is equally important to establish an informed understanding about the condition and its handicaps at the same time. To bring this about requires a concerted effort to educate both individuals and groups of individuals within the community on the causes of retardation, its effects on the individual and on his family, the level of functioning that can be expected from different levels of disability, and from this the potential for social participation of each individual, given the opportunity. At the same time the retarded themselves and their families may have to be taught how to take advantage of the new status that society is prepared to offer.

This task involves a skillful utilization of all the basic social work concepts and techniques as they apply to such different areas of involvement as *individual personal* relationships, *group attitudes,* and the wider complexities of *interactive patterns within social systems.* For example, the retarded individual who has experienced a long record of failure (whether in school, at work, or in social relationships) or the family who is still numbed by the advent of a retarded baby will both need intensive help through the *individualized social casework* approach to prepare them to accept wider social involvement and the resulting therapeutic influences. Concurrently, the skeptical and suspicious reaction that mental retardation often evokes in normal members of the community may need modifying by *group discussions and involvement* before they can arrive at a compassionate understanding of the problem and the deviances it entails. In a situation which demands so much contrived manipulation of the social environment, *community organization* will unquestionably play a large part in creating and supporting the therapeutic milieu. The following chapters will discuss in greater detail how these three methods can be used to provide the triple-faceted pattern of social care for the retarded and their families delineated in this chapter as the fundamental approach to their problems. Although they will be treated separately, each method of social work will be considered in terms of its relevance to the therapeutic milieu.

Once this frame of reference is accepted, many of the current techniques of social work and the other helping professions involved in mental retardation will be seen to contain elements that reinforce the concept. The notion of specially devised regimes runs through all forms of care for the retarded. In the beginning this was expressed in the geographically segregated institutional establishments described in Chapter 2. Later on, colony[18] and family care,[19] which developed out of the custodial system, made a limited attempt to extend the intramural therapeutic milieu beyond the institution's walls to the world outside. Today the continuum of care, which envisages a comprehensive pattern of rehabilitative services for the mentally retarded of all grades of disability at successive phases of life, has moved a step further and is shifting the therapeutic milieu into the heart of the community at large.

4 THE APPLICATION OF THE THREE SOCIAL WORK METHODS

IN THE foregoing chapter an overall frame of reference has been postulated within which social services and social work on behalf of the mentally retarded might be most effectively conceived and executed. This is the concept of the total therapeutic milieu, which has the dual purpose of compensating for the specific functional difficulties of the retarded and of reinforcing the caretaking efforts of normal individuals and groups in their environment. The vital role of social work in promoting and maintaining such a milieu was projected briefly, and the remainder of the book will explore the ways in which casework, group work, and community organization can be most effectually utilized. First, however, we need to discuss briefly two special features of mental retardation that apply to all three methods: (1) certain characteristics of the condition; and (2) the necessity of employing the generic social work approach to the variegated problems associated with the handicap.

The account of mental retardation in its many forms given in Chapter 1 has indicated the complex origins and manifestations of the condition and its potential presence throughout an entire lifetime. This chronological span combined with the complexity of the disability results in a wide gamut of social dysfunctioning on the part of the retarded and in an equally wide assortment of adjustment problems among normal individuals and social institutions upon whom the disability impinges. The variety of problems and stress that may be associated with *one* category of the condition at *one* life-stage—for example, those surrounding a severely retarded child of school age—are extended in several different directions when there are four separate grades of social malfunctioning to consider and when the disabilities within these categories are complicated by age groupings. The interweaving of the two important components of social adaptation—chronological maturity and functional capacity—results in a complex mesh of adjustive patterns and problems requiring a broad, imaginative, and flexible range of social work stratagems.

There is additional confusion in the use of the term "mental retardation" to denote a condition of implied homogeneity; in fact, two major categories are subsumed under this common name, which though subject to the same legal criteria actually present very different types of problems. It is necessary to distinguish clearly between them because each presents a different kind of maladjustment and different requirements for rehabilitation. They are (1) the category of mild retardation, which accounts for around eight-tenths of the identified retarded population; and (2) the remainder, comprising the three lower grades of more severe handicap.*

Individuals in the first category, who resemble their normal peers in appearance and behavior, have a much greater potential for social rehabilitation. If retardation of the mild variety is assumed to be at least partially a response to gross social deprivation, the problem takes on another dimension in that there is a possibility of reversing the condition by appropriate interventive measures.[1] Furthermore, it is important to realize that both the etiology and manifestations of mild retardation have much in common with the other socially disabling conditions that occur in sociopathic environments—e.g., delinquency or psychiatric disturbance. The social problems presented by this segment of the retarded are closely related to those of the cultural group to which they belong, and the principal difference between them and their peers of *normal* intelligence may be inferior resources for surviving the impact of stresses to which they are exposed. In these circumstances, what in effect constitutes retardation is the differential susceptibility to massive negative social influences and an idiosyncratic response which is manifested in

---

* Figures in the 1966 Report of the President's Committee were 89 percent for the mild group and 11 percent for the three other grades combined.

depressed intellectual functioning rather than emotional disorder. The possibility that some minimal biological impairment contributes to, or determines, this susceptibility has been postulated by clinicians in the field,[2] but from the social worker's vantage point it is the combination of this susceptibility (whatever its origin) interacting with gross social hazard that is the principal focus of concern. Alleviation of the social problems of this numerically large and mildly disabled client category must therefore include a preventive as well as a rehabilitative aspect.

In the other category of retardation, comprising the more severely handicapped, the disability is almost always organic in origin and accompanied by physical components. The social problems of this category are in general qualitatively different from those of the mildly retarded and tend to be more specialized. Another socially significant difference is that in this more impaired group the handicap, although it is often susceptible to training and behavioral therapy techniques, is basically irreversible; and the problems it creates are chronic and often impose serious adjustments, both for the affected individual and for the normal individuals in his social environment.

The family with a seriously retarded member invariably has to adapt its pattern of functioning to encompass the unusual care that the retarded child requires, and where there is an additional serious physical handicap, actual management may impose serious stresses. There is also the psychological difficulty of accepting a defective child with conspicuous disability and marked social deviance.[3] In contrast to the mildly retarded who *share* the social problem of their entire cultural environment, the more obviously retarded and their families experience social difficulties that tend to *separate* them from their group.

The different nature and origins of the social stress associated with these two major categories of retardation lead to differences in the forms and goals of social work. Social work with the more seriously retarded may need to focus on helping their families adjust to certain aspects of their social situation, such as chronic disability and dependence, and to live with it as comfortably as they can. In dealing with the mildly retarded in culturally deprived families, the opposite aim is necessary and the emphasis should be on community action to mobilize clients' efforts to change their adverse social situation. The very fact that mild retardation, when it is of sociocultural origin, is potentially preventable and can be remedied to a marked degree demands that the negative current social conditions affecting the mildly retarded *not* be adjusted to. By contrast, a certain degree of resignation to the irreversible nature of organically determined retardation is necessary if a family is to achieve a balanced acceptance of the unusual social problems that the handicap creates.

When considering the social problems of the mentally retarded, it is important to bear in mind this rather marked dichotomy between the mild and the more serious grades of handicap and to be clear about the groups to which specific problems apply. Otherwise, observations lose their relevance and in some contexts may be downright erroneous. To talk about the *chronic dependence of* the mentally retarded without specifying that this applies principally to the more seriously handicapped evokes an incorrect picture of universal dependence and inadequacy. For the mildly retarded this is not generally substantiated by documented employment records or by the more significant, if less tangible, fact that after leaving school many of them melt into the community at large.

This point leads into the second important consideration for social work with the mentally retarded, *which* is the *chronic* nature of the disability as it affects the *second* category of retarded described above (that is, the less than 20 percent in the three lower grades whose defect is invariably organic in origin) and the way this inherent factor determines the approach to their social problems. While chronicity is not exclusive to mental retardation but is also a part of an increasingly large number of conditions which produce problems in social functioning and adjustment, it has to be recognized that the chronicity of retardation has certain features not found in other chronic conditions which give it a distinctive character.

The first of these distinguishing features is that the disability is of lifelong duration and often reveals itself at birth or in early childhood. This early beginning adds a dimension of *acute immediate shock* to that of *chronic stress* which is implicit in the handicap, and therefore demands a double and simultaneous adjustment on the part of the family to meet the two different traumatic factors. The second point is that this innate chronicity of mental retardation is accompanied by a fairly severe degree of impairment, producing both quantitative and qualitative disability which is rarely— if ever—found in such a formidable combination in other conditions or situations of social handicap. To illustrate: an adult suffering from a cerebral accident may be reduced to the same state of helplessness as a severely or profoundly retarded child, but this trauma does not usually occur till late middle-age. Likewise, though certain physical illnesses, such as cystic fibrosis, hemophilia, or the sequelae of poliomyelitis, occur in childhood, the areas of impairment are more circumscribed than those affected by the pervasive condition of retardation, and overall development is not stultified. Further, the chronicity of dependence resulting from chronic handicap is different in the two conditions: with the former it is limited to physical needs, whereas with the latter there is also psychological dependence which prevails throughout life. Management and care of a child with a serious health problem whose intellectual capacity is unimpaired is very different from that of a retarded child. The child with a health problem can in some respects simulate the social role of normal peers and physical maturation will eventuate in the social status of adulthood, however circumscribed. This the retarded child will never achieve.

Stemming from this long-term disability and its social concomitant of chronic dependence is a third dimension of chronic stress—the persistent vulnerability of the family or constellation of other individuals by whom the retarded member is protected and sustained. In contrast to the *supposedly static* nature of the handicap itself, the complex of social stresses that can result from the interaction of the retarded individual's chronic disability with the shifts in psychological pressures, social roles and life circumstances within the family presents an extremely *dynamic* situation. This is not only an appropriate target for professional skills but also an inescapable responsibility in that a much larger area of social interaction and potential dysfunction becomes involved when the initial problem of retardation is seen in the context of the total environment.[4]

These triple components of chronic stress—disability, depend-

ence, and family vulnerability—present the social worker with the
challenge of meeting the special social needs of the retarded client
and of providing support for the significant adults (usually immediate family or relatives) who have the long-term responsibility
for his care. For the latter there must be readily available intensive
help to meet the potential crises which surround this precariously
placed social unit and which may be set in motion at any moment
by the high vulnerability of the chronically retarded and their low
margin of social adjustment. *In some respects it can be said that the
essential characteristic of social work with the retarded is determined
by the chronic nature of the handicap, the duality of the problems
it creates, and the resultant need for special stratagems to cope with
the constant interplay of chronic and acute needs.* In considering
this unusual facet of the handicap it becomes imperative to distinguish between the *comprehensive chronic "problem condition"* of
mental retardation, and its accompanying social dysfunction, and
the *acute problems of social adjustment* that may arise from it. The
nature of these acute problems varies with the degree of adaptive
impairment, age of the individual, and sociocultural and physical
environment within which they occur. They will be examined more
closely in the subsequent chapter on casework.

To encompass the potentially wide spectrum of deviant functioning inherent in mental retardation and the social crises it is liable
to precipitate, social work must operate on two planes. For the
acute and emergent aspects of need it must be able to disentangle
from this complex of factors the exact pressures that constitute the
immediate problem at any given moment, and by identifying their
most vulnerable point of impact, define a circumscribed area for
effective helping. The segmented approach implied in this must,
however, be carried out within an overall diagnostic perception of
the total problem-complex or service will be uncoordinated, frag-
mentary, and inadequate. When, for example, a family has difficulty
in accepting the fact that their school-age child needs a special
educational regime, the immediate focus of help has to be the
psychological pressures that this traumatic news has created for
them and the crisis into which they have been precipitated. However, the child's limited intellectual functioning is likely to be a

long-term problem which may never be completely solved and which will bring other difficulties in its train. Effective help in the situation will therefore depend on a recognition of the chronic components present, since denial of handicap on the part of parents invariably springs as much from anxiety about the future as from the current shock factors. The extent to which long-term aspects can be actively introduced by the social worker depends on how much the parents need to cling to their defensive denial at the current phase of stress and on whether they can be helped to move toward a more realistic appraisal of the situation, with the prospect of ongoing help as and when future hazards and needs are revealed.

The need to partialize the problem must also be tied in with the client's perception of it and the particular aspects he or she is ready to acknowledge and accept help with. If the impact of retardation and the tragedy it represents for the family are to be tolerated, its multiple pressures must very often be handled piecemeal, and it is incumbent upon social work to shape itself to this approach, even though it may not appear to be satisfactorily meeting all the different interlocking aspects of the whole problem. The fact that services are predicated upon the concept of a continuum covering all phases of development and functioning is an implicit acceptance of comprehensive need, but this does not necessarily mean that the retarded and their families can or should adopt such a complex or long-term view of their difficulties. In general, their coping resources are more effective when they are invested in meeting one aspect or phase of difficulty at a time. There are several reasons for this. First, the slow rate of development of a retarded child, together with the recent rapid increase in diagnostic and remedial techniques, now makes it difficult to predict competence of functioning over more than a short time span. For example, plans for a moderately retarded four-year-old cannot be projected beyond the next phase of social development, which is the educational period. Second, the extreme dependence of a retarded individual on the environment in both childhood and maturity means that significant change in life circumstances—for example the death or serious illness of a parent or a broken marriage—may substantially alter his existing life situation and necessitate fresh arrangements for his care. Furthermore, the environment may significantly affect his level of development and capacity for social adaptation according to whether it provides optimal or minimal opportunity for growth and learning. These factors underline the paradox inherent in retardation that while the problems it causes are long term, their alleviation invariably has to be conceived within much shorter periods.

Mental retardation, however, has its own particular momentum which dictates the need for help in a logical sequence. This momentum derives from the concept of developmental crises which punctuate the pattern of chronicity with recurrent stress phases for which intensive assistance may be required. The first and most crucial of these points of pressure is the initial discovery of the disability and its social implications, which can seriously damage the adaptive resources of the normal individuals concerned if skilled help is not immediately available. Next come the developmental stages of entry into education, onset of adolescence merging into chronological adulthood without corresponding social maturity, and finally the crisis of separation when the nuclear family group has, for one reason or another, to relinquish the care of the retarded individual. This inevitable succession of critical phases and events links the problem of retardation with the crisis theory of help. This will be explored more fully in the following chapter on casework.

In considering this significant component of chronicity it is important to remember that current social work thinking and practice are placing an increasing emphasis on chronic social problems of all kinds. Bess Dana[5] has drawn attention to changing health patterns in modern society, which make it imperative for medical social work to develop skills that can deal with chronic diseases, their social consequences of long-term disability and dependence, and hence the necessity for psychological adjustment to changed life patterns. In another sphere of social maladaptation, Carol Meyer cites isolation, social pressures, social injustice, social breakdown, depersonalization, and identity confusion as the major problems for social work.[6] This orientation toward chronic pressures that can be relieved or reduced but never entirely reversed or eliminated makes retardation an appropriate target for professional commitment as it is shaping up today.

A further important feature to be noted in regard to social work with the retarded is that—owing to the variations in social dependency among retarded individuals—the client role is less clearly defined in this area of handicap than in many other social problem areas. A necessary preliminary to discussing social work in all of the three methodologies is a consideration of who represents the primary client in this field and under what circumstances this primacy prevails. The social work client can be defined as the individual (or group of individuals) who is aware (or can be made aware) that he or she has a social problem, and who has enough incentive to accept professional help in trying to reduce its stressful effects. The capacity to make some changes in thinking and behavior that will favorably affect the situation which gave rise to the difficulty is included in motivation. Within this definition of being aware of a problem and having the will and capacity to work actively toward its solution, it is clear that many types of retarded individuals who are in need of social work help cannot in fact fulfill the client role properly. It is therefore important to redefine who constitutes the client when the major problem concerns mental retardation, and the extent to which each individual can participate in solving his problems has to be carefully assessed.

This capacity is inextricably bound up with the degree of impairment in social functioning that results from the subaverage intelligence which denotes retardation, and also with the way in which it manifests itself. Social dysfunction in a mildly retarded adult or adolescent may be revealed in a reactive behavior disorder, in delinquency, or in the chronic inability to remain employed. His chronological counterpart in the moderate or severe grades of retardation presents another type of social dysfunction which is expressed in a limited ability for independent self-care and impaired perception of his social role and the normal demands of his environment. Of these two types of mentally retarded individuals, the former probably can be treated as a client in his own right because his capacity for social involvement and communication is minimally impaired, while the latter, with his more serious degree of defect, is unable to assume this self-directing role. Instead, he is relegated to a *secondary* or *passive* client status, imposed upon him by his

disability and the social problems it evokes but in whose solution
he cannot have much active part. *Primary* or *active* clientship in
this situation therefore devolves upon the normal adult who has
responsibility for the retarded individual in those areas of functioning
he cannot manage for himself. With regard to the various social
work methods, the mildly retarded of adult status can usually function as clients in casework and group work settings, whereas individuals with more serious impairment may have only marginal and
mainly passive participation in casework but can assume a limited
active role in group work. The severely and profoundly retarded
have a totally passive client status, and active social work involvement falls entirely upon their families or other supporting adults.

This situation is best described as a *client-nexus*, in respect of
which there are two separate but closely involved sets of problems.
These are represented by the deficits of the retarded individuals and
the specialized needs they create, and the stresses that the normal
caretaking adults experience in the process of trying to meet these
needs. An example of this dual process is a retarded adult living with
elderly parents who requires some form of substitute care to relieve
stress in the home. The decision to request this is made by the
parents and they are most actively involved in the ensuing arrangement. However the end-product of the decision—namely, placement
in a specialized residential facility—is geared to the needs and disability of the retarded individual, in respect of which he or she
is a client. Social work measures to solve these situations must take
into account the needs of both sets of clients and wherever possible
should keep an even balance between the well-being of both. Plans
for relieving the family of a grossly defective member must have
built-in safeguards for the latter's welfare, not only on the ethical
grounds that as a client his well-being is of professional concern
but because the family may be unable to cooperate if they feel that
their difficulties are solved at the expense of the retarded member.

The special features of mental retardation that we have outlined
will exert some influence upon the way all three methods are applied
in practice, but there is a closer connection between certain of these
distinctive features and a particular method than others. The component of chronicity, for example, can be more easily dealt with

in the community organization frame of reference, because the provision of institutionalized social services, to which this method of social work is in part directed, is by its nature long term in character. By contrast, casework, in which the traditional goal has been client movement toward problem-solving, must accept several modifications to its theory and practice in order to absorb some of the insoluble problems with which retardation is surrounded. On the other hand, the strong individualizing component of casework makes it relatively easy to deal with the problem of differential clientship. The multidisciplinary aspect of work with the retarded, which involves a cooperative partnership of several people with different skills, has some features in common with group work; and this method, as we have shown, is useful in encompassing clients in the primary and secondary roles. These specific points support the contention that in the area of mental retardation social work must retain an essentially broad-based and flexible character which will permit all its methods to be utilized interchangeably, as well as the skills and resources from the other disciplines.

This leads us to the second part of our discussion, which is concerned with the modifications and innovations needed to make our current patterns of social work practice effective in dealing with the problems in this field of handicap. The first, and perhaps most important, determinant of social work must be a recognition that the multidisciplinary approach is essential for tackling the comprehensive adjustment problems created by this disability and that, because of the condition's complexity, rehabilitative measures must embrace as wide a range of therapeutic disciplines as possible. Interdependence among professional workers with different skills is an important feature of social and clinical rehabilitation in all fields, but for retardation it is an overriding necessity because the amalgam of factors that are involved in its etiology and in the resultant social pressures produces a problem-complex that cannot be effectively tackled by any one discipline alone.[7] Further, the adverse effects that retardation exerts upon *social functioning* at all levels demand that the ultimate aim of all remedial programs—regardless of what disciplinary field they derive from—must be to compensate for this *social deficiency*. Compensation may be expressed in regard to a range of developmental achievements—as, for example, in orthopedic care for a doubly handicapped child which enables him to walk and so increases his scope of developmental activity, or in psychological counseling to help an adolescent adjust to the norms of adult life.

The collaborative approach has considerable significance for social workers because of the particular role it imposes upon them. That is to say, within this broad context of social rehabilitation, the values and objectives of social work must inevitably wield a special influence. Thus it is necessary to identify and highlight the social implications inherent in all the therapeutic modalities that are concerned in the rehabilitation of the retarded, and it falls to the social worker operating in the multidisciplinary framework to do this. This will involve interpreting to colleagues with other professional orientations the social dimensions that must be considered when formulating overall treatment goals. These social factors may concern the social role and functioning of the retarded individual, factors in the environment that may help or hinder treatment, or the implications that the treatment program will have for the entire family group to which the retarded child or adult belongs. To give an example: It may be necessary to clarify the social value of treatment to a medical colleague whose primary focus is clinical, as illustrated in the case of a moderately retarded boy who developed a hearing loss in late adolescence. The specialist to whom he was referred did not initially recommend a hearing aid, as he questioned the boy's capacity to manage it and also did not appreciate the extra limitations that deafness placed on the boy's social adjustment. When the social worker explained that the boy was particularly fond of music and that his family were convinced they could teach him to use the appliance, it was prescribed and he soon mastered it perfectly. Without this extra dimension of understanding about the social factors involved, this boy's rehabilitative treatment would have been negated, his level of social participation and functioning greatly diminished, and the frustrations and difficulties of being deaf would probably have undermined his emotional adjustment and created extra stress for his family.

In order to ensure acceptance of her professional contribution by colleagues in other disciplines the social worker must be able to elucidate the precise nature of the social work approach, the skills involved, and its value to the overall treatment plan. It is often necessary to clarify why a social evaluation is vital to a treatment program which seems completely valid and straightforward to the professional colleague concerned with one specific treatment modality but does not in fact take into account dynamic social factors. For example, the cooperation of a mother in following through on a difficult but essential diet to counteract phenylketonuria in her baby may hinge on her personal emotions surrounding food, on the cultural attitudes toward scientific intervention in such a basic primitive activity, or even on the practical difficulties attached to the operation. It is the social worker's task to emphasize the importance that these factors may have for the success or failure of the medical regimen, and to see that they are also dealt with as crucial components of treatment.

Besides identifying and demonstrating her own specialized contribution, however, the social worker involved in the multifaceted problems of retardation must also develop a thorough appreciation of the part that other disciplines play in the rehabilitation of the retarded and must accept an understanding of their particular skills as a necessary adjunct to her own professional competence. In counseling around the psychological and social problems associated with schooling, for example, the social worker may need to know a good deal about the goals and techniques of special education in order to interpret its rehabilitative function to parents and secure their active cooperation. Working in a multidisciplinary context, therefore, demands a strong awareness of professional identity in that it poses the problem of preserving intact the unique and essential components of social work while keeping them open for the infusion of skills from other disciplines when the latter can appreciably add to the therapeutic endeavor.

Further, although it is legitimate to perceive social work as the core profession for helping the retarded because of the social character of their handicap, its contribution must also be recognized as partial and at times subordinate to the more cogent claims of other treatment modalities. It may, for example, be more important for a mother to devote her limited time to taking her child to a day care center for *his* training than to come to the social worker for counseling on *her* problems. One would hope that these two services would be synchronized to avoid the necessity of choice, but where they are not, the casework may have to receive lower priority. Likewise, the social worker may have to make sure that important social considerations are not overridden by those of older, more established disciplines that have a more clearly perceived value and role. For example, if bringing a child to a training facility imposes undue strain on the mother which redounds adversely on the rest of the family, this may have to be pointed out and the program suspended until some practical solution can be worked out. While other disciplines may be more preoccupied with the individual patient or client and the extent to which his disability will be alleviated by treatment, social work has to be concerned with its effect on everyone intimately associated with the primary client, and how it influences their interaction and social functioning.

Lastly, it is necessary to realize that very few of the treatment approaches are exclusive to one profession and that within the interdisciplinary team some functions are interchangeable. However, this recognition and the cooperative professional stance it implies may be seen as representing the maximum expression of social work's unique function since it underpins the conviction that the complex social phenomenon which is mental retardation is handled most effectively when the separate but interrelated efforts of several professions are coordinated into one complex effort rather than being applied as separate individual therapies. The social worker can be invaluable in reinforcing this situation by providing consultation to other colleagues when their special tasks encroach upon the area of social problems. Thus the public health nurse who visits a family to initiate a home-training program for a young retarded child may find herself drawn into dealing with social problems normally outside her immediate area of knowledge and competence. While this may sometimes necessitate referring the family directly to the social worker if the problems raised are very complex, it may often be better for the nurse to handle them since she has the most vital relationship with the family because of the help she is providing for the child. In such instances she may be able to do this in consultation with the social worker.

Similary, the social worker may need to draw on the different areas of expertise of her colleagues in her own special tasks—for example, bringing the nurse or doctor's expert knowledge of nutrition into counseling a mother on how to handle a rigid and dictatorial feeding pattern that a child has developed. Unless the mother can feel assured by an expert that withholding food will not *physically* damage the child, she is unlikely to cooperate in breaking through the *psychological* impasse that exists between them. Neither of these examples implies an abdication of the social worker's special function but rather an extended use of it.

The second significant feature affecting social work practice is that mental retardation, because of its diverse etiology and various manifestations of social disability and stress, cannot be treated as a single clearly delineated problem for which one or another specified form of social work help can be prescribed. Instead its complex range of problems is likely to require the application of all *three methods*, either *simultaneously* or as alternative plans *in sequence*. For example, within one family a moderately retarded school-age child may need group work services, his parents may need counseling around their attitudes toward him, and if a service the child may require later (for example, an industrial training facility) is lacking, the family and the community to which they belong may need help to involve themselves in community organization to obtain this facility. *Sequentially*, a married couple who feel very defeated at having a retarded child may move from individual and family counseling to group counseling with other parents similarly placed, out of which situation they may become actively involved in community organization to improve material conditions for their child. This *simultaneous-method approach* demands a flexibility of attitude toward the problems of retardation on the part of individual social workers, the agency providing the immediate service, and beyond these two the wider network of community services organized for the retarded. This reflects trends that are developing in social work practice in other problem areas. Services to children in their own homes, which is in the process of being defined as one of the emerging and significant services offered in the child welfare field,[8] emphasizes this same need to mobilize resources on a broad front by utilizing all three professional methods. This development contains important implications for training, professional identification with specific methodologies, and the way in which social service facilities are organized and coordinated.[9]

The third point at issue, which, like the previous ones, stems from the complex nature of retardation, relates to the question of whether the social problems associated with it are best dealt with in a *generic* or a *specialized* setting, and, from this consideration, whether the professional skills and resources required to meet the particular needs of the retarded should be derived from generic or specialized training and experience. Contrary to recent opinion in the social work field, which has been inclined to relegate retardation to its own esoteric corner, it is now being realized that social problems associated with this disability are most effectively combated by a judicious combination of generic and specialized skills and resources, whether this combination is in terms of the professional orientation of individual workers or in arrangements for reciprocal cooperation and consultation between generic and specialized agencies.

Since this is a very controversial issue, it may be helpful to examine briefly the arguments in its favor. First, the exclusive provision of separate specialized services for the retarded has contributed significantly to their social isolation, and fostered the stereotype of individuals fundamentally different from the so-called normal population. Involvement of retarded clients and their families in social services of a generic nature helps to reduce this alienation. Second, the encapsulation within a specially devised facility tends to narrow the scope of service potentially available for the retarded both in diversity of progam and amount. This in turn limits a perception of their needs. For example, the alternative forms of care provided by special schooling within the community or institutional placement offered very restricted regimes of therapy or rehabilitation which catered only to the component of subnormal intelligence and rarely dealt with the more complex symptomatology which we now recognize as part of retardation. Third, the wider scope of needs that has been revealed in recent years by the scientific knowledge emanating from the many disciplines concerned with retardation has demonstrated a massive gap in corresponding services; this can only be filled if existing social service structures incorporate the needs of the retarded into their repertoire. Fourth, mental retardation is now recognized as a problem that affects the entire family rather than the retarded individual alone;[10] and it is highly appropriate that the needs and problems of this wider client-nexus be served in a generic setting initially, even if the retarded individual requires different care which necessitates subsequent referral to a specialist agency. Further, since many of the characteristics, needs, and problems associated with retardation are common to other social problem areas and client groups, it is an economic disposition of resources for these common elements to be handled within a generic context instead of being siphoned off for specialist treatment.

This point becomes apparent when we examine the specialized services for the retarded and realize that they are primarily centered around a specific aspect of the handicap—i.e., the evaluation of medical and psychological factors which requires special diagnostic techniques, vocational training that utilizes particular training skills, institutional care that provides a special living regime. While all these specialized services should have an orientation to the family as well as to the retarded individual himself, it is a skewed approach to expect them to be the sole—or even the most effective—resources for meeting more generic problems associated with retardation. Family adjustment, residential placement, and protective care should be handled by agencies that have developed an expertise in dealing with these problems, and the wider area of social need—i.e., the need for placement for a child or counseling for the family on the difficulties of living with a retarded member—should determine the sort of service that is provided instead of the narrower criterion of the individual's retardation. This service should be given by the type of agency that has maximum competence in this area.

The generic social agencies or, to be more accurate, agencies not directly specializing in retardation, such as medical social work departments, child welfare agencies, family agencies, and institutions dealing with the psychiatrically disturbed and the delinquent, can in fact become the major resource of social work help for the retarded if they choose to assume this role. They are in a very good strategic position for case-finding, particularly in regard to clients with mild retardation who do not always come to specialized facilities or require specialized treatment. It can therefore serve as an effective first line of treatment through meeting the client's request for help when it is most needed, instead of referring him elsewhere which has such a damping effect on motivation and cooperation. The rationale that a nonspecialized agency is not equipped to deal with the problems relating to retardation is not valid, and when proffered as the reason for withholding service, it is likely to have an extremely discouraging effect on the distraught family since it implies a condition so esoteric and unamenable to normal helping procedures that special equipment is required to handle the very human needs and problems it gives rise to. This tendency to reject is slowly diminishing, and both the literature of social work and innovative projects indicate that the generic agencies are becoming much more receptive to the idea of serving retarded clients.[11]

This fact introduces our final point, which concerns the adaptations that social work and the social agencies in which it is practiced must make in order to meet the needs of the retarded and their families. This is little more than an extension of the two points already cited, in that the generic social work agencies must adopt the same approach toward the complex problems of retardation as is embodied in the multidisciplinary frame of reference within which a specialized retardation agency must operate. Thus the generic social agency or unit, as representing the core professional discipline most intimately concerned with retardation, must assume a primary responsibility for this handicapped group, and reinforce their own basic skills and expertise by borrowing the skills and knowledge that the specialized agencies have developed for handling this complex handicap. This may involve seeking the expertise of another discipline to clarify aspects of the problem that are currently outside of their existing body of professional knowledge and skills or the resources of the agency, or it may mean consultation from a social worker who has experience in retardation. For example, counseling a mildly retarded adult about his employment difficulties and the emotional and social problems associated with this area of failure is an appropriate function of a family agency and well within its competence if an evaluation can be obtained from a vocational rehabilitation center on his employment capacity. A child welfare agency can handle residential placement if they have access to skilled diagnostic data indicating what sort of residential care will best suit the child's intellectual and psychological needs. Counseling around parental feelings about a young retarded child and how to cope with the problems of management is well within the scope of generic casework provided the worker can obtain some basic information on the clinical basis of the child's condition and the development levels that can be expected. A representative of a special clinic— for example, the pediatrician or public health nurse—could provide such guidance which would serve as the baseline from which generic casework techniques would be applied to the common as well as the specialized aspects of the situation.

These arguments should not be regarded as denying that mental retardation has special, and sometimes unique, characteristics or that the retarded in certain circumstances have needs which require highly specialized help. Rather, their purpose is to correct a distortion in perspective and to highlight the fact that the different and potentially separating characteristics of the retarded represent specific and prescribed aspects of their condition and not its *totality*. The three following examples illustrate the generic nature of many of the problems which are associated with specific situations created by mental retardation. A mildly retarded adolescent girl with a poor self-image and difficulty in making social relationships has a similar adjustment problem to that of a girl of normal or superior intelligence who cannot make friends. Although their social maladjustment may have different causes and the methods of handling it will not be quite the same, the underlying psychological stress and its manifestations in social behavior are identical. Similarly, the task of looking after a retarded adult relative with limited capacity for self-care may not be very different in the essentials of management from the care of an elderly person with failing physical and mental powers who needs sustained care and supervision. Lastly, the grief reaction of parents to discovering that their young child is markedly retarded has many resemblances to the mourning process that all parents experience when an offspring has a serious disability with long-term implications. On the other hand, in order to maintain a proper perspective it is important to realize that all three examples contain factors that are special to the mentally retarded. The retarded adolescent faces greater realistic handicaps in making social relationships because of her limited social skills and ability to communicate than her brighter counterpart, who has more to offer once she has surmounted the psychological hurdle of her low self-esteem. The family with the dependent retarded adult has carried this burden on a long-term basis, whereas the geriatric care of an elderly relative is a task assumed later in life and is of briefer duration. In addition to their grief, the parents of a retarded young child have to cope with the peculiar psychological stress associated with the stigma of intellectual defect, which does not apply in the same way to physical disability.

All three, however, crystallize the points emphasized in this chapter that there are specialized and common components to the problems of retardation, and that the total condition and the social maladjustments it creates can only be helped by an equal recognition of these two elements. This will be illustrated in greater detail in the chapter on casework.

5 SOME CONCEPTS OF CASEWORK

CASEWORK in its particular applicability to mental retardation has two dimensions. As one of the three traditional methods of social work practice, it is the means of providing a particular form of help with the problems in social functioning and adjustment that beset individuals who are themselves retarded or who have the responsibility for others suffering from this disability. Beyond this immediate and direct function, this particular social work method serves the secondary but equally valuable purpose of supplying a blueprint of principles and techniques which, while not directly utilized by the two other methods, influences the way in which both group work and community organization are carried out. Because it was the earliest method to develop a theoretical (as opposed to pragmatic) basis, casework embodies the essential philosophy and ethical considerations that underlie all social work practice; and its emphasis on the professional relationship as a primary tool has created the practical medium for expressing some of the profession's most important tenets. The belief in the unique value of an individual and in his inalienable right to be treated in a way that sustains this inherent concept of human dignity is essential to the practice of casework but also extends to the whole arena of social work. Although these attitudes find their most coherent and explicit expression in the personal interaction between individuals, they are also the basic ingredients of a broader social cohesiveness, because individuals compose the wider social group and influence the way it develops and operates. For the retarded and their families who have the two great needs to be assimilated into the general cohesive fabric of society and to be perceived and treated in terms of their individuality, regardless of their handicap and its social limitations, casework is a very important component of social work. For this reason a good deal of space will be devoted to discussing how its techniques can be applied to the retardation field and the modifications required to make them especially effective for this area of social handicap. To provide a general background, it will be useful to examine some of the current definitions of casework that informs social work practice today.

Since its inception at the beginning of this century, casework has evoked a wide range of definitions, each representing a particular bias in the method's development and application.[1] This variety and the different emphases implied for practice make it difficult to decide on a particular definition as the starting point for a discussion of the application of casework to the retardation field, since no single one is capable of covering the complex mesh of problems and needs associated with this handicap and of clarifying their essential and sometimes unique nature. After much deliberation, the four definitions set forth below were selected to represent an amalgam of ideas on the topic.

The most generalized and comprehensive definition, by Helen Harris Perlman, states that the "essence of social casework help is that it aims to facilitate the individual's social adaptation, to restore, reshape or reinforce his functioning as a social being.[2] This is a succinct summary of the overall objectives of this method of social work for the mentally retarded and their families, and also offers scope for including within the purview of this one process the wide variety of social problems associated with the handicap. *Facilitating* the social adaptation of individuals whom the disability adversely affects, either directly through their own defect or indirectly through close contact with a retarded person, is a broad concept which relates to the total client group described in Chapter 4; and the activities of "restoring," "reshaping," or "reinforcing" social functioning can be applied along the whole range of problems that they experience. Families with a retarded child, for example, may need help in *reshaping* their social functioning to meet the special demands involved in his care, and if the shock of his disability has threatened the parental role and undermined their capacity to fulfill it, this specific aspect of their social functioning may have to be *restored* through outside help. Similar objectives can be applied to the mildly retarded youth who may need help to *reinforce* his functioning as an independent, adult wage-earner, while the social functioning of a more handicapped client must be *deliberately created* through the provision of a special milieu in which his positive capacity can find some expression.

The second definition, put forth by Bertha Reynolds thirty-eight years ago, asserts that "social casework has two poles of interest . . . the individual and his environment . . . the function of social casework is not to treat the individual alone nor his environment alone, but the process of adaptation which is a dynamic interaction of the two." [3] This is particularly relevant to mental retardation in which so many of the pressing social problems arise out of the negative interaction between the retarded and their environment.

The third definition, from another angle by Werner Boehm, elaborates on the process of adaptation between the individual and his environment by introducing the concept of social role performance "which requires reciprocal activity or social interaction between individual and individual, individual and group, and individual and community." In line with this approach, casework is defined as "the method of service which seeks to intervene in the psycho-social aspects of an individual's life for the purpose of helping him to improve, restore, preserve or enhance his functioning in the performance of any social roles he has to fulfill." [4] This added dimension is also very pertinent to the retarded for whom social roles are often ambiguous, improperly perceived, or even denied, and whose social functioning is therefore unnecessarily confused or diminished.

Fourth, the concept of casework put forward by Herbert Apthekar,[5] in which the administration and provision of concrete helping services is seen as the essential distinguishing characteristic of this particular process of social work, is of major importance to the social problems of retardation. The performance of the retarded in prescribed roles, their successful interaction with their environment, and their total social adaptation depend in large measure on concrete services being easily accessible to offset the stresses and deficits in functioning that the condition gives rise to. In regard to Apthekar's definition of casework it is important to realize that the emphasis on concrete practical services does not imply less value for help of a psychological nature, which he includes as an essential component in administering a practical service. This dual emphasis is particularly significant for retardation. Because of the psychological issues that accompany the practical burdens created by this disability, there must be a skillful intermingling of services catering to both the practical and the psychological components of the problem.[6] The first is met by a concrete service and the second by skilled counseling, and the maximum effectiveness of both depends on the separate contribution that each can make. Most families with a retarded member require some counseling round their feelings before they can mobilize their emotional resources to cope with the psychological problems arising out of their situation, but the full value of counseling will not be realized unless relief is provided for the practical difficulties of management. For example, teen-age siblings will find it easier to tolerate a moderately retarded adolescent if he or she is involved in a full-time educational or training program instead of hanging around the house, and parents' very real fears concerning the development of their preschool retarded child are as much allayed by the professional help of a home-training program as by ventilating them in counseling. Conversely, many clients require counseling to help master their psychological resistance to the social and emotional implications of retardation before they can fully utilize practical help. A mildly retarded adolescent or young adult in the employable range may refuse special industrial training or job placement if the offer is not accompanied by some counseling based on an implicit recognition of the psychological stresses that asking for help may evoke and the opportunity for the individual to express anxieties associated with this special placement.

The great contribution that counseling can make to casework is to facilitate the best use of services and in this way to grease the wheels of a comprehensive service for the retarded. In addition to reducing the psychological resistance to utilizing a particular service, counseling is also invaluable for interpreting the precise nature of specific services being recommended, for explaining their purpose and their hoped-for effect on the social functioning of the retarded individual, and finally for enlisting the active cooperation of the family in the service program. When a severely retarded child of school age is to be enrolled in an Activity-of-Daily-Living program at a day care center, his parents must understand that its immediate goal is the development of basic self-help skills (such as feeding, toileting, and simple dressing and undressing); that the longer-term objective is to prepare the child for possible entry into a trainable program in the school system; and that both these objectives will be possible only if the training regime and techniques of the center are rigidly reinforced by a similar routine at home.

Again, we see the close interdependence of practical and emotional factors in that the success of the training program depends heavily on the family's full cooperation at home, and this in turn may be affected by a wide variety of emotional factors, not all of which are immediately obvious. These may include anxiety about separating from the child, fear about his exposure to a new and more demanding experience that will highlight his inadequacy, and unwillingness to permit him to be identified with a service that clearly denotes the handicap of retardation. At a more unconscious level there may be reluctance to involve the child in treatment which will *improve* social functioning because this recognizes his developing social role as a chronically and conspicuously handicapped person. Thus, as long as the preschool retarded child remains in the seclusion of his home, his parents can minimize his disability or attribute it to immaturity; but this defense cannot be maintained when he enters a training facility in the outside world.

The emotions surrounding mental retardation are invariably subtle and complex, and require skill and insight to penetrate and expose their nature and origin. The case of Mrs. Fanara is illustrative. She was having great difficulty toilet-training her seven-year-old doubly handicapped girl and seemed unable to follow through on the guidance provided by the public health nurse's training program. Suspecting some emotional block, the public health nurse referred the mother to the social worker. An exploration of Mrs. Fanara's feelings revealed that in childhood she had felt inferior to a preferred younger sister, that she had always experienced her mother as a critical rather

than a supportive figure, and that in the present difficult circumstances this undermining attitude was felt acutely. Her inept response to the home-training program could be interpreted as expressing at least three things—a hostile reaction to a critical authority
figure whom she associated with her mother, an unconscious wish
to affirm the "badness" that she felt adults ascribed to her, and a
realistic sense of inadequacy in meeting the special needs of this
atypical child, which stemmed from her own experience of being
improperly mothered. Mrs. Fanara's deeper feelings about the child's
defective condition and what this meant in regard to her earlier relationships and family attitudes were preventing her from utilizing the
home-training service. This added to her sense of defeat because the
child could not be considered for an educational program until she had
mastered this basic self-help skill. Once Mrs. Fanara realized that she
did in fact have the capacity to train the child and that this step
would open up other possibilities for help, she was able to overcome
her hopeless attitude and begin to tackle the problem. Symbolic of
her changed feelings was her spontaneous suggestion to her husband
that they do over their kitchen; and the two of them repainted it and
put down fresh tiles. The child very soon mastered toilet-training
and was enrolled in a trainable class.

Another mother—Mrs. Levy—exemplifies the opposite situation,
in that she could not benefit from counseling until it was allied with
a direct service. She was only able to discuss her deep sense of guilt,
disappointment, and frustration after her five-year-old, mildly retarded boy was involved in educational play therapy with the special
teacher and showed improvement in functioning as a result. Mrs.
Levy had also experienced toilet-training difficulties and was feeling
very guilty about the harsh punitive methods she had resorted to in
order to break through the boy's resistance. At this stage she needed
reassurance that her firm methods were well-meaning and in some
measure effective since the child had achieved this important stage
of self-control. When Steven showed marked progress in other areas,
his mother was able to relax, to feel more comfortable in her maternal
role, and to devise better ways of handling the boy's limited behavior.
She also began to interpret his needs to her husband and mobilize his
interest in helping the child.

Until recently, casework in the mental retardation field has not been maximally useful because of lack of adequate and appropriate services to back it up. When, as Schild points out,[7] the only service available to parents of a retarded child below the educable level was long-term institutional care, the social worker dealing with problems of family adjustment to this situation had very little room for maneuvering. The two negative alternatives in this situation were to keep the child at home, with inevitable stress for the family when they had no services in the community to draw on, or to consign him to an institution with the inevitable trauma of separation and disrupted family life. This lack of practical services to buttress casework has placed the profession of social work at a serious disadvantage vis-à-vis other professional disciplines that provide a more visible service. It comes as a shock, for example, to find in the study carried out by Ehlers[8] that mothers of retarded children attending the evaluation clinic in Cambridge, Massachusetts, ranked social work among the lowest of the professional disciplines which they found helpful. Further—and this is the more cogent point—the study shows that the traditional helping methods of social work were both appreciated and utilized by the mothers in their contacts with representatives of other professions—notably the public health nurse and the teacher. These staff members were seen as maximally helpful because they represented a practical service directed immediately to the child's deficiencies. Because of this benign association mothers tended to use them for help with their other problems; that is, they ventilated their feelings and fears about the less tangible factors of their situation. Social workers, whose contribution was limited to dealing with the intangible emotional difficulties and divorced from practical help, were not regarded as prime repositories of support.

Associated with this painful finding and its undeniable indictment of our professional role (which can undoubtedly be amply confirmed by other agencies dealing with the retarded) is another factor which needs to be discussed briefly before we move on to the more positive task of exploring how casework can redeem its lost reputation and become helpful to this hard-pressed segment of the population. This relates to the subtle effect that the lack of practical services has had on the style of casework with the retarded and their families, and to the distortions that have developed about the outstanding problems associated with this disability. The main consequence has been an undue emphasis on the psychological components of the total problem, particularly on the emotional reactions of the normal family members to the abnormal situation of a retarded child or relative.

The resurgence of writing on retardation by social workers and psychologists in the past ten or fifteen years has been concerned principally with this topic. This trend has not been entirely negative, since it has helped to present the complex problem of retardation more precisely and has been partly responsible for ousting the stereotype of retardation entertained by many professional workers. Early papers such as that by Solnit and Stark on the mourning reaction of parents to the birth of a defective child[9] and Mandelbaum's skillful analysis of the psychopathological reactions that are encountered in *some* families[10] have made a great contribution to the understanding of retardation and its problems by disclosing the complex dynamics of feeling and behavior that can be triggered by the advent of a retarded child. The knowledge and insights produced by this psychologically oriented approach have had an important effect on social work practice in that planning for the care of the retarded child or adult now includes a consideration of the emotional factors that are inevitably present.

The mechanistic approach of advising a family to place a retarded baby for life and replace it by an early new pregnancy has been changed to the more realistic approach of helping the parents to work through the emotional shock of such an event at the same time that they are planning practical steps for coping with the external difficulties it raises.[11] And though placement for a delinquent, mildly retarded adolescent with behavior problems may still have to be done through a court order, there is now an awareness that both the individual and his family will need casework help in adjusting to this disrupting event if it is not to be experienced as a punitive and destructive measure. This development of a psychodynamic approach to the social problems of retardation has had a positive influence on the direction and quality of social work. It has been one of the major forces for bringing the retarded client and his family into the ambience of common human needs and problems and for counteracting the tendency to reject them as inappropriate clients for social work help.

Along with these acknowledged advantages, however, certain negative effects have grown out of this overemphasized psychological approach. There has been an incomplete and biased perception of the emotional components to retardation, and resulting from this, certain inappropriate emphases in treatment. The latter have developed out of a failure to distinguish the difference in etiology between the emotional factors associated with retardation and those which have a functional basis in the personality and previous psychological history of clients whose problems are of a different order. More explicitly, the main body of emotional problems encountered in the conventional, psychiatrically oriented casework agency stem from the personal psychopathology of the clientele involved and the maladjusted pattern of relationships to which *they themselves contribute*. For families of retarded individuals the core of their problem derives, not primarily from this type of interpersonal maladjustment and its *intrapsychic* source, but rather from the *external* pathology of the deviance and incapacity associated with the disability. Because their problem originates from outside, this group of clients (that is, the normal relatives) do not inevitably present a functional type of pathology; in fact, many of them demonstrate normal— and often, exceptionally sound—psychological and emotional health. This is not to deny the fact that stable individuals and families are always shaken by the traumatic event of a retarded child and that their behavior may temporarily disintegrate into a disturbed pattern under the impact of shock. Furthermore, as the literature indicates, for some families or individuals the presence of a retarded member may produce a severe emotional disturbance: in such situations, however, the retardation is usually a trigger that sets in motion a psychopathological tendency which could have been reactivated by any other form of severe stress.

This preoccupation with psychodynamic theory has introduced a bias into social work with the retarded by translating the unique problems of this handicap into the same pathological terms as apply to other areas of maladjustment dominated by psychological issues of functional origin. Thus articles on family reactions toward retardation in the past two decades have focused on negative aspects, with emphasis on parental guilt evoked by the child's defect and on the neurotic and depressive reactions that this traumatic experience sets in motion in the family. Much less attention has been paid to healthy adjustive reactions which are encountered in practice just as often as pathological responses. The result has been an overemphasis upon identifying the pathological elements in the personality and family structures of clients involved with a retarded child or adult and an inclination to treat as sick what may be essentially normal individuals reacting to realistic stress. The indiscriminate use of the psychotherapeutic approach not only represents a misevaluation of the total situation in many cases (since the majority of families do not want or need therapy in its conventional psychiatric sense) but also increases the total negative content of the problem by investing the family with their own pathology. Since the situation is already heavily weighted with the intrinsic pathology that stems from the retarded individual's disability, placing the parents in a *patient role* does not constitute constructive help. Rather, they need to be treated as the healthy components of a vulnerable situation and their positive coping capacities need to be highlighted. This very important point will be expanded in Chapter 7 when the professional relationship with their retarded and their families is discussed.

A further distorting effect of this approach is that it adds a heightened psychological tone to a problem-situation that is predominantly social, and converts into a matter of individual psychopathology feelings and reactions that are in reality a normal social reaction to an external traumatizing event. Different ways of viewing the problems of retardation in the family are illustrated by the writings of Solnit and Stark,[12] and Mandelbaum[13] on the one hand, and by Olshansky[14] on the other. The former writers deal with the parental reaction to this experience in terms of an individualized psychological response to an ego-threatening event. Olshansky, by contrast, has conceptualized the reaction to the tragic event of retardation as a social one that is found almost universally among those individuals who have been visited by it. Just as a delusion ceases to be a psychotic symptom when it is held true by an entire culture, so "chronic sorrow" ceases to be a pathological response when it is admitted to by the bulk of parents with retarded children.

The present-day expansion of more varied and plentiful service facilities for the retarded is enabling casework to shift from this individual-focused position, with its pessimistic, pathology-oriented dimension, to the broader functions of providing for the retarded client group a rounded social work service which meets both practical and emotional problems. This trend gives the method of casework a proper social, as opposed to psychiatric, orientation and permits its indispensable skills to be directed toward improving the overall social functioning, assimilation, and acceptance of the retarded and their sustaining families.[15] In this context of practical provision, the psychological counseling component of casework becomes an effective reality geared to facilitating the psychological processes that underpin social functioning and adjustment instead of remaining an unrealistic preoccupation with internal stresses that can too easily become an escape from confronting external difficulties. Since these difficulties may be very severe in connection with retardation, this danger needs to be guarded against vigilantly.

Having established this social orientation to casework, we will now examine some of its traditional concepts and modes of practice to see how they can be converted into a pattern of work that will reinforce and extend this approach. A primary point for emphasis is the wide range of stress that retardation gives rise to, and the resultant need to evolve a variety of working styles to meet this complexity. For clarity it is useful to divide these pressures into separate categories, each of which, while overlapping at many points, has a distinctive character.

The first of these is the chronic problem-condition, which contains within itself recurrent crisis points that are mainly associated with the developmental phases and their corresponding social pressures. Second, there is a group of problems of a more acute and circumscribed nature that are not integral to the chronic problem-condition but are apt to occur as an outcome of the stress it imposes. Third, there is a more diffuse and heterogeneous cluster of problems that are neither peculiar nor directly ascribable to retardation but are exacerbated by its presence. Fourth, there are the types of social problems that derive primarily from poverty and the social and material deprivation this condition imposes. These social problems are often involved in the genesis of retardation or are a strong contributory cause. The second and third group of problems can be termed *secondary* in that they are not integral to retardation but rather a by-product of the condition. The long-term adjustive problems that are an inseparable feature of the more severe forms of retardation and the various social pathologies that form part of the condition's etiology can be styled *primary* problems. Using this arbitrary division we shall discuss both groups in more detail.

It is helpful to visualize the different manifestations of stress inherent in the chronic problem situation as three distinct phases that characterize the emotional and practical response that most families experience with retardation, and to conceive of these response patterns being handled according to three corresponding modes of operation. First, there is the acute reactive phase when the family first discovers the child's handicapping condition; this phase may recur at subsequent developmental points in the child's or adult's life when the social failure due to retardation is more cogently demonstrated. The families of more seriously handicapped children whose deviance becomes obvious early experience this critical impact of revelation more severely; but the revelation of retardation in its less disabling forms and at later phases of development may produce a situation of crisis just as disturbing in its way, even though its long-term and qualitative pressures may be less severe.[16] The family of an adolescent with mild or borderline retardation may be very shocked to discover that he or she needs special vocational training as a preliminary to employment, while the boy or girl concerned may be threatened by the social inadequacy this implies and react with difficult behavior.

The theory of crisis intervention,[17] whereby appropriate assistance given at a critical phase may prevent serious and lasting psychological damage, has particular relevance for the families of a retarded child because of the immediate and grave threat to emotional and social stability that the disability generally represents. Furthermore, one of the main objectives of crisis intervention is to salvage individuals with relatively sound adaptive resources who have been over-whelmed by their problems and the extraordinary demands imposed. Many families who are temporarily traumatized by the presence of a retarded member are able to cope with the ordinary (as opposed to the extraordinary) pressures of life, and possess resources which can be mobilized for a constructive response to their situation. This approach is especially suitable for them. It must also be recognized that these families are in a peculiar situation of maximum risk in that the event precipitating the critical reaction is not of itself soluble (as many other crises of functional origin are) and will continue to exert chronic emotional and practical demands on the family. They will therefore need exceptionally strong and resilient coping resources, and it is essential that they be given adequate and properly directed help at these crisis junctures in order to build up their long-term capacity for handling this permanent problem. The severity of the crisis of discovering mental retardation stems from the fact that it requires a multiple adjustment. That is to say, the initial shock of learning about the presence of the condition is exacerbated by the recognition that serious long-term disability is the inevitable sequel; this dual blow adds another dimension beyond that found in the crisis situations. There is the third, equally disturbing, factor that it is not merely a normal or pre-existing state of equilibrium that is disturbed but the more emotionally dynamic one of positive aspira-tion and hope which surround a new baby's birth. This adds a third, more poignant and shocking facet.

The casework approach to problems of mental retardation based on crisis theory comprises many things. Summed up briefly, it involves close psychological identification with the family's emotional re-sponse to their problem, emotional support from a concerned but uninvolved outsider to sustain them during their reaction to the shock, and the offer of external resources to reinforce their own coping mechanisms which will be called into play. This source of support includes planning for the relief of the serious practical diffi-culties connected with retardation. It may not take any more definite form than informing the family of the range of available facilities to which they can turn if so minded; but the introduction of prac-tical services, even when they are not immediately desired or applicable, adds a dimension of external reality to a situation which is momentarily dominated by overwhelming internal emotional forces. The agonizing impact that Down's syndrome makes upon the family very early in the child's life may be slightly alleviated by the knowledge that children with this type of disability have a good potential for training and that a suitable facility will be available when the child reaches that stage of development.

The therapeutic pattern derived from crisis theory is limited in regard to both goals and time involved in achieving them, because the very nature of crisis implies a confrontation with pressing emergent problems that demand some sort of resolution. In the case of retardation no final solution can be planned for the overall problems which the disability creates, so assistance must be focused on the shorter-term and more soluble hazards of the situation as represented by the immediate response of the normal family members to this disturbing event. To illustrate this point more explicitly, the chronically disabling effects of the retarded child's innate biological impairment cannot be fully remedied, but their negative influences may be modified or exacerbated by the attitudes and resultant behavior of his family toward him. If parents are not helped to come to terms both emotionally and practically with the ineluctable reality of their circumstances, their emotional maladjustment will express itself in inadequate or inappropriate management of both the handicapped child and the total family economy. This will inevitably curtail the already limited developmental capacity of the child, and the social development of the entire family may be equally warped by the negative patterns of relationship and interaction. Since the latter are theoretically open to help, they represent the growing points in a situation which has many static components, and as such must be the target for effective intervention.

This brings us to the second phase of help to be offered in the total adjustive process affecting families of the retarded. This phase is a necessary sequel to the more intensive help provided in the crisis situation, and its major aim is to stabilize the family in its long-term situation of assimilating the child and his problems, whether this acceptance takes the form of rearing the child at home or placing him in residential care. The quality and focus of help are therefore different from those that characterize the crisis-intervention process. While that process is concerned with highly disturbed and disintegrating emotions, the second phase is expressed in a more protracted support for the newly acquired emotional equilibrium which, hopefully, has resulted from the concentrated help of the preceding phase. The focus of help must also shift from the acute distress feelings of the family to the longer-range need to adjust to their role as parents of a handicapped child, and to the emotional and practical implications this carries. This second phase or pattern of help derives primarily from a *supportive* relationship through which the parents are helped to develop to a maximum their emotional resources and practical skills in caring for this retarded member. It is principally concerned with the parent-child-family complex, and its objective is to create the most propitious environment for the retarded child's social growth and development by building up the family's competence to care for him.

Parents often feel themselves to be extremely deficient in their parent roles because of having produced a defective child and not knowing how to cope with his special needs. Hence this function of casework has an important therapeutic significance because it is directed to mobilizing their healthy and normal resources to compensate for the deficits of their specially vulnerable child. Raising a retarded (or any other sort of markedly deviant) child should be likened to a challenging and highly specialized technical operation which demands the learning and practice of special skills. If parents can view their task in this guise, they may perhaps come round to seeing that their child's deficits and unusual needs are the means by which their own skills can become both enlarged and refined. Although the help offered at this stage is less intensive in content than that which is provided in the crisis situation, it must also be regarded as a relatively limited operation in time and in objectives. Its main aim is to assist the family or relatives to achieve some sort of emotional and practical equilibrium which will permit the assimilation of the retarded member into its midst while preserving its own integrity. Within this orientation of *progressive acceptance* it is important that the caseworker's supportive helping relationship not become a permanent feature, since its principal goal must be to strengthen and foster the family's own coping resources for the task and enable them to develop their own independent skills for managing their unusual situation.

However, the chronicity of retardation and its built-in susceptibility to stress also demand that some form of permanent sustaining social work help be available for the families and individuals who have to function within this precarious context. This can be envisaged as the long-term and *readily accessible provision* of advisory and practical services to be drawn on as necessity requires, and its special value lies not in its specific application to current identified problems but in its permanent availability for dealing with them when they erupt. This type of assistance logically follows the two preceding forms of help, and it is geared to another dimension of needs, namely those which stem from the chronic vulnerability to stress of the retarded and the crises that will inevitably occur when there is a marked shift in their life situation. This type of crisis may be precipitated by changes in the environment, such as the birth of a new baby, the illness or death of a parent figure, marital disruption or a change within the retarded individual himself; for example, deterioration in health which affects social functioning may convert a stable situation into one of major crisis. Such hazards, which are part of normal life experience, necessitate a readjustment in living that will strain (or even exceed) the impaired adaptive capacity of the mentally retarded and will represent an additional hazard for his family when they are superimposed on the atypical stresses that go along with caring for a retarded person.

To meet these long-term potential needs for help, it is necessary to evolve a new pattern of relating between social worker and client which will permit an indefinite unintensive contact to be maintained by both—one that can be converted promptly into a more intensive form when a crisis occurs. Here it is important to emphasize the difference between the *supportive* pattern already referred to and this new type of help because the essential characteristic of the latter is that it does not provide long-term active support (which implies a dependency need that is not necessarily present in the families of the retarded) but the guarantee of it as needed. This is not a *supportive* relationship in the generally accepted use of this term; it can be more accurately described as a *retainer* relationship in that the client retains the right of prompt service from the social worker or agency and a "live line" contact is maintained between the two by casual occasional visits or phone calls initiated by either party. The essential value of this type of operation is that it provides an assurance of help from a familiar source when needed without foisting it upon individuals who can normally be expected to manage their affairs alone. Within this retainer frame of reference situations will occur that may need to be treated by the two previous methods of help. A serious illness in the mother, for example, entails a crisis situation which may have to be countered by an immediate change of plans, such as the admission of the retarded individual for institutional care, or it may involve the family in a long-term reshaping of their pattern of life for which supportive help over an extended period may be needed. Another type of crisis that may emerge within the retainer situation is when a mildly retarded young adult loses his job, either because of his own inadequacy or because of economic circumstances that render him redundant. Knowing where to turn for prompt advice and understanding help may spell the difference between his surviving this upset or degenerating into a progressively worsening state of social failure. Critical situations of a different type can also develop. These are not caused by an external occurrence which disrupts an existing mode of functioning (as we have just described) but come about when a sequence of minor pressures leads to a fresh phase of understanding, acceptance, and decision-making. Such an example is the decision of parents of a profoundly retarded child to place him in residential care because of the increasing difficulty of caring for him at home as he gets older and larger but remains equally dependent.

This triple-faceted continuum of service we have outlined should be the model on which help for all the social problems associated with retardation should be based because it represents the three stages through which the family must move in order to achieve acceptance of, and adjustment to, the long-term and potentially recurrent hazards of retardation. The relative weight given to each phase of help in this continuum will vary with individual problems and situations. The shattered young mother who brings a new baby for clinical evaluation may require a long period of intensive help before she can absorb the critical shock of the diagnosis and prognosis. By contrast, the older relatives of a moderately retarded adult who go to a family agency for advice on how to solve newly emerging difficulties in intrafamily relationships may benefit from the supportive help which will enable them to readjust their approach to the retarded relative. Although these three phases have been treated separately, their inter-dependence must be appreciated because none of them is sufficient to meet the depth and severity of the problem of retardation. The re-laxed *retainer* situation is only viable if the family or individual have previously been given *support* during the time when they are learn-ing to adjust to the long-term social implications of their situation, and this adjustment is rarely possible unless the emotional impact of the preceding crisis situation has been sustained and worked though. Generally speaking, most problems associated with retardation— because of its chronic nature and the recurrent crises it causes—re-quire all three phases of treatment in turn, and the lasting efficacy of the final phase will be determined by the quality of help that has been made available in the preceding two.

To this point the problems discussed are an intrinsic by-product of mental retardation, and the pressures they create can be predicted for any family with a retarded member. A second type of problem that is also inherent in the condition are those known (or strongly suspected) to contribute directly to its causation. These are the social hazards stemming from poverty which create an environment of deprivation that stultifies normal emotional and psychological development in early childhood.[18] The more basic approach to situa-tions of this nature is to features in the environment which produce these stultifying conditions, either by establishing compensatory services or over a longer range by dealing with the underlying prob-lem of poverty. These tasks primarily utilize the techniques of com-munity organization which are examined in Chapter 10, but at the same time as this more fundamental approach is being pursued there still remain many problems of interpersonal adjustment which re-quire the skills of casework.

A third category of problems are those that are in no way specific to retardation and can crop up in any area of social work but which have an increased impact when they are present in combination with this condition. For example, chronic ill health in one of the parents imposes a strain upon the family that is greatly exacerbated if there is also a retarded child. This sort of case is exemplified by the birth of a boy with obvious mental defect to a family in which the father had an active and often florid psychotic illness. This traumatic event created a serious additional stress because assimilating the baby and his handicap required a high investment of emotional energy from the mother, which had hitherto been absorbed by the father's illness. Further, the father identified the child's impairment with his own condition and tended to interfere with practical management tactics when these became involved with his delusions.

For this group of secondary problems that may be associated with mental retardation but are *not* an inevitable feature of the condition, the same generic casework techniques can be used that are employed for most social problem areas; and the special considerations that have just been discussed in regard to the specific retardation problems assume less relevance. That is to say, the specialized considerations required for dealing with the components of chronicity and irreversibility and their implicatons for limited movement and solution have much less significance for the secondary problems because the latter are by-products of mental retardation rather than an integral feature. They can therefore be detached from the central, overall problem-condition and can be treated in their own right. Further, when such problems can be relegated to a circumscribed area of difficulty that is amenable to help, they contain a potential for change and improvement which may be absent in the central problem-area.

For example, a disturbance in parent-child relationships, which is expressed in conflicted handling of the child and a negative reactive behavior disorder on his part, can be tackled primarily through the underlying dynamics of the parents' attitude—i.e., what factors in their own past and present psychological backgrounds are contributing to their current feelings and behavior and how these can be modified into a more constructive pattern. In such a context casework utilizes its traditional problem-solving process and techniques, and its goal is the circumscribed one of improving the distorted interactive patterns between the adults who are suffering a *temporary* disturbance in their parental functioning and the child who has a *chronic* impairment. The latter must be taken into account since it may well be the precipitating factor behind the parents' problem, but the focus of help is on their reactions to the situation rather than on the handicap itself, which cannot be fundamentally changed, though its manifestations may be modified for better or for worse.

This approach is illustrated by the case of Martha Neumann. This seven-year-old, mildly retarded girl was closely involved in a manipulative and infantilizing relationship with her mother which contained serious neurotic overtones. The emotional factors that influenced the mother's behavior were complex and related to the following sequence of traumatic events in her own life. First, she had become separated from her own mother during the Nazi Occupation in Europe, so that at thirteen she had been forced into assuming responsibility for several younger siblings, at first in their own home and later in a concentration camp. The death of a younger sister during the long and hazardous journey to the camp had evoked an intense reaction of guilt and impotence, which was reinforced by extreme anger toward her mother for abandoning the family. Although Mrs. Neumann, her father, and three other siblings survived intact and the whole family was reunited in America, her early adolescent doubts about her adequacy in the maternal role remained unsolved and, in spite of a satisfactory marriage and two healthy children, they were acutely reactivated when her third child showed signs of deviant development in early childhood. The diagnosis of a progressive, deteriorating neurological condition induced an extreme depressive reaction which was expressed in coddling and indulging the child on the grounds that her short life should be made as easy as possible and that, with no future, there was no point in bringing her up with the same training as the other children had had. When this fatal prognosis was questioned and eventually reversed three or four years later, both she and the child were inextricably involved in a highly protective life-in-death relationship which was interfering with the child's training and social development and had also become an increasing source of resentment to her mother. Mrs. Neumann needed help in recreating a fresh maternal role for herself, geared to preparing the child for life instead of death, and to achieve this she had to work through her depression and the preceding events in her early life in which were its origins. This was accomplished by fairly intensive individual casework, which gave her the opportunity to identify with the social worker (who was well versed in the idiosyncratic behavior and needs of the child's mildly retarded condition) and, through this relationship, to learn how to cope with "mothering" this atypical child whom she had unconsciously identified with her dead sister. When she could associate her sense of being betrayed by the mother and her feelings of guilt and loss toward the little sister with her current feelings toward her retarded daughter, she began to separate from the child and apply her quite competent child-rearing skills toward her training. The casework techniques successively utilized were reinforcement of her obvious positive abilities as a mother as revealed in her handling of her two other children; exploration of her earlier relationships within her own family; drawing out of hostile feelings toward her own mother, in terms of describing them and also demonstrating them by displacement on to the worker; interpretation of her identification of the retarded child with the earlier "loss" situation; and finally, acceptance of her present sense of loss in having an impaired child.

This case has been chosen as an illustration because it shows how the interaction between the problem-condition of retardation and the individual personal difficulties of the mother created a circumscribed but potentially serious functional problem. If the child's relatively mild handicap (as it turned out to be) had occurred in a family which had not been exposed to an earlier tragic experience, the disturbed pattern of relationships and behavior would have been less likely to develop, just as the mother's psychological vulnerability might not have been reactivated by a third normal child. This problem-complex cannot be described as inherent in mental retardation but the condition, with its symbolic association with loss, contained specially potent ingredients for catalyzing the mother's earlier experiences into a uniquely destructive pattern of behavior. In terms of imagery, she was employing her overprotective neurotic drives to swaddle the child in premature grave-clothes, and if there had not been intervention, in the shape of special schooling for the child and simultaneous casework for the mother, the child's already limited capacity for growth and development might have been effectually smothered into a state of permanently infantile neurotic dependence.

Identification of these secondary problems is a very important, and frequently taxing, function of casework. Whether the problems are expressed as a direct and idiosyncratic reaction to the condition, as in this instance, or are an aggravation of existing pressures which originate from other sources, or represent causal factors in the etiology of retardation, it is always difficult to distinguish between extrinsic reality reactions to the pathological situation created by this condition and what may be an exaggerated response which derives its main impetus not from the retardation per se but from some deeper psychological maladjustment on the part of those concerned with it. Often it is a question of very delicate balance of these relative weights, and properly directed casework depends upon a very precise and careful assessment of this point. It is as dangerous and unproductive of good professional practice to assume that every problem in an individual or his family stems automatically from his retarded condition as to ascribe every maladjusted situation to intra-psychic forces operating within individuals and independently of external environmental pressures that are produced by mental retardation. In reality there is a constant dynamic interaction between these two major components of any problem-situation, and even when one of them is singled out as the primary focus of help, the contribution of the other must be borne in mind. The following is an example of how serious difficulties of external origin were aggravated by retardation, and also of the part that psychological factors played in reinforcing the pressures associated with retardation.

Richard Cooke was a moderately retarded five-year-old with some brain damage which expressed itself in hyperactivity, perseveration, and occasional tantrums. His family, consisting of three older siblings between the ages of seven and twelve and his mother, lived in substandard housing in a neighborhood which had poor transportation and no facilities for retarded children of his level. The mother, who was divorced, had chronic poor health from a neglected gynecological condition, and kept the family together with difficulty on a marginal income from public assistance. She found the care of a retarded child (the illegitimate offspring of a liaison which she subsequently regretted) extremely burdensome and handled him with impatience and inconsistency. As a result he became a serious management problem and his difficult behavior aggravated her poor physical health, undermined her psychological resources, and upset the other children in the family. Most of the social problems experienced by this family were of external origin: inadequate income, crowded housing, no adult to support the mother in her difficult task of handling a deviant child, and no special services to take over part of the child's training. These pressures were, however, exacerbated by certain psychological factors which derived from the mother's basic ambivalence toward the child and her feelings of guilt about both his condition and his illegitimate status. Her own long-term frustration at belonging to an underprivileged minority group and her deep conviction that she had always come off second-best in life also increased the tensions produced by the situation and made it extra difficult for her to adjust to the external stresses he created. The symbolic meaning that the child's defect had for her was once vividly expressed when she described a childhood memory in which she had coveted a fairy doll from the top of the Christmas tree but had in fact been given a broken one instead.

In this chapter we have seen that the problems encountered by retarded individuals and their families run the entire gamut of social adjustment. To make it easier to relate these to the different factors of retardation with which they are specifically associated, this array of problems has been separated into different categories based on the different methods of approach and emphases in work which they demand. From this baseline we shall go on to examine in greater detail the principal processes of casework that can be most aptly applied to the problems of the retarded. These are the social diagnosis and the use of the professional relationship and other techniques of interaction. They will be dealt with in the next three chapters.

6 THE SOCIAL EVALUATION AND ITS SIGNIFICANCE FOR MENTAL RETARDATON

THE SYSTEMATIC evaluation of factors in the environment that significantly affect an individual's social adaptation has been an integral part of modern social work since 1917 when Mary Richmond formulated her famous concept of social diagnosis in the book of that name.[1] Much of its content is still pertinent today for social workers who are primarily concerned with the adjustment problems between individuals and the external factors of their environment, and it has a special relevance to mental retardation because of the serious practical difficulties this handicap creates. Although the social diagnosis originated in casework, it is also an integral feature of group work and community organization even if these two methods emphasize different facets of investigation.

We are assuming that the basic elements of this social work process are familiar to readers, and therefore this book will concentrate upon certain aspects that have a particular relevance for retardation. Briefly the main areas that we see as most important to explore are those components of the environment which impinge most critically upon the social development and functioning of a retarded individual, the role that he fills within this social milieu, and the impact that his disability makes upon the normal individuals with whom he is in closest and most significant contact. To understand these three vital constituents of the retarded client's social situation it is necessary to look at him and his characteristics, at the complex psychological and material influences in his background, and at the patterns of interaction that these two complementary elements set in motion. As a preliminary to dealing with these more focused facets of the task we must also briefly look at some of the broader social developments that have had an effect upon the retarded and influenced their social adjustment and assimilation.

In the half century since *Social Diagnosis* appeared there has been a gradual change in the social philosophy toward mental handicap with an accompanying increase in the quantity and variety of social welfare services for retarded individuals of all ages and most levels of functioning. As a result, the social horizons of this handicapped group have widened, and they now have a greater opportunity to remain in the community at large and to participate in some measure in its normal activities. The moderately retarded adult who, with training, can be taught simple industrial processes and can learn to travel to a sheltered workshop where he does a full day's paid work, performs essentially the same wage-earner role as his normal peers. This situation invests him with a very different social status from that of his counterpart of thirty years ago, when the alternatives were to remain at home with his family as a chronically dependent quasi-invalid with conspicuously deviant behavior or to be placed in an institution which provided custodial care within a medical framework and, only under very favorable and rare circumstances, carefully devised occupational diversion.

This new trend has significantly extended the social worker's scope of responsibility for helping the retarded and their families in that she now has to relate to a clientele with a wider range of disability, and she must be knowledgeable about, and able to manipulate, the much more complex array of rehabilitative services that are available to meet these broader needs. She must also have a precise understanding of the social roles that now devolve upon these hitherto socially inactive clients and be able to identify the factors in their social background that will sustain and develop these. Closely associated with this is the very important task of assessing the interaction between the retarded client and the significant normal individuals in his background in the light of this more viable social role, and evaluating not only the contribution that the environment makes to his satisfactory social adaptation but also the effect the retarded individual may have upon his environment, particularly in terms of the stress his handicap may impose. This is important to bear in mind because by increasing the retarded individual's scope for social participation and interaction, we also increase the potential for stress in himself and in those normal individuals who support him. For example, attending a sheltered workshop makes substantial demands on the social adaptive capacity of a moderately retarded adult; the necessity for keeping to a time schedule, the give-and-take with other retarded employees, and the acceptance of criticism for substandard work are all liable to be a strain on the individual which may be expressed within the family and impose extra stress on them. Likewise, if a severely retarded child is accepted for day care, this will help his development and relieve the parents of total responsibility for his care, but the main long-term burden remains the same and the availability of *partial* help may in fact increase pressures in the family by subverting an alternative decision for placement.[2] In both these instances the wider opportunities for retarded individuals may create problems that did not exist when their handicapped dependent status was clearly defined and their area of functioning more limited.

A third significant factor which underlines the importance of the social diagnosis is that the social difficulties associated with mental retardation are complex and pervasive and affect all areas of the client's life as well as that of his family. They cannot, therefore, be eased by professional services alone but require the active therapeutic involvement of the entire social group to which the retarded individual belongs. This may be expressed in a tolerant understanding of his deviance, his being accepted in the community's social institutions (as illustrated by membership in a church group or trade union), or in emotional and practical support for the normal individuals who are responsible for the retarded one.

On this account the social factors are not merely vital components of rehabilitation (as they are with many other handicapping conditions); they are in fact often therapeutic agents in their own right. That is to say, it is the social acceptance of the retarded individual's disability and deviance which minimizes the handicap, and this acceptance is closely related to the capacity of the environment to contain the retarded person. The main diagnostic task, therefore, must be to assess the interaction between these two constituent parts

with particular emphasis on how far it promotes the healthy functioning of both. We are highlighting the relevance of this sociological
model for mental retardation because it would seem to offer a much
more constructive way of approaching the problems associated with
this disability than the more traditional pattern. It also harks back
to some of the principal factors in the original conception of what
goes into a good social diagnosis.

When this term was coined, it represented a much-needed attempt
to introduce a more rational and disciplined element into the process
of social investigation, which was the necessary preliminary to
social work assistance. Emphasis was given to acquiring *accurate* information, but the dynamic interpretation of these data as an interacting whole represented the *essential* professional skill involved.
Both *Social Diagnosis* and *What is Social Casework* [3] have a strong
sociological orientation, and even a brief glance at either book reveals the fact that the client, whether he is represented as an abstract
construct or figures in a case history, is rooted firmly in a material
milieu and that his personal difficulties are closely tied to an unsatisfactory interaction between this and himself. This frame of reference
had an important influence upon the kind of data sought, and while
the history and causal factors of a social problem were considered
crucial, equal emphasis was placed on the personal and social assets
in the client's life which could be immediately realized to help
him back on his feet. The main ingredients of a good social diagnosis
spelled out by Mary Richmond were "a general description of the
difficulty; . . . a statement of those peculiarities of circumstances
and personality which differentiate the case under review from all
others; . . . an enumeration of the causal factors in order of their
importance; the appraisal of the assets for construction discovered
in the course of enquiry . . . those within our client, those within
his immediate family and outside." [4]

This positive sociological approach offers a useful perspective on
mental retardation because it shifts the focus away from the individual pathology implied in the medical model of diagnosis to the
new and more competent social role of the mentally retarded. It also
emphasizes the importance of understanding the interaction between
the retarded individual and his environment, particularly in regard

to reciprocal roles. For example, although an individual may suffer from a severely limiting degree of physical and mental impairment, this does not relegate him to a completely passive role since this very passivity is part of an interactive process in that it evokes a proportionately strong measure of reciprocal response. Moreover, its catalyzing action may be just as disturbing to the equilibrium of the environment as more overtly destructive behavior. For example, family relationships may become warped and mutually destructive if a child with gross neurological damage absorbs too much of his mother's time and energies, if the father wants residential placement, and if the normal children become enmeshed in marital disagreements to the detriment of their own legitimate needs.

An effective assessment of the social environment of a retarded child or adult must therefore be approached along two lines— namely, the emotional and material resources it contains for the protection and stimulation of the retarded client, and at what cost to the normal members of the family (or substitute family) these are provided. The health and viability of the normal individuals are of utmost importance for two reasons. One is that the overall welfare of the retarded individual depends on the coping strength of those around him, and the other is that the pervasive dependency of the retarded does impose very heavy burdens. Good social work practice must be aware of the potential threat to family life that this stress represents, and must realize that the vulnerability of the normal family members is as vital an issue as the retarded person's actual handicap.[5] The simultaneous concern for the welfare of the disabled client and for maintaining the integrity of the environment that sustains him is the key contribution of social work in this situation, in that it does not foster the exclusive interests of a single individual but balances them against the equally valid claims of the social unit of which he is a part.

The concept of maintaining this sort of equilibrium is perhaps one of the distinctive features of social work in the retardation field because the many different but interrelated factors in the situation must be constantly weighed to determine at what point their interaction results in a positive or negative outcome. The first important stress factor to be measured is the relationship between the *extent* of the patient's disability and the *capacity* of his environment to provide social tolerance and support; effective social planning for both the retarded and his family will depend on an accurate assessment of this equation. The components of this relationship may have many different permutations: at one end of the scale a hopelessly disabled child may be satisfactorily maintained in a family setting with emotional and material strengths, while a client with a much milder degree of basic impairment may become a social casualty because of the adverse social conditions with which he is surrounded. The relative stresses set off by the *material* and *psychological factors* in the situation are the second point that needs careful assessing. A family with good material resources may be unable to care for a retarded member because of their disturbed psychological response to having a chronically handicapped child with a recognized social stigma, while another family in more modest circumstances but with greater emotional integrity may be able to assimilate this disability. Some families have the emotional capacity to care for even a seriously disabled child but cannot cope with the practical problems involved because these are a further drain on their limited resources and exacerbate other practical difficulties of living, such as inadequate income and substandard housing. The last complex of related factors which determine how successfully the retarded individual can be absorbed into the pattern of normal social life is the three-way relationship that exists between his degree of social dysfunctioning, the ability of the family to tolerate this, and the supportive social services that are available to compensate for these stresses.

From this overview of the social diagnostic process we must move to a more explicit scrutiny of the social components which will influence the social adjustment and growth of the retarded. Since the primary focus of social work help is the client's disability and the interference with social functioning it creates, we shall start by examining the role and status he is invested with, his innate characteristics and the way in which the significant people in his background (usually the family) perceive and respond to them. The client's level of social functioning needs to be studied in conjunction with status and role because status depends a good deal on an individual's level of development and social competence; a child with severe multiple handicaps, for example, is likely to retain baby status throughout his entire childhood because of his helpless dependence. Conversely, developmental levels may be partly determined by the role the child is expected to fill.

If the family of a moderately retarded child persist in treating him as the not very efficient but highly lovable pet, this infantile role may seriously hinder him from learning practical social skills and from developing in social maturity. Therefore, in order to make an accurate prediction of the retarded individual's capacity for social adjustment, it is necessary to learn about the role that he is expected to play within his social milieu, how realistically this accords with his capacity and potential, and also how easily it can be reinforced by those around him. If these three factors do not synchronize smoothly, the adjustment of the retarded individual is inevitably impeded. For example, a mildly retarded adolescent whose parents expect him to function as a near normal in a regular educational setting is being ascribed a role that is beyond his capacity; the strain resulting from this disparity is likely to create anxiety and other psychological defensive reactions which will adversely affect his performance in almost all areas of functioning.

The social behavior and functioning level of a retarded child or adult will vary in detail according to differences in age and degree of disability, but certain broad areas provide good indices of level of social development. For the *preschool* child it is important to find out his capacity for self-feeding, toileting, helping to dress himself, handling toys, and the sort of response he makes to overtures from other children. These activities will indicate how much in arrears he is with these important milestones. For the *school-age* child the type and extent of involvement with siblings and other children (such as those belonging to relatives, close friends, or neighbors) will be a good indication of his capacity for social relationships. This same criterion can also be applied to more highly organized social activity, and membership in the Cub Scouts or being part of a religious group are also indications of how well the retarded client is accepted socially and of his ability to benefit from this. For the older child it is useful to know whether he ever stays away from home overnight, either with relatives or friends informally or on a more organized basis at camp, since this is a good indication of emotional maturity as well of the social opportunities he has. Other manifestations of social competence which the social evaluation should pick up are whether the retarded child or adult can do small jobs around the house, be sent on simple shopping errands to nearby stores, and how he comports himself in these situations. The twelve-year-old boy with moderate retardation who learns to buy the evening paper and to distinguish which coin is needed for payment is building up a good reservoir of vital social skills for the time when he is of employable age and starts industrial training.

The social involvement of the retarded child or adult outside of his own home can also reveal the perception the family has of his social functioning. Parents who refuse to let a retarded child mix with peers or younger children of normal intelligence *may* do so on the reasonable grounds that he cannot hold his own with more able children. Their reluctance may also be a subtle expression of their feeling that he is socially different, unacceptable, and likely to be rejected. On this account the retarded client's social life has very important implications for both himself and his family because it provides a way of breaking into the intensely dependent relationships that will form between the retarded child and his family if his social satisfactions derive mainly from them. Such an exclusive pattern of relationship not only restricts the retarded child's emotional and social growth but makes it very difficult for him as an adult to assume an independent mature role. These observations apply mainly to moderately and severely retarded individuals who have some potential for development if it is recognized and encouraged. As we have already indicated, the individual's own capacity is an important factor in determining what role he will fill but the perception of him and his handicap by other people, especially the family, is also crucial. Therefore, to understand fully the social situation of a retarded client it is important to explore the factors within his family that are likely to influence the sort of role they prescribe for him. These factors may be of psychological, cultural, and sociological origin.

In regard to the first it is important to have an understanding of the dominant psychological characteristics of the normal people who are most intimately involved in the care of a retarded individual. Thus a retarded child may assume a certain status because he complements the psychological idiosyncracies or needs of one or both parents. A mother with very strong nurturing drives may take special satisfaction from the invalid role of a profoundly retarded child. Alternatively, the chronic burden of care demanded by some levels of disability may reinforce a latent streak of masochism in either parent. The reciprocal parent roles, which are an outcome of their combined psychological drives, may be another influence which shapes the role of the retarded child or adult. To illustrate, if the total psychological economy of a family rests on the notion that the mother's role is exclusively related to home-making and child-rearing, a severely (or even moderately) retarded child may be invaluable in reinforcing this scheme. Further, if this function is threatened by societal trends (for example, the pressure on married women to go into industry), there may be a strong unconscious vested interest in keeping the retarded individual in a permanently dependent status, regardless of his latent capacity for greater development.

In such an instance the role of the retarded is influenced by societal trends; it is therefore important to look at cultural influences which may also play a part.[6] Thus, if the prevailing cultural values sanction a particular form of social inadequacy—for example, long-term economic dependence through ill health—then the retarded child or adult, with his conspicuous disability and its corollary of chronic dependence, will tend to be regarded as quasi-invalids. This will ensure the tolerance and acceptance that accompany the sick role as well as sympathetic support for the family who have to meet the extra and unusual needs of this role. Further, this particular role will be more likely to be accepted if the family belongs to a subculture which encourages an attitude of philosophical resignation toward major misfortunes, and mental retardation can be accepted as a phenomenon that falls within this religious or philosophical frame of reference.[7]

In order to understand the quite complex relationships and patterns of interaction that can develop in a family that has a retarded member it is helpful to conceptualize some of the roles and status that have been, and still are, assigned to the retarded. A varied range of such role ascriptions has been described by Wolfensberger,[8] but for our purposes we can identify three that recur frequently and exert a good deal of influence on how the retarded individual is assimilated into the community to which he belongs. They are the role that is *actually benign,* the role that is *benign by intention,* and the *malign* role.

The *actually benign* role accords most closely with the individual's innate capacities, has greatest resemblance to that same role when it is performed by a normal individual, and is aimed at developing the retarded individual's abilities in the direction of the norm. The *intended benign* role depends more upon society's view of the retarded individual than upon his innate competence, and seeks to achieve compassion and tolerance for his disability rather than ways of compensating for it by external help. The *malign* role is an expression of hostile and devaluing attitudes toward mental deficiency; it accentuates the deviant qualities of the retarded individual and usually leads to his ejection from society rather than his successful integration. The most blatant example of this is the perception of a conspicuously retarded child as less than human. In today's culture this does not get explicit recognition but when placement at birth is recommended for a baby with obvious retardation, the physician, nurse, social worker, minister or whoever initiates this suggestion is implicitly reflecting this attitude. The effect is often to evoke a similar frame of mind in the family because when parents are advised to take the totally unnatural step of immediately separating themselves from the newborn child with whom they have the closest biological and psychological ties they are liable to assume that the baby is so extremely abnormal as to forfeit all normal claims to nurturing and parental concern. Many parents of children with Down's syndrome who have survived the psychological trauma of such *untimely* advice have subsequently expressed amazement at the relatively normal appearance and behavior of the child as it develops.

The actually benign role is not an entity of its own but rather a modification of the role performed by normal people to suit the limited capacity for social functioning that is an inevitable by-product of mental retardation. This role offers the best prognosis for rehabilitation since it means that the family or relatives recognize the social potential of the retarded individual and will therefore be motivated to utilize services that will further this.

The intended benign role is exemplified by the "invalid" role, the permanent "innocent child" role, and what may be termed the "cherished idol" role, which sets the retarded child apart and insists on his being given a hallowed place within the family set-up. All of these roles ensure compassionate treatment and a measure of happiness for the retarded individual in that his limitations are catered to and he is protected from the major stresses that might otherwise occur. They are, however, essentially static roles and do not assist him to develop his potential to its fullest or to take a realistic part in the social life around him. The intended benign role has partly evolved out of the lack of rehabilitative services to help the family in their management of the retarded individual; when the latter is a dependent adult who has made an adjustment within this frame of reference, his family may be reluctant to consider outside help which will challenge this social status and his niche in the family. This point is illustrated by a moderately retarded man in his late twenties who lived alone with his parents who were of retirement age. Although he was capable of learning to travel on his own and could have done well in a sheltered workshop, the parents would not accept this facility but preferred to keep him at home where they themselves undertook to keep him occupied with useful tasks about the house. These were not particularly suited to his normal male role; he had no contact with peers; and as a result he was extremely fearful about social contacts. The parents themselves began to feel the burden of keeping him busy but could not make the necessary adjustment in their perception and management of him to let him have a trial outside of the home. In such situations social work has the responsibility of redefining the role and status of the retarded client in more realistic and effective terms and of helping the family to accept and reinforce it.

The malign role is much more difficult to analyze and modify because it expresses deep-seated, unconscious psychological and cultural factors that are not usually accessible to the individuals concerned. A very dramatic example of this sort of role, the behavior it evoked in the child and her family, and its complex origins is the case of a nine-year-old girl with Down's syndrome who was born to a middle-aged couple who had come to the United States as refugees from Europe after the Second World War. At this child's birth the parents already had a large family of half-grown children and an addition to the family was unwelcome, aside from her handicap. Because of the language barrier and other marked cultural differences the family lived in social isolation and so were unaware of how to get help with raising this child. When she eventually reached a diagnostic center she had no self-help skills, and was uncontrollable and extremely unhappy. The parents were then desperate for help because she was becoming an extremely disruptive force within the family which had now stretched to include a second generation of grandchildren.

A detailed exploration of the family's history provided by two grown-up sons and a daughter-in-law yielded some penetrating insights into the situation. The family were Jewish and had originally lived in a provincial town where the father owned a small but secure family business. When the country was occupied by the Nazis, the entire family fled into a remote mountainous area where they were kept in hiding by non-Jewish families. The mother was in an advanced stage of pregnancy and the birth of the baby precipitated a major crisis because it coincided with an impromptu visit of German soldiers and the villagers were afraid that its crying might give away the presence of the refugee Jews. In fear of reprisals the suggestion was put forward to smother it, but the mother could not tolerate this and hid in the woods until the danger was over. Though both survived, the episode made a tremendous emotional impact upon the whole family and was felt to crystallize the totality of destructive experiences that they had been subjected to on account of the war. The advent of an unwanted and visibly defective child after arrival in the promised land of America seemed to revive all the negative valences associated with the earlier experiences and was taken as a sign that the ill luck had not been left behind in the past. Because of this massive displacement of hostility and fear, none of the family were able to relate to the child on a realistic basis and when her behavior became difficult they were paralyzed and could not attempt any control. At the time of their request for help there were no community facilities that could cope with such a difficult child, and the family could not contemplate institutional care and its implied rejection. In addition the cultural and language barriers made it impossible to deal effectively with the family's distorted emotional involvement.

This case is a good illustration of many of the points that we have made about evaluating the retarded individual, his place in the social environment to which he belongs and his interaction with it. Starting with the child, we see extremely negative behavior patterns which seriously disturb the psychological and social life of her family as well as impeding her own maximum social development. These patterns can be related to the role into which the family has fitted her, which in turn can be seen to derive from a series of extremely shattering psychological and social experiences. These resulted in part from the family's cultural and historical status—i.e., being Jewish in a country when it was overrun by an invading army with a formidable policy of racial persecution.

In this instance the exploration of the family's personal history, cultural origins, and current attitudes was related primarily to the pathology of the situation and the contribution made by these factors toward the central problem of the child's unmanageable behavior. This represents the *etiological* or *diagnostic* facets of the social evaluation which are important for interventive treatment. It is, however, equally important to assess the family and its total environment from the *prognostic* angle and to discover what strengths it possesses that will assist the retarded client's social adjustment and more particularly the rehabilitative measures being considered for him. Social work is portrayed in this book as functioning within the conceptual framework of the therapeutic milieu. The remainder of the chapter will examine the various factors that constitute this supportive environment and those that are liable to undermine it. In this context the environment means the family or significant people with whom the retarded child or adult is closely involved, the extended family network from which the nuclear family is derived, and the wider community to which both relate. All three will be assessed from both psychological and material or practical angles.

The nuclear family is the most vital, and also most vulnerable, component of the retarded individual's social milieu, and its composition, structure, and functioning pattern need very careful analysis.[9] The actual number of individuals who make up the family is important for many reasons as is the way they are distributed along the age continuum and the place at which the retarded child or adult fits in. If we look at the nuclear family as the primary protective shell within which the handicapped member lives and develops, the first feature that is essential to his stability is the presence of both parents. Though a single parent family can cope with a retarded member it usually does so with greater stress. To some extent the same is true of families in which the retarded child is an only child. Here, although the parents have more time, energy, and material resources to devote to the demands of the retarded child, they nevertheless face a lonely task in which rewards are inevitably limited since their total emotional investment as parents is in one child with a handicap. In larger families the number, sex, ages, and ordinal place of siblings is important because these factors help to determine the degree of strain the parents encounter in coping with total family needs and also affect the role that the retarded child has. Several young children close in age to the handicapped child make the task of his care that much more difficult whereas one or two older children may be an asset in providing some companionship and helping to train him by example and shared activity.

This leads us into the type and pattern of relationships within the family, particularly the way they have evolved to cope with a disabled member. Various factors affect this area of family functioning but probably the most crucial is the parents' basic attitude toward the phenomenon of handicap and the child who embodies it, and how this affects their role and behavior as parents. An evaluation of the parents' feelings toward the retarded child and of the mechanisms they employ for dealing with these emotions is a first and most essential step in the social diagnosis because they set the feeling tone for the entire family which will influence the relationships between all members.

Many factors influence how parents feel about and respond to their handicapped child—namely broad societal attitudes, the approach of their immediate community, the reaction of family and close friends, and, at the heart of the matter, their own personal sense of identity and self-esteem. These are all interrelated in their impact, but we shall be discussing the first three items at greater length later on so at this point the focus will be on the psychological make-up of the parents. A most crucial point to bear in mind is that the advent of a damaged offspring is a serious blow which strikes hard at the ego of the individuals to whom this event has occurred. To understand the nature of each individual parent's vulnerable areas it is essential to know what his or her current social aspirations are, on what the maintenance of their self-esteem depends, and the origins of this emotional security or insecurity. For this an exploration of some factors in the parents' developing years is vital because the shock of having a defective child almost invariably activates old and earlier stresses. The nature of these earlier psychological experiences, how successfully the conflicts arising out of them have been resolved and the extent of their residual effects will all have a bearing upon the way the parents respond to this new crisis. Furthermore, in making this sort of analysis it is necessary to take into account that it is not simply the psychological idiosyncrasies and residues of each parent that must be assessed but also—and more important—the new psychological amalgam that is created by the fusion and interaction of the two separate entities.

Generally speaking we can divide early psychological events into two groups, those that are an intrinsic part of normal development and those that have been peculiar to this individual or family. In the first category are the type and quality of family relationships that the mother and father experienced as children with their own parents and siblings; the advent of any new baby re-creates these earlier family patterns and the feelings associated with them, and an unusual or unresolved situation in the past assumes a heightened significance if the baby in the present is himself abnormal. The woman who still feels a strong sense of sibling rivalry with a sister (as in the case of Mrs. Fanara in Chapter 5) will have more difficulty in accepting a deficient baby than someone who has worked through these earlier feelings and is able to view her plight in more objective terms instead of investing it with emotions left over from another situation. Equally if a father has not been able to establish his own identity as an independent, competent male vis-à-vis a more potent father figure, he is likely to perceive a defective offspring as manifest proof of his innate inferiority or his permanently immature status.

The parents' record of achievement will also throw useful light on how either of them is likely to react to the implied failure of having a defective child. Failure in school may make a parent especially sensitive to intellectual deficit, and for the father his achievement in his professional or work sphere may be very significant since these are both important sources of self-esteem in today's society as well as indications of the level of economic or material security he has achieved. There is the added point that a child with a severe degree of handicap may make exceptional demands upon his financial resources because of the need for extra and specialized care, and these demands can represent a serious threat to the father's role of family provider. The father in the Christie case (which is described in Chapter 7) illustrates how this particular stress factor can affect adjustment to having a retarded child.

The medical histories of both parents and their families are another important area for exploration on two counts. First, information on clinical pathological conditions in family members may assist the diagnostic formulation of the medical components in the child's overall condition. Second, even when there is no known or apparent relationship between a certain illness that the family has experienced and the retarded child's specific handicap, it may be a fertile source of latent anxiety, particularly with regard to hereditary or etiological factors. There is also an irrational component in that a fantasied connection is often thought to exist between illness (or a surgical operation or obvious handicap) and the defect in the child, since both carry the implications of non-wholeness and spoiled identity.[10] This point is exemplified by a woman with a congenital anomaly manifested in deformed hands and forearms. Because of this, she had been sent to a special school for the physically handicapped and this educational segregation, together with her obvious and unsightly disability, had led to an unhappy childhood of loneliness and teasing by other children. Although her eight-year-old son had clearly not inherited this condition, she became very upset when his school referred him for special educational placement because of some learning disability and behavior problems associated with his frustration of not being able to keep up in class. Her intense need to deny anything wrong in him completely prevented her from relating realistically to his learning problems and his need for help.

Another example of a similar misconception of origin is the case of Mrs. Ronan whose mother had been hospitalized for an acute mental illness following a hysterectomy when Mrs. Ronan was fifteen. Although this event did not affect the practical aspects of Mrs. Ronan's life (since her grandmother lived in the home and could carry on its management), it gave her a special sensitivity toward mental disorder, and when her first child was found to have brain damage with some retardation, she reacted with a great deal of anxiety, directed particularly toward causation and the possibility of a hereditary factor. Her anxiety undermined her competence in handling the child's atypical behavior, and at four-and-one-half years of age he presented a quite serious overlay of neurotic disturbance on top of his mild retardation. This reinforced Mrs. Ronan's belief that the child had inherited mental instability from her side of the family.

The parents' basic attitude toward the retarded child is one of the main factors that determines how efficiently the total family economy is managed to meet this unusual and often stressful situation. Next in importance come the normal children and the type of relationships that they are helped to build with their retarded sibling.[11] These should be carefully evaluated because they are a good indication of how effective the family is in meeting the retarded child's needs and also of how well it is able to maintain its own viability and integrity in discharging this responsibility. The roles that may devolve upon the normal children because of a defective sibling are varied and not necessarily harmful but they inevitably contain elements that are not found in family setups which do not have to cope with deviance and excessive dependency. Whether the roles of the normal children are healthy and conducive to normal development or pathological and distorting depends largely on the parents' adjustment to their problem and their realistic perception of the difficulty it creates. It is particularly vital to explore carefully this aspect of family dynamics because many parents are unaware of the effect that the presence of a retarded child can have upon his siblings and need help in recognizing and dealing constructively with the conflicts that are likely to ensue.[12] The ideal resolution of this charged area of interpersonal relationships occurs when the parents have themselves reached the stage of frankly recognizing the social implications that retardation has for the other children and are able to devise a modus vivendi for the whole family that compensates for the inevitable disadvantages. This level of emotional integrity and maturity is not achieved by all parents. Therefore, social work with the family must concern itself with the less constructive roles into which the normal children may be thrust. If, for example, retardation has been a special blow to parental aspirations, there may be an exceptionally strong emphasis on achievement by the normal children to compensate for the retarded child's lack of success. This can produce disturbing repercussions within the family in that it may make the normal children ashamed of their retarded brother (or sister) as well as stimulating a destructive competitiveness aimed at showing up his inadequacies. The compulsion to constantly excel can also create anxiety for the normal children about their capacity to sustain these standards, and it is also a subtle way of robbing them of their individual identities since their value to their parents is felt to be dependent on the compensatory success they can demonstrate.

An equally detrimental role is created for the normal children when one (or both) parents cannot acknowledge negative feelings about the child's deficits and displaces this hostility onto the normal siblings in unreasonable and constant criticism of their behavior. This scapegoating device occurs more frequently when there is only one normal child to sharpen the contrast with the retarded one, and it creates very serious problems for the former because his parents' demands are not related to his intrinsic qualities but to the deficiencies of the handicapped child. This situation inevitably produces disturbed behavior in the normal sibling and completes the destructive cycle by reinforcing the parents' conviction that he is difficult and justifies their punitive handling. It also supports their unconscious feeling of failure as parents since neither child develops normally.

A third role that the normal children may be expected to fill is that of "parents' aide" or support, in which they are expected to identify with the parents' special concern for the retarded child's well-being, often at the expense of their own legitimate needs. This approach interferes with the fraternal relationship that normally develops among siblings, and inhibits them from expressing normal feelings and behavior (including hostility when it is appropriate) toward the retarded child. It is important for the social history to uncover these atypical patterns of family behavior: unless they are modified by outside help they will not only deprive the retarded child of potentially valuable allies who will provide a unique opportunity for social and emotional development, but are also likely to have a negative influence on the social and emotional development of the normal children, giving them a permanently warped view of family life.

Outside of the nuclear family unit the most important component of the social environment is the extended family of grandparents, aunts, uncles, and cousins. The social evaluation should explore the relationship between these concerned individuals and the nuclear family, particularly in regard to their current involvement with the problem of retardation. Support from the kinship group is of inestimable value to the parents because they can handle their distress and bewilderment better if they feel that the retarded child and the attendant difficulties are sympathetically accepted by their close relatives. The active psychological support from grandparents is especially necessary in that it fortifies the parents' identification with effective nurturing roles and increases their sense of competence in coping with the demanding task of rearing a retarded baby.

It is therefore not only important to discover how much contact the nuclear family has with the extended group but also to understand whether this interaction is fundamentally benign in intent and supportive to the parents. Thus if an active grandmother with free time on her hands lives within easy access of the nuclear family, she can be a major source of support, by being on hand to advise on management, to baby sit, and to share generally in the task of handling the retarded child and other children. However, if this assistance takes the form of a complete takeover of the nuclear family's problems and responsibilities, the parents will be unconsciously forced into a dependent position to a more competent and powerful parent figure. This will either create resentment and conflict or an abrogation of responsibility which will prevent their own coping abilities from developing. It is also important to understand the attitudes of the relatives toward retardation and its presence in the family, because excessive mourning over the tragic event or rejection and denial of its presence can have a very adverse effect upon the parents.

In addition to these complex emotional factors there are many practical issues connected with the extended kinship network and its relationship with the nuclear family unit, in that the former provides a readily available source of help in the management of both the retarded child himself and the whole family. Conversely, if the family has no such contacts, either because it has physically moved too far away from the parents' home or because the two households are emotionally at loggerheads, it is in an extremely vulnerable position for coping with the inevitable strains imposed by retardation through having no one on hand to offer emotional support or to be available in an emergency.

Aside from their direct influence upon the parents themselves, the extended family, if it is in regular contact, has a valuable socializing function in providing an additional set of people with whom the retarded child can relate and develop his social skills and experience. This applies particularly to the more profoundly handicapped, who are very much cut off from outside contacts. A case in point is a multiply handicapped boy of four with cerebral palsy, almost no vision, and a severe degree of retardation but whose social responsiveness was developed far beyond what his intellectual and motor capacities would have indicated. This was mainly due to the fact that he lived in the center of a warm extended family group; the constant attention he received from grandparents, uncles, and aunts, and young cousins of varying ages provided a high level of affectionate stimulation. This also meant that he was not relating exclusively to his mother, so that the intense, almost symbiotic relationship that is liable to develop between a severely impaired child and the parent most closely involved in his care was diluted by the many emotional and social contacts he experienced with other family members. This is an important factor in preserving the mental health of the parents as well as preventing too close an attachment which can create major difficulties of separation and adjustment if the child subsequently has to be placed in residential care.

Another cogent reason for studying the extended family is that they embody the cultural values in which the parents have been reared, and these are often a key to understanding how the family will adjust to the trauma of retardation. From the diagnostic angle it is of prime importance to know whether these values still dominate the thinking and behavior of the parents because they may have an important influence on treatment plans.[13] This point is especially critical in a pluralistic society such as the United States where the social and geographical mobility which characterizes today's living can create serious gaps between the cultural values with which a family was brought up and their adherence to them in later life. For retardation (and many other obviously handicapping and deviant conditions) this has a special significance since the way a generation steeped in one culture approaches the problems may not be suitable for the next one. For example, if a parent of a retarded child comes from a family that emigrated from a technologically backward and less complex society, the older generation of relatives may not understand the origin of retardation or what remedial measures are feasible, and the status with which they endow the child may be inappropriate. This is particularly true when a conspicuously damaged child is prescribed treatment that shatters the conventional conception of the sick role and seems to be harsh rather than compassionate. If this cultural dilemma is not properly comprehended and worked with, it can create a conflict in the parents' mind about the value of treatment; and even when they remain convinced of its efficacy, they are faced with having to oppose their family's views. In extreme circumstances this may amount to curtailing the contact between the retarded child and the older-generation relatives if their approach cuts across the parents' management stratagems for handling the retarded child's problems. Because it is much easier for the nuclear family if they have the support of their families, it is important to explore these areas of potential cultural discrepancy and help the significant people concerned to resolve their conflicts. An illustration of this sort of situation is the Martinelli family where the six-year-old girl was severely retarded with strong autistic symptoms. The parents were very eager for any sort of modern therapy to be tried; but the older members of their families tended to be skeptical of these efforts, preferring to put their trust in prayers for a miracle and even suggesting the "horns" to ward off the evil eye. Since the child's impairment was very severe and her progress extremely slow despite intensive and well-coordinated help from several disciplines, it was very difficult for the parents to make a convincing case to their skeptical relatives that the modern, scientific treatment was likely to be more effective. This was a situation in which a great deal of supportive counseling was needed from the psychiatrist, the play therapist, and the social worker, all of whom together functioned in the role of the extended family kinship group. (This technique of supportive counseling is described more fully in Chapter 7.)

The third feature of the environment which needs exploring is the way in which the family that contains a retarded member fits into the community of which it is a part. This is a vital sphere of social interaction to investigate because it has both diagnostic and treatment connotations. Diagnostically the relationship between the family with a retarded child or adult and the wider community will throw light on how they view their child's handicap and how they react to the particular social situation it creates for them. For example, if the stigma of retardation is felt acutely, a family may defend itself against feared ostracism and rejection by having minimal contact with outside individuals and groups. This is an understandable but essentially unhealthy reaction which can only lead to distorted social growth and functioning for the entire family including the retarded member. It is pathological because it fosters an excessive concentration on the negative and socially deviant elements in the situation, and the ingrown conviction that mental retardation is socially unacceptable can never be put to the test if the family and the retarded individual keep their distance from the normal families around them. It is therefore a crucial area for social work intervention, and the social diagnosis should try to discover the full range of social involvement and activities that the entire family engages in. It is important to know how much social life the parents allow themselves, whether their activities are formal (such as a weekly bowling or bridge group) or informal (visits to friends or relatives), and whether they play an active part in the running of their community, through affiliation with a religious or political group. The social life of the normal siblings is of equal concern, particularly whether it has to be curtailed because of the retarded child's limitations and if so what compensations are offered. It is particularly revealing to know whether the normal children have many friends, whether they bring them to the home, and how they interpret the retarded child's deviance to them.

The therapeutic aspect of community involvement should cover the social life of both the parents and the children. If the latter have an active and varied social life and find that they are accepted by their peers, this will counteract the feeling that they are socially different because of having a handicapped sibling. By the same token the normal child who is timid about making friends and does not like to introduce them to his family may develop a strong sense of social inferiority which can adversely affect his personal relationships throughout his life. The friends of the normal siblings may also be helpful to the retarded child in providing him with an additional social dimension and reinforcing his sense of personal acceptability. The initial sense of being socially different that the normal family is likely to experience because of the presence of a socially devalued handicap is most effectively overcome by the practical demonstration of acceptance, which is really best provided by normal members of society in day-to-day social intercourse. The wider social group or community is therefore an important therapeutic agent, and on this account it is essential to know what its resources are for neighborliness and what capacity the family has for utilizing these. Moreover, the emphasis that the social evaluation puts on the day-to-day normal social functioning of the family has an additional value to its diagnostic one in that it demonstrates the social worker's concern for the normal as well as retarded family members and therefore places the handicap of the latter in an essentially family-oriented context. Because retardation has traditionally been treated as a medical problem, with primary focus on the disabled retarded patient, it is essential that social work in its operation balance this perspective by reinforcing the social interactive aspects of the situation.

So far we have concentrated on the intangible components of the environment as they are expressed in the psychological and social attitudes, roles, and relationships that develop around the handicap of retardation. Now we need to consider the practical elements in the retarded individual's milieu, since they too exert a very important influence upon his own development and upon the capacity of the environment to contain and support him. First in importance are the *economic* circumstances because the disabling conditions associated with retardation frequently impose unusual expenses upon the family. From babyhood the slow developer will probably require more frequent and often specialized medical attention. In later childhood extra social services (such as day care, special camping facilities, tutoring, homemaker service) are all a potential drain on family resources.

To the immediate financial pressures is added the prospect of having to provide against a lifetime of partial or complete dependency. Anxiety about these long-term commitments is often a major source of stress, particularly for the father who may feel that he cannot meet these unusual and heavy demands. If this area of potential conflict is not recognized and ventilated, it can lead to marital tension. The employment conditions, as well as the earning capacity, of the wage earner are also significant factors in a family's ability to adjust to retardation. If the father has to work very long hours or travel a great distance to work, his share in the actual care of the retarded child is necessarily curtailed. This prevents him from becoming familiar with the child and developing an attitude of acceptance based on a growing acquaintance with the child's special characteristics. It also places responsibility for the retarded child's actual management on the mother alone, giving her a feeling of isolation. The emotions generated by this situation may lead to a preoccupation with the child to the exclusion of the rest of the family, particularly the nonparticipating husband, or it can cause great resentment and a marital conflict. In any case there is a physical strain on the mother if she has no one to take the child off her hands.

The close association between mental retardation, whe
severe, and poor socioeconomic conditions is another re
is so important to investigate a family's economic status. I
lies with the special problem of retardation also have to
the broader and more basic stresses of a marginal budget, a
meager resources are to be mobilized to help the retarded c
must get help with their day-to-day living expenditure
aspect of their lives is overlooked, the special remedial t
for the retarded client may be impeded by such things as
carfare to keep an appointment or of ready money for me
or other special treatment. It may even affect the ability to
through on a prescribed routine because the parents are to
occupied with the mere survival of their household.

The physical environment is another area of special relevai
mental retardation, particularly the developmental and functional
problems the handicap gives rise to. It is therefore important to
obtain a fairly detailed picture of the child's home and how it is
arranged to neutralize some of these disadvantages. It is, for example,
necessary to have adequate living space which will give the retarded
child the opportunity of developing in his slow and maladroit way
without interfering too much with the rest of the family. A major
focus of conflict exists when the normal children do not have privacy
to do their homework or engage in other activities without interruption from the retarded child; a place where they can keep their own
possessions intact is also essential. The training of the retarded child
is made easier or more difficult by the physical layout of the household. Thus it is difficult to instill good sleeping habits into a hyperactive toddler if he has to share sleeping quarters with another child,
or if his room is too near to the main living area for seclusion at bedtime. The floor level on which the family lives is also of crucial importance on many counts. For a family that lives three or four floors
up it is a physical effort to take a child (and probably his stroller
too) down several flights of stairs. Even when this problem is overcome by an elevator, there still remains a restriction on his going
out of the house to play unaccompanied, which might be feasible
from a ground floor living accommodation. The presence of a yard

also makes management, social training, and play stimulation easier. Beyond the home it is useful to know whether there is a public park or playground within walking distance, what public transport is available, and how close the main road and its traffic hazards are. Accessibility to stores is another important feature, first, because this makes it easier for the mother to do her shopping, and second, because it provides a small sample of the outside world for the retarded individual to become familiar with. For the older individual it offers an opportunity to practice the important social skill of shopping, exchanging money, and so on. By emphasizing the significance of the ordinary material and geographical environment, the social worker is conveying to the family how it can be exploited to develop the social awareness, skills, and capacities of the retarded individual.

Inevitably the utilization of these hidden (or informal) social assets will depend on the family's attitude toward them. For example, the mother who takes her retarded child to the housing project play area when it is empty does not help him to learn to play with other children, nor does she give other adults outside of the family an opportunity to become familiar with the child (in both his usual and unusual aspects) and observe her way of coping with the problem. Similarly, the father who is apprehensive about letting an older child explore his neighborhood on his own is losing the chance for the child and his neighbors to get used to each other. The quality of the locality must also be understood because this will inevitably influence parents in how much independence they permit the child to have. If the family lives in a dilapidated neighborhood that is due for slum clearance, there may be justifiable hesitation about letting the retarded child out alone because of the incipient hazards associated with drug addiction, alcoholism, violence, and other forms of social pathology. Again it is not the physical environment alone that counts but the individuals, for some very poor districts often exhibit neighborliness and communal responsibility for a handicapped child's welfare. The same applies to a large-scale housing project in which a child of limited understanding could easily get lost; if he is known to most of the other residents, however, this danger is greatly reduced.

Parents who are realistic about the problem will often cope with this hazard by asking their neighbors to notify them if they see the child wandering too far away from his own home.

The final factor that must be studied if an effective diagnosis of the social environment is to be made is the network of health, educational, and social services that the family and their retarded member need to mitigate his disability. This represents the formal and organized welfare effort of the community, which is an essential factor in social adjustment. This is neither a new idea nor one that is unique to retardation. Mary Richmond has cited the importance of the social institutions to which the client under diagnosis must be positively related. For the retarded client, however, they assume even greater significance because without specially devised help his impaired capacity for social development and functioning will stand permanently in the way of long-term social adjustment. The type and range of services needed will depend on the client's disability and his family's social needs, but the concept of a continuum of interrelated and sequential services should be the model against which this particular segment of the client's background should be assessed. The scope, source, and pattern of such services will be dealt with more elaborately in the final chapter on community organization. In addition to finding out what services are available, it is also necessary to discover the parents' attitudes toward using them because the family which metaphorically "keeps itself within doors" with its problem is likely to be less motivated to seek out special help or cooperate when it is available.

This chapter has concentrated so far on the evaluation of the social factors that have greatest relevance to retardation in its more pronounced and disabling forms. We have devoted so much space to this aspect of the social diagnosis because it illustrates most clearly the specific and unusual attributes of mental retardation and the different approaches social work must adopt in order to deal with them. Before closing, however, we must look at the differential use of the social diagnostic procedure in contexts other than those involving severe retardation. These fall into two main areas: first, that which concerns the social adjustment of the mildly retarded in both childhood and adult life, and second, those situations in which mental retardation is not the primary or central problem but a serious secondary one that complicates or exacerbates a broader and more basic social maladjustment.

In the latter situation many features of the traditional social history will be utilized since primary focus must be on the total problem. When retardation is one of the crucial components, it is equally necessary to utilize some of the more specialized aspects already described. A first essential is to analyze the particular contribution that retardation makes to the genesis and maintenance of the acute problem and give it a proper perspective. In such situations the assessment must focus primarily on the pathological forces that have converged to create the core problem; within this frame of reference the social factors that further or hinder the long-term adjustive patterns of the retarded individual are of less immediate importance than the current maladaptive patterns of relationships and interaction. The assessment of the part played by the retarded individual in the situation, irrespective of his age or degree of defect, should be directed to his current level of functioning, the role he has been ascribed, and the relative strength of the contribution that his handicap and social impairment make to the main dislocating elements. The case of Maria Navarro, described toward the end of this chapter, will illustrate these points.

When the presenting problem centers on the social maladjustment of a mildly retarded child or adult, the social evaluation should combine its conventional techniques for uncovering the cause of the current difficulty with an exploration of those resources in the environment that have provided support in the past and can be mobilized for the future. Thus many of the guidelines already laid down in this chapter for the more severely retarded can be utilized in relation to the mildly retarded, with some different emphases being noted.

The first significant difference is in regard to social role and the interaction between the mildly retarded, of whatever age, and their peers. For the obviously retarded the ascription of a special role associated with his handicap helps the environment to absorb him because this role reduces ambiguity about his deviant behavior and the level of social competence that can be expected. Role is, therefore, an important assimilating mechanism. For the mildly (and less conspicuously) retarded, role ascription is more complicated, mainly because the majority of these belong to the poorest sectors of society where their impaired adaptive behavior (in the vernacular "slow ways") does not automatically stand out amid the general low level of social functioning that poverty imposes upon everyone. Further the specific disability of retardation is to a great extent a function of standards and attitudes that derive from the value system of the dominant society and are not necessarily recognized by, or applicable to, those of the subculture to which the mildly retarded belong. That is to say, a child whose intelligence on testing falls below an arbitrarily imposed norm is designated as retarded and in need of special education, even though his overall social performance within his own group may be perceived as perfectly normal.[14]

In these situations there is a discrepancy between the social role *imposed* from outside of the subculture and that which has naturally evolved within it. This contradiction, unless understood and carefully handled, may serve to isolate the mildly retarded socially. In addition it is liable to create identity confusion which will have repercussions in all spheres of social interaction. For example, within the family there may be confusion about norms of behavior to be expected, what constitutes atypical (or retarded) features, and how they should be handled. Instead of a sympathetic understanding of the retarded child's shortcomings, the bewildered parents may fall back on a more punitive approach designed to make him try harder and shape up. Alternatively, they may reject the dictum of authority, persist in ignoring some of the child's real difficulties, and refuse to cooperate in help which may be both necessary and potentially effective. Neither of these ways of responding to the situation is conducive to building the benign and supportive milieu that a retarded individual needs.

The material components of the environment have already been cited as factors which have an important bearing on the social development and adjustment of the mentally retarded and their families, regardless of degree of handicap. In the case of the mildly retarded economic factors loom especially large because the general precariousness of life that results from poverty not only adds to their basic difficulties but is often a strong causative factor. The economy of the home is therefore a very vital area for exploration: what income maintains it, who provides it, whether it is adequate for the family's needs, and to what extent the actual physical home provides at least minimal security and comfort. These basic ingredients of survival will dictate the type and quality of care in the home, the degree of stimulation or deprivation that the children (whether normal or retarded) are exposed to, including such extraordinary (but not always rare) experiences as physical neglect, abuse, and even cruelty. In this connection it is also essential to explore the mental and physical health of the parents, and their resources for meeting the needs of the family within the demoralizing framework of poverty and social alienation. The question of a single-parent family also has particular significance in the context of poverty because there is less likelihood of relatives or reliable friends being available to help in the care of the children; if the mother has to go out to full-time work, this will probably mean that the children have to be placed in family day care. If this arrangement does not provide adequate stimulation or supervision (and the *informal* arrangements that poor families invariably have to depend on cannot usually meet adequate standards of child care), there is very real danger that the child's development will be hindered. When signs of retardation are already present, this will reinforce the deficit, and with normal children potential may be stultified and functioning become retarded.

The concept of the therapeutic milieu for individuals with more severe degrees of impairment is essentially a protective one within which their limited developmental capacity can be maximized. For the mildly retarded the therapeutic aspects of the environment must operate to reinforce their normalcy and develop their independence. On this account the institutions within the community, both formal and informal, are important. For the child, the school and how it relates to his needs is vital, as are facilities for leisure-time activities. For the adolescent and adult, employment prospects and social and recreational outlets are important. Beyond these formal sources of social support, the mores, structure, and operational patterns of the total culture must be understood since these are very influential in helping or impeding the adjustment of the mildly retarded. For example, in a locality ridden by poverty where the prevailing mental

climate is one of severe frustration and anger, the mildly retarded
individual runs the risk of being the scapegoat because his slower
adaptive capacity and the personal insecurity that accompanies it
may symbolize the collective sense of inadequacy that pervades the
whole community. An equal hazard is that he may, by virtue of being
naïve and easily led, get caught up in antisocial activities which end
in police charges and the attendant penalties. For the mildly retarded
adult other sociological factors may be significant in determining
how well he will be able to cope with independent adult living.
Where social mobility is limited and employment patterns remain
fairly constant, the retarded adult with relatively poor intelligence
may make out well because he has a prolonged opportunity to get
to know his neighbors, his job is likely to remain stable, and there will
not be a high turnover of workmates to tax his capacity for forming
new social contacts. Where the physical environment does not
change much, carrying on the ordinary affairs of living will be less
confusing because of being familiar. Moreover, in communities
which have low social mobility (in terms of population shifts or
opportunity for job advancement), psychological and social energy,
which is expended in the process of social movement, is so-to-speak
ploughed back into the existing network of social institutions and
relationships so that they are likely to be stronger and to involve
concern for all the members. This provides a sturdy social fabric
from which the more vulnerable retarded adult can derive a measure
of implicit and unconscious support as well as practical neighborly
intervention when occasion arises. An example of this is a man of
forty-five who lived in a small semirural town and worked at a
simple factory job in a well-established firm within cycling distance
of his home. Among his circle of workmates, one assumed responsibility for his budgeting and removed a portion of his weekly wage
on payday for long-term savings. Others assisted with such bureaucratic pitfalls as income tax and social security; and on social occasions, such as the firm's summer outing, there was a general benign
conspiracy to ensure that his consumption of alcohol was carefully
regulated. This man had a marginal intelligence; and without this
support, which was built into the pattern of his daily life, it is doubtful whether he would have survived outside of an institution.

Because of the varied range of acute problems and long-term stress created by mental retardation, the social evaluation must assume a complex and flexible pattern. In this chapter we have attempted to define the more important facets of this process, and to illustrate the points made we shall conclude with a description of three cases which demonstrate different types of problems and the different diagnostic emphases each requires.

The Mansfield family brought their three-and-a-half-year-old son Gerard to a special day care center for evaluation and, hopefully, preschool training. His history of birth trauma and high bilirubin level in the neonatal period suggested the presence of cerebral injury, which was subsequently confirmed by consistently slow development in all areas. On testing, the child was found to be well within the moderate range of retardation and, despite his hyperactivity and perseverative tendencies, he had achieved a fair degree of social skills. He could feed himself, was toilet-trained, and related well to other children, though his idiosyncratic handling of play material prevented his joining in cooperative play for more than short spells of time. Gerard was the second of three children, the eldest of whom had been born when Mrs. Mansfield was nearly forty. Before marriage she had worked as a trained nurse and had met her husband when he was in the hospital with a serious bout of pneumonia. Currently Mr. Mansfield was employed as a supervisor in a factory, which provided a steady and adequate income but not much financial margin. His health was precarious, owing to his having had T.B. as a child, so that his earning capacity was liable to be reduced by spells of sick leave in bad weather.

In spite of these setbacks the marriage was a basically happy one, and Mrs. Mansfield's strong nurturing tendencies were complemented by her husband's need for extra care. This gave her a dominating role without detracting from his, and he was able to assume responsibility and authority within the family. Mr. Mansfield originally came from another state so there were no paternal relatives close at hand, and Mrs. Mansfield's mother was elderly and unable to offer much practical assistance though she gave a good deal of emotional support. However, several married sisters and brothers and their spouses lived within reasonable distance, and the family shared many social activities with them and could rely on them for help in minor ways. Both parents were active in their local Catholic church and had succeeded in interesting the priest and congregation in the problems of retardation. Although this family had certain vulnerable features, such as the fact that both parents were relatively old for bringing up a young family and that the father had a chronically recurring health problem, it provided a very satisfactory environment for a moderately retarded child. The mother's professional background gave her a special expertise in dealing with the child's atypical health and training problems, and both parents derived a great deal of pleasure from having a young family. The normal children (who were both girls) were taught to relate to the retarded child as though he were normal, and from this he received both acceptance and stimulation. The presence of maternal relatives helped to dilute the full pressure of emotional and management strains, and the parents' early application for the child's admission to day care reflected their strong concern for obtaining whatever professional help was available and relevant. This in its turn would ease the management difficulties and so reduce stress that might be expected to impinge upon the family as a whole. It would also ensure that the retarded member was started on a consistent regimen of training which would stand him in good stead if the family were unable to continue with his care at any time in the future. The social diagnosis of this situation rested on assessing the potential efficiency of the environment for giving the most protective and stimulating care to the retarded child, without depleting its own resources too seriously.

In the next case the evaluation was focused on the complex of pressures associated with the seriously maladjusted behavior of a mildly retarded school girl that both stemmed from and contributed to serious family dislocation. Maria Navarro was referred to a child guidance clinic by the school medical officer for a psychiatric evaluation and assessment of her intelligence, on account of extremely disruptive behavior in school and near-delinquent activities reported by her mother. She was twelve-and-a-half years old and had been placed in a special class eighteen months previously because she was consistently disruptive in a regular class and had marked learning difficulties. When her behavior did not improve in the much easier academic setting, it was proposed to evaluate her further for neurological damage or severe emotional disorder. The child had a very bad relationship with her teacher, carried on an endless feud with the other children in school, had no friends, stayed out late, had been caught in a minor sexual misdemeanor, and was, on her mother's admission, entirely beyond her control. Her social background was as follows. Her mother (Mrs. Phillips) had come from Puerto Rico at the age of sixteen to stay with an aunt in one of the large eastern industrial cities of the United States and had married her first cousin two years later. After Maria was born, the father began drinking heavily and did not provide a stable income to support the home. On this account the baby was placed in the care of a grandaunt, and her mother returned to factory work. The marriage persisted in a very turbulent way (with frequent assaults by the father which resulted in police intervention) until Maria was eight, at which time the parents were divorced. Two years later the mother married a Negro man from one of the southern states who had himself been married before. He had been abandoned by his mother in early childhood and raised in a succession of poor, badly supervised foster homes, and at the time of Maria's referral to the clinic he suffered from severe asthma and bronchitis and made a precarious living as a cab driver. This job involved long working hours which did not help his health, and he was consequently very moody and difficult. Maria's existence had not been disclosed to her stepfather before the marriage, so that he was extremely resentful toward her, criticized her endlessly, and made invidious comparisons between her and his own daughter of the same age who lived with his first wife. He also showed outright favoritism toward the two-and-a-half-year-old boy of this second marriage, which provoked Maria to jealousy and at times very aggressive behavior toward the child.

Maria's mother was an emotionally immature and narcissistic woman whose growing up experiences had not developed her capacity for adult relationships, particularly that of motherhood. Her two disastrous marriages indicated an un-insightful and pathological way of trying to solve her many problems and currently she was extremely hostile toward her daughter whom she regarded as the major reason for her present marital difficulties. She had cut herself off from her own relatives when she remarried, and her second husband had no family living near enough to offer any practical help or advice with Maria. Mrs. Phillips had no reliable friends to turn to, and the chaotic pattern of life that the entire family was enmeshed in alienated them from the neighbors. An evaluation of this milieu showed that it was quite incapable of providing any sort of protection or care for this disturbed girl of subaverage intelligence, and further it was obvious that her presence was an added factor of aggravation to a seriously pathological home situation. The causes of this situation were not purely, or even primarily, the retardation but the unhappy chain of social experiences to which the child and her mother had both been exposed for most of their lives. Had Maria's social environment been healthier it is unlikely that the slight degree of retardation would have resulted in such seriously disordered functioning, and it can even be postulated that without the social stresses she experienced from an early age her intelligence might have developed normally.

The third case illustrates the interplay between the negative functional factors that are deliberately responsible for maladjusted behavior and the positive factors in the environment that can be mobilized to reduce the stress and reinforce more constructive functioning. In this context the social evaluation does take into account factors in the past that have had a significant part in precipitating or building up to the current critical situation since they will have to be dealt with in order to solve the acute pressures. It is also concerned with the positive factors in the past that have contributed to the client's more satisfactory aspects of behavior, since part of the therapeutic goal will be to recreate healthy conditions in which the client has flourished to compensate for his more vulnerable aspects.

Howard Burton came to the probation officer through a police court charge for petty larceny. The social history revealed that he had lost a fairly good factory job two months previously on account of persistent unpunctuality and finally for talking back to his supervisor when criticized about this. As a result of this upset, and the ensuing lack of money, he had quarreled with the aunt and uncle with whom he lived and had been turned out of their home. Since then he had been "sleeping rough," picking up meals in cheap eating places when he could and stealing in a small way for spending money. His record of delinquent activities was of long standing but not serious. At the age of eleven he had been committed to a State School partly because of a theft charge but mainly because of the lack of order and control in his home, which was supported by his unmarried mother and a restrictive but nearly blind elderly grandfather. At the State School he had responded well to the more stable routine and, as he grew older, demonstrated good work habits, a desire to please, and an outstanding ability for athletics. At nineteen, after a year's trial in work in the community near the school, he was discharged on parole to a married sister of his mother's (since the mother had died in the interim) where he made a good adjustment to work and fitted into the household.

Three years later a slightly younger male cousin returned home from service in the armed forces and a serious rivalry developed because the cousin had more money to spend, was able to get better jobs, and was altogether more of a social success. The feud was also of long standing since the boys had played together a good deal as children (including some joint participation in delinquent activities) and Howard had not understood why he had been sent away from home and his cousin had not. Further probing showed that the aunt and her family looked upon themselves as being the prosperous and successful branch of the family whereas Howard's mother had not only been regarded as dull-witted but was also under constant criticism for managing her life and family so ineptly. These strong emotional forces had to be uncovered in order to comprehend properly Howard's complex adjustment problems, but an equally important task of social work was to try to reinstate in the here and now the sort of social situation in which he had hitherto done well.

It was found, for example, that though he had originally resented being sent to the State School, over the years he had formed some good relationships in the community near which it was situated and that he had felt comfortable in the small town and the easier pace of its country environs. This included a satisfactory period of work with a local firm of builders.

In evaluating the features that appeared to be specially significant for his social adjustment, the following seemed among the most important.

First, the small town setting and the opportunity for working in a local firm where there was continuity of personnel to supervise him and with whom he could identify in the male adult wage-earning role.

Second, a family setup in which he figured as a useful male in the home. This was the role he had aspired to as a small boy in his mother's household and later had partly filled in his aunt's home until the return of the usurping cousin.

Third, scope for organized recreation which gave him a chance to develop and display his athletic ability.

Social work intervention, based on this assessment, took the form of helping him to get work in one of the local firms in the town near the State School. Arrangements were also made for him to lodge with a middle-aged widow living in the town who had a spare room because her youngest son had recently left home to get married. She had a number of relations, including an elderly father living next door who took his meals with her, so that there were many other individuals with whom Howard could relate. He was also permitted to join the recreation club of the State School where his participation gave him the added status of being no longer under legal jurisdiction but an independent member of the outside community.

In this case the problem was acute and emergent (in that it involved a police court charge), and relatively circumscribed (in that it need not happen again); but it was also partly related to the boy's innate social vulnerability which stemmed from his mild retardation and from his unresolved emotional conflicts of long standing. Social work had to engage both these aspects and to unravel past and current psychological pressures which were hindering his social adjustment, as well as to build up his present social situation so that it would offer specific protection against these types of stress.

7 THE PROFESSIONAL RELATION- SHIP WITH THE DEPENDENT CLIENT AND HIS FAMILY

THE PROFESSIONAL relationship is one of the most vital components of social work in the field of mental retardation. This chapter will describe certain features of this process that have a particular (or in certain instances, unique) applicability to the retarded client and his family. Primary emphasis will be on the relationship as utilized in casework, but many of the features under discussion will also have relevance to the other two methods of group work and community organization.

For the client group whose presenting problem is mental retardation the establishment of a professional relationship assumes a special importance because it is the medium through which the social acceptance of the handicap that was discussed earlier is conveyed by the social worker to the client. Moreover, the relationship with the worker and her agency embodies the concern of the whole profession for the social disadvantages that retardation entails, and provides the framework within which help for these problems can be set in motion. It is also the means of mobilizing and maintaining the necessary psychological energy in clients to cope with them. The professional relationship that develops between the social worker and clients for whom retardation is the major problem includes many of the ingredients that invest the relationship in any problem-focused situation that draws on social work help. It also possesses certain elements that are peculiar to this disability which must be understood. For example, some of the problems that arise out of the chronicity factor are different from those related to other types of social disability and influence the nature of the relationship in several directions. The triple-phased pattern of help described in Chapter 5, comprising *crisis-focused, supportive,* and *retainer* operations, will utilize a varying shift of emphases in the relationship, ranging from the intense and frequent to the casual and sporadic. From another angle, casework help that involves the three different levels of client-participation (designated in Chapter 4 as the fully *independent* retarded adult, the fully *dependent* retarded adult or child, and the *responsible adults charged with the latter's care*) will require different aspects of the relationship to be used in varying degrees according to different client needs. For example, in her dealings with the independent retarded adult the social worker may assume a predominantly supportive role or may have to exercise her authority more frequently, whereas her work with responsible relatives will probably draw on a fuller repertoire of approaches to match both the greater adjustive capacity that their normal intelligence makes possible and the special features of their responsible role. With the third type of client we have identified in this field—the dependent retarded child or adult of limited powers of comprehension and communication—the relationship may rest primarily on a sustained and overt expression of interest and goodwill, but it may also have to fall back on its authority aspect if circumstances necessitate more direct and active intervention.

Because of these important but different emphases and their ramifications in practice, we are spreading the discussion of the professional relationship over two chapters. That with the dependent client and the supportive family constellation will be dealt with now. In the following chapter we shall examine how this professional tool is utilized in relation to the more self-sufficient client within the mildly retarded range of handicap.

THE FAMILY AS PRIMARY CLIENT

It is important to remember that the family or normal relatives who assume the client role in casework are not essentially different from the normal range of clients encountered in any situation demanding social work help. Their potential for solving their problems is not affected by the intellectual impairment that the retarded suffer from, and though their overall situation may contain chronic and irreversible difficulties, their own capacity for readjustment is not necessarily subject to similar limitations. On the other hand, the normal relatives who are clients are liable to the same range of social and personal maladjustments as affect the community at large, and may therefore bring to the casework situation other factors besides the central one of retardation that hinder their effective involvement in help. Among relatives of the retarded may be found neurotic and psychotic behavior, immaturity, character disorder, disturbed interpersonal relationships, economic pressures, as well as varying degrees of emotional and social stability. Most of the techniques currently in use in social casework can be applied to this category of "normal" clients, and in general they are able to utilize the traditional type of professional relationship without any special modification. (In some families the so-called responsible relative may also be intellectually deficient but this factor will be covered in the next chapter on the retarded adult client.)

In considering the use of the professional relationship and other techniques of interaction for families of the retarded, we will start with those emergent and relatively circumscribed problems identified in the previous chapter as *secondary* problems. These contain many elements common to other social work situations in which the difficulties are clearly demarcated and sufficiently focused to make an eventual solution theoretically feasible. For example, the marital disturbance that has been precipitated by the shock of a retarded child's birth, though it may be long-standing and may take a long time to work through, still remains potentially open to resolution if the couple can mobilize their energies to involve themselves in casework help. In such a situation the usual approaches and techniques for developing and maintaining the professional relationship can be employed. The "sustaining process" of Hollis[1] and her "six sustaining procedures," which are directed to reducing the anxiety, bewilderment, and discomfort that a client feels when confronted with a problem sufficiently severe to require help, will be appropriate, along with the many other components of relationship that have been analyzed and identified by other writers. However, it is necessary to realize that the more circumscribed and potentially reversible difficulties occur in the context of the chronic, pervasive, and insoluble problem of retardation, which produces a double stress. In order to dispel ambiguity about the nature of the feasible help available, the social worker must take great pains to clarify for the family what their workable problem is, to what extent it can be modified by help, and the nature of the change envisaged. Otherwise the clients' expectations will be unrealistic, they will be unable to relate themselves to a meaningful goal, and the casework process will be blocked.

This dual stress has several aspects which may confuse or subvert the objectives toward which casework is directed. First, the strong feelings of despair and defeat that parents of a retarded child experience at one point or another are liable to invest any offer of help with an excessive amount of optimism and hope. This is often in inverse ratio to the disability and its problems; the social worker and the promise of help she may embody are therefore frequently perceived as much more potent than they really are, so that the sense of disappointment is correspondingly acute when unrealistically conceived goals are not realized. To avoid this, the social worker must be able to convey to the family that the treatment goals will touch only limited aspects of their problem and that assistance, in whatever form it is offered, can never be commensurate with the total needs of the case. However greatly a child's functioning is improved by training programs, or family attitudes modified so that they can handle their difficulties with less stress, in the final analysis both the child's basic defect and the regret this evokes in the parents still remain. The fact that the chronic stress situation remains unchanged, even though immediate pressures are relieved, imposes upon the social worker the difficult task of providing the family with the sort of relationship that will sustain them in their acceptance of the long-term stress at the same time as it motivates them to become involved in the active process that is needed to solve their more acute emergent problems. In such situations families have to engage in two almost opposing psychological processes—on the one hand, resignation to an insoluble problem and, on the other, mobilization of energy to attack one soluble portion of it which only amounts to a partial solution to their difficulty. Because of this double tension a family's resources for dealing with the more acute aspect of their problem may be absorbed in meeting the chronic strains that retardation creates, and their motivation for a limited solution will be undermined.

An illustration of this type of problem within problem is illustrated by the case of Mrs. Hylton, who asked for an interview with the social worker of the day care center where her three-and-one-half-year-old retarded son Donald was receiving preschool training. She expressed concern about her six-year-old daughter, who was reported to be very nervous in school, had severe nightmares, and suffered from a succession of minor somatic ailments. All these manifestations of disturbance were attributed to the child's anxiety over her brother. However, further exploration revealed that the father was excessively preoccupied with the girl's health, spent most of his spare time with her, and ignored the boy. The mother also disclosed that her husband was terrified of having another defective child and as a result their sexual relationship was fraught with tension and frustration. The shock and disappointment at having a retarded son were further aggravated by a fear that the boy's condition was due to an inherited factor which the father secretly thought came from his side. This highly disturbed family situation, which involved the normal sibling and was reacting adversely on the retarded child's development, demanded extensive casework treatment, but it was difficult to involve the father in this process because he could not see the point of help unless it could make an appreciable difference to the fundamental problem of his son's chronic defect.

Another important point to be recognized about the limited reactive problems that occur within the chronic and wider context of retardation is that the condition is often used to mask other more complex and serious functional problems within a family. Because of its alleged irreversibility mental retardation lends itself easily to being exploited as a smoke screen for more deep-seated and pervasive maladjustments, and the serious character of the reality problems associated with it provides a socially sanctioned opportunity for adopting a resigned attitude to the status quo. The most obvious example of this is when one parent becomes unrealistically invested in the care of a severely retarded child in order to work out an unresolved marital problem. It may be expressed by the mother who insists on giving round-the-clock care to a grossly impaired child so that she has no time for meeting the husband's needs at any level, or by the father who imposes the care of a very handicapped child upon his wife by refusing any sort of outside help, such as temporary placement or leaving the child with a relative or baby-sitter. In either situation there is almost invariably collusion from the apparently victimized partner, who receives as much protection from the threatening factors in the relationship as the one whose behavior is overtly responsible for the disturbed situation.

This point inevitably leads into another aspect of the casework process which is of special significance for the social worker's relationship to the normal family members. This is the importance of diagnostic acumen with which to identify the real character of the problems found in the family constellations, where there is retardation. Tied in with this is the equally important function of understanding the individual roles of separate members of the family as well as the place they fill in the total nexus, and of assessing how the dominant personal and social characteristics of each meshes with the overall problem of retardation, with either positive or negative results.

An illustration of the interplay of the parents' own personality problems around retardation is found in the Christie family, who were referred to the social worker initially to discuss placement for their seven-year-old son Norman who was moderately retarded, with some organic impairment. This apparently circumscribed topic of placement opened the discussion to other more complex anxieties, chief of which was the poor school record and social inadequacy of an older brother of twelve. Mrs. Christie was particularly concerned because her husband constantly complained about this boy's behavior and was obviously undermining his confidence. A psychological and psychiatric evaluation was suggested, and it showed the boy to be functioning within the borderline range of intelligence. He also had a poor self-image and a good many fears, as might have been expected from the family's account of his behavior and their attitudes toward him. Family counseling was offered to sort out attitudes and management tactics for both children, and in the course of this treatment a great many facts about the parents emerged that were highly pertinent to the focused problem of retardation. The father had lost his mother when he was fourteen and entertained an overt fantasy of being a nurturing and supportive figure himself, while also looking for this type of relationship in his wife. She had been a delicate girl, frequently missing school through illness, and grew up overshadowed by her own mother and a younger sister to regard herself as very inadequate in the coping feminine role. The overt problem of the more severely handicapped child threatened her ability to raise him adequately, and also the father's provider role because of the extra expense involved in special medical care and education. This sense of being hindered from providing proper economic support, plus the feeling of not being mothered by his wife (who was a very poor housekeeper), undermined the father's chosen self-image, and the inadequate behavior of the oldest boy was a threatening duplication of his own fancied ineptness. The only intact member of the family—the second boy of ten—was also threatened by the pathological network of relationships that was evolving because he was perceived as the perfect child, bore the brunt of displaced parental hopes, and was encouraged to adopt a slighting and rejecting attitude toward his brothers. To improve the lot of the two obviously vulnerable children it was necessary to work through the parents' own relationship in order to shift displaced affect and help them to accept a realistic appraisal of both retarded children's prognoses, and to adjust their handling of them to maximize their actual potential. Within this family the problems can be seen at different levels of modifiability. That of the parents' relationship was *theoretically* open to full solution. The limitations of the less retarded boy could be minimized by improving the emotional atmosphere of his home and so ensuring him the psychological support he needed to face adolescence. The more severe disability of the younger child could not be radically changed, but his position within the family and community could be made more secure if the parents were helped to achieve a more realistic acceptance of his limitations which would enable them to handle him more competently.

This case illustrates the value of approaching the total problem-complex in a succession of phases which deals with the more emergent and acute problems as a preliminary to mobilizing and fortifying the client's resources for long-term toleration of chronic stress.

The supportive type of relationship that is needed for the second phase of help is principally concerned in aiding families to weather the strain of living in the shadow of this disability, and it utilizes somewhat different emphases from those that color the relationship in a more direct problem-solving context. As we have previously pointed out, the central problem in this long-term situation is not the result of maladjusted personal relationships and behavior; therefore, the casework process is not *primarily* involved in probing attitudes, current and past patterns of relationships, and emotional experiences of the family in order to understand the dynamics of the present situation. Furthermore, this professional relationship, instead of being directed toward engaging the client family in working through their problems, has the different purpose of bolstering them up as they mobilize their resources for the long emotional and practical siege that is involved in caring for a retarded offspring or other relative. For the pressures of this chronic situation certain approaches and techniques are specially useful. One is the *authority* derived from knowledge that Perlman[2] cites as an important aspect of the helping relationship, and which has a particularly sharp relevance to the families of the retarded. Although the severity of this handicap is universally recognized, it is very doubtful whether those not directly involved with it can properly appreciate the degree of bewilderment and isolation that parents or relatives experience when confronted with the unfamiliar task of having to care for a retarded individual of whatever age. Being able to draw on the professional expertise of the social worker may help to stabilize a family when overwhelmed with confusion and despair at the enormity of the task. This enabling authority will be found in the social worker's knowledge about the condition's origins and manifestations, the special needs of retarded individuals, her accumulated experience of how to handle the more deviant aspects of their behavior and functioning, and also her awareness of the emotional reactions that these evoke within the family and also in other individuals and groups outside of the home.[3] Knowledge about facilities that are available to help the family in their task is also invaluable in diminishing the sense of isolation and impotence that the difficulties arouse.

The authority of knowledge has significance in helping families of the retarded because it replaces the social support for child-rearing that in normal circumstances is provided informally by relatives and friends and other private individuals, who form the immediate social network to which the family is linked. In the case of the retarded child, who is often thought to have different and specialized needs, this common currency of child-rearing advice may be withheld, for fear it is inappropriate or somehow deleterious and might aggravate the condition. Moreover, the grief, shock, and disappointment that the child's handicap evokes invariably invades the extended family as well, so that often there is no emotionally stable person available to provide psychological support for the parents at the critical time when they are having to acknowledge and adjust to the condition. In such situations as these the social worker, and the agency she represents, may take on the function of the supportive kinship network within which the nuclear family unit can be actively supported in their difficult task of adjusting to a deviant child and learning how to meet his needs. When this happens, the social worker sometimes becomes invested with the status normally accorded the grandmother or other close family members—and is related to as a helpful and sustaining authority figure.[4] This approach utilizes the transference aspects of the professional relationship, and it can be a very vital means of shoring up parents in their own nurturing role. If the social worker can demonstrate her acceptance of the child and his defects—however gross they may be—with sympathy, but without the conflicted emotional involvement that family members often display, this offers parents a model with whom they can identify in caring for the child's needs. This identificatory process stems partly from the social worker's genuine concern for the damaged child and for the parents' desire to meet the demands his care makes, and partly from the authority which close familiarity with the intricacies of his condition bestows.

Besides the reality aspects that make up this *model* relationship (which is expressed through support and advice on the myriad practical problems that surround retardation), it is important to be aware of the dynamic and unconscious elements that may also be present and the different degrees of reality and fantasy that will be operating. In some cases, where the occurrence of retardation has disrupted relationships within a family that had hitherto been relatively healthy and benign, the social worker may not need to do more than provide the help that is not forthcoming from the family. She achieves this by permitting and encouraging the parents to express feelings that have to be repressed before relatives because of the disturbed response they evoke; by giving guidance on handling the child and his relationship with other family members; and by underwriting at every opportunity the parents' demonstrated capacity for coping. In one such case a fundamentally stable young couple were able to ventilate their recurrent feelings of despair about their brain-damaged two-year-old daughter and test out their management tactics with an outsider who not only understood the massive difficulties of their situation but could also clarify for them the very constructive ways in which they were trying to meet them. This gave them enough support to withstand the constant lamentations that the grandparents on both sides of the family tended to indulge in, and also to follow through on rehabilitative measures that were distrusted and even openly disparaged by these older members.

In other situations this *model* relationship may be more complex, if the mother or father or, as sometimes happens, both have not worked through the relationship with their own parents, and disagreements over the practical problems of managing the child revive or mask earlier unresolved conflicts. What happens in such cases is that the immature parent has to work through these earlier difficulties, using the complex task of managing the retarded child as the learning ground. The case of Mrs. Berman illustrates this sort of situation. Her only daughter of four-and-a-half was mildly retarded, and her slow development was due to a genetically determined condition which had associated gastrointestinal complications. Mrs. Berman had great difficulty in following the somewhat difficult medical regimen required to stabilize the child's nutritional status, and her fears about the child's atypical development made her both overprotective and inconsistent in handling her. Consequently the child had developed a reactive behavior disorder which was seriously impeding her mental and social functioning. Both these manifestations of inept management were attributed to interference by the paternal grandmother, who openly sabotaged the child's diet and encouraged defiance of the mother's control. Mrs. Berman at twelve years of age had lost her own mother from a lingering and painful illness which she still remembered with unhappiness. The care she subsequently received in adolescence had been patchy, and when she was sixteen her father remarried. She had a very poor relationship with her stepmother and harbored a permanent grudge against her father for having, as she thought, abandoned her interests for his own. Her marriage at twenty to a dull but steady older man was overshadowed early on by the birth of a very defective child, who died in the hospital after a harrowing six months in which both the emotional and the economic resources of the family were depleted. When the second child was found to suffer from the same condition in a much milder form, the anxiety about her survival created tremendous tension within the home, which was exacerbated by the emotional reaction of both parents to the genetic nature of the disability.

Mrs. Berman's basic insecurity, which stemmed from her sense of loss of parents in adolescence, was thoroughly undermined by the knowledge of having produced two defective children, and her lack of confidence in her maternal role played right into the domineering tendency of her mother-in-law. Further, Mrs. Berman's need for a parent figure with whom to identify was so great that she submitted to the older woman's controlling behavior, even while she realized it was not helpful and resented it. To counteract this situation, which was equally damaging to both the child and the parents, the social worker set out deliberately to displace this negative influence and to create a more benign advisory figure upon whom the mother could model herself. Although this process involved an exploration of early relationships and of her long-term depressive reaction to the loss of her mother, the main focus was on providing Mrs. Berman with a positive experience in the here and now which would compensate for this lack and help her to develop not only better child-rearing capacities but also a better image of herself. This was primarily achieved by hammering home the many positive features she manifested in her care of the little girl, and by distracting her attention from the negative aspects which had been so fiercely underlined by the anxious but unhelpful grandmother. The goal was in fact to force the mother to give up her conception of herself as inadequate, and to insist on her adopting a more positive self-image. The improvement in the child's health, which resulted from sticking to the diet, earned approval from the physician who was following the case, and noticeable improvement in behavior and functioning (which incidentally made it possible for the child to be enrolled in a preschool program) convinced the mother of her competence. This enabled her to take a firm but less hostile stand against her mother-in-law, who in turn began to control her interfering when she realized that her daughter-in-law could handle the child and her problems quite efficiently.

Whether one subscribes to psychoanalytical theory, which would associate defects in a child with punishment for Oedipal rivalry and presumption, or accepts the fact that being faced with meeting the unusual needs of an atypical child automatically rouses parents' anxiety about their competence, a retarded child is unquestionably an undermining experience and parents urgently require reassurance that they have the ability to function adequately in the difficult situation created by the handicap. This insecurity is often expressed in questions on aspects of child management that are not strictly within the social worker's repertoire of information or skills. It is nevertheless important to recognize the symbolic nature of these requests for guidance and to respond to them in reality terms by referral to another expert in the subject. When a mother, for example, asks advice on feeding or some other health problem, she *may* be wanting practical information, but it is just as likely that she is unconsciously tapping the resources of the social worker, who is perceived as a supportive authority figure.

Parents' doubts about their ability to cope with the needs of their retarded child may also be associated with a sense of personal immaturity, and they sometimes express a desire to be given implicit —or even explicit—permission to assume the mature status that is inherent in looking after any child, let alone a handicapped one. This underlying attitude may be the reason for the persistent demands of parents for reassurance or for their seeking advice on aspects of care which in reality they are quite able to carry out themselves. When this sort of situation recurs frequently, the social worker must be able to recognize these hidden intentions and, if the supportive relationship is strong enough, she should try to confront the parents with the fact that they are perpetuating a false dependency by pretending to seek help in an area in which they are really quite competent. In such situations the refusal to give support that is not really needed is tantamount to graduating them from the apprenticeship of learning how to be a good parent to the handicapped child, and their repeated requests for advice can represent an unconscious demand to be free from this tutelage. In some cases this unconscious desire should be explicitly interpreted if the parents find it easy to relate on a verbal level. Otherwise the implicit message can be conveyed by the indirect method of pointing out factual evidence of the parents' coping ability.

This helping device is very well illustrated by Mrs. Davis, who was a young and rather insecure mother of a hyperactive, perseverative three-year-old girl with moderate retardation and some brain injury. Mrs. Davis was receiving intensive counseling on how to manage this difficult child in the home, and between the weekly interviews she would telephone at least once to express her despair at the child's most recent and disturbing escapade and to demand advice on how to prevent its recurrence. One day, as she was recounting the ups and downs of the past week, she commented that three days earlier she had been very upset, and as usual had gone to the telephone to call the social worker. As she began to dial the number, she heard the worker's voice in her head saying: "Now Mrs. Davis, you know as well as I do how to manage Lydia when she will not stop turning the gas taps on." On the strength of this she put down the receiver, locked the kitchen door, put the child into her stroller and walked her round the block for five minutes. On their return the child was ready to be diverted by a more constructive activity; Mrs. Davis had not become over-whelmed with exasperation as usually happened; and she suddenly realized that it was within her competence to manage the child, even though it was difficult.

This process of transferring expert knowledge (and the self-con-fidence it evokes) from the social worker to the family introduces another type of relationship which is essentially reciprocal in char-acter. This is a *cooperative* relationship, which derives from a perception of the family that does not view them as applicants seek-ing help for difficulties that denote social failure or inadequacy, but rather as individuals upon whom a problem not of their own making has been visited. The implication of this is that their own stability and capacity for adjustment is *basically* unimpaired by the problem of retardation for which they need help, and in this capacity they relate to the social worker as equal co-solvers of their problem. This new concept of equally shared involvement was pre-sented by Elliot Studt in 1965 [5] when she discussed the anachronism of the traditional social worker–client partnership in which the worker was always in the superior giving position and the client at the receiving end. This idea has special relevance in the retardation field because in the course of such a cooperative transaction there may be an equal exchange of skills and abilities between the social worker and the family through which the family's expertise as caretakers closely involved in the day-to-day routine of a retarded child may contribute as much as the social worker's specialized knowledge derived from other sources. Moreover, the concept has application over a wider area because most of the newer services for the retarded have been initiated by parent organizations, and the personal involvement of individual parents has enabled them to bring a good deal of first hand experience into the field.

Interaction of this sort has great value for both sides in that it augments the social worker's store of knowledge and skills in this still rather unfamiliar area of disability, and also gives the parents the psychological boost of feeling that they are not only able to meet the difficulties of their problems but can in fact create something of considerable social value out of their experience. The cooperative relationship can be demonstrated in practical terms by utilizing parents of one retarded child to help other families who are facing a critical situation similar to their own. One social agency* bases its main operation on this and makes special use of parents to counsel others when they are first faced with the shock of a young, obviously retarded baby. Parents are particularly useful in interpreting the value of a specialized service to families who may be hesitant and fearful of the implications. In one case parents who were very reluctant to send their child who had cerebral palsy (plus a moderate to severe degree of retardation) to a day care center were eventually convinced about the value of this program by another mother whose child was already enrolled there. This mother was felt to be an impartial advocate who also possessed cogent evidence in the improvement she could personally vouch for in her son, and because of this her persuasion was more effective than the combined efforts of the center staff.

Another very great advantage of this form of relationship is that it introduces a predominantly *social* note into the context of retardation, which is so often an isolating phenomenon, and it helps to mobilize many other resources beyond those offered or mediated by the social agency. In this way it has much in common with the policy of antipoverty programs whereby local members of communities are employed to help their neighbors with their social problems. This approach is based on the conviction that people with firsthand experience of poverty will have more insight into how to help other poor people, and as such, they will be more acceptable. It also supports the equally valuable assumption that viable help with social problems must be mobilized from within the community at large and not just emanate from a social agency. All these aspects apply to retardation and the families who have to cope with the difficulties it produces. This fresh approach leads

* Retarded Infants' Services Inc., New York.

nicely into the next phase of our theme, which is to describe another facet of the professional social work relationship that is useful for the retarded and their families.

This is the relationship that prevails in the context of *retainer* help, when the link between client and social worker remains constant but is maintained in a very loosely organized way. The function of this relationship is to meet the needs of a situation that it is dominated by chronicity and has little potential for fundamental movement. This type of situation fits less well with the professional relationship that has developed within a problem-solving context and which contains an implicit dynamic quality that is geared to set in motion forces which will lead to change in the client. When a family has achieved a reasonably satisfactory equilibrium in meeting the chronic stress of their situation, a movement-inducing relationship can be a damaging factor; and the sustaining devices that Hollis[6] cites for holding the client in the tension-filled casework situation may in fact be more disturbing than reassuring. Families who live with the permanent stresses of retardation do not always find it helpful to ventilate feelings or reflect upon the precise nature of difficulties that cannot be altered. Indeed, in many instances they are better off when helped to contain their reactions to stress. The relationship in this situation often provides more support when it is not directly concerned with the problems but is geared instead to the norms of life within which the retarded and the family have to function. Because families with retarded members are liable to feel (or in fact be) isolated from society at large, one of the social worker's major functions may be in just supplying the opportunity for normal social intercourse and the exchange of ideas and experience along broader lines. Some parents, for example, like to discuss the philosophical aspects of retardation, the place of the retarded in society, their relationship to current values, and the religious implications of suffering and disappointment. Sharing of such ideas can be extended by suggesting to interested parents relevant literature about retardation. This focusing on the intellectual aspects of the problem serves two purposes: it recognizes the parents' claim to equal expertise and implicitly conveys that the social worker's authority deriving from knowledge can be reinvested in the parents.

This is in direct contrast to the usual descriptions of the professional relationship in which social exchange is not regarded as appropriate. For creating the long-term support which is needed to meet the problem-situation of the retarded, a casual contact in an informal context may be more comforting to families than a more self-consciously professional one. Without dwelling too purposefully upon the problems which may necessitate professional help, it serves to remind them that it is available if need arises; it can also offer implicit reinforcement to the normal aspects of the family's social role, which otherwise is liable to become distorted by the unusual circumstances of having to care for a retarded child or adult. This point can be illustrated by the mother of a profoundly retarded girl of seventeen who insisted on giving the social worker hot milk when she paid a home visit one cold winter day. By accepting this demonstration of concern for *her* well-being, the social worker was implicitly acknowledging the mother's strong desire and capacity for nurturing which were so chronically frustrated by her own defective child. This also put her on a footing of equality with the social worker and minimized her status as a dependent client with the implications of inadequacy in this role. Since the mother had to feel adequate to meet her very realistic problems, her acting this out with the social worker and the worker's acceptance of *her* temporary dependency were a much more effective affirmation of the mother's competence in the nurturing role than any discussion would have been. This client did not want verbal *recognition* that she felt inadequate; she needed proof that she was *not*.

Another rather amusing illustration of how clients find their own way of using this flexible contact is the case of Ernest Perry, a moderately retarded man of fifty-three living with a widowed elder sister of 68. The sister had given her mother a deathbed promise not "to put Ernest away," so she had provided him with a home in the close-knit working class community in London where both had been brought up. He helped in a local greengrocery to earn spending money and generally made himself useful with the rough jobs about the house, but from time to time his behavior would "get out of line" (for example, he would lie in bed instead of going to work or spend his small earnings on drink instead of giving it to his sister toward his keep). On such occasions the sister threatened to summon the community social worker who visited the family "To take him away." So effective was this magically invoked external control that eventually the sister did not have to declare her intentions; she merely glanced significantly toward the clock behind which the letter with the omnipotent address reposed and that was sufficient warning. Although question might be raised as to what particular role or skill of social work this gesture utilized, in dynamic terms it gave the sister enough support to feel *she* could control her brother. This enabled *him* to function in *her* home and in the wider community as a deviant but fully accepted individual, because his behavior did not transgress generally accepted social norms.

This truly social aspect of professional social work has tended to be overlooked in recent years because of the greater concentration on the intensive interpersonal involvement that is required to solve more acute and circumscribed problems, but with the increasing concern for chronic problem-states that has been referred to in an earlier chapter, this extended-over-time and more diluted approach is receiving more attention. A claim for its revival was very cogently expressed in relation to the English professional scene by Waldron[7] several years ago, but its applicability to certain areas of social work is now just as relevant in America. The effusiveness with which a moderately retarded child may greet the social worker when she meets him and his family in a grocery store or on a public bus or subway demonstrates to people round about that it is possible to interact socially with the retarded, and it is probably a more dynamic force in assisting the family's sense of social assimilation than any number of more private interviews in which this theme is discussed. This approach ties in with the type of relationship mentioned earlier, which provides a therapeutic experience within the reality situations of life, and it is to some extent a derivative of therapeutic patterns that other writers have described. In England Irvine[8] and in the United States Garrett[9] have both written about aspects of this process, and Timms[10] extends the concept by suggesting that the social worker may utilize a variety of roles through which to interact with a client. Although Irvine describes the use of this method to modify the psychological dynamics and resultant behavior of individual clients in the professional one-to-one relationship, the concept can be stretched to apply to the wider context of social interaction. In this respect it is relevant to the retainer relationship when it provides a socially expanding and reinforcing experience.

THE DEPENDENT RETARDED CLIENT

The complementary facet to the family in what we have termed the client-complex is the chronically dependent client—that is to say, the retarded individual who is past the stage of childhood (the normal phase of dependency) but still requires full protection and supervision from adults to ensure his well-being and survival. By the very nature of his handicap, which is expressed in significantly impaired adaptive behavior, this type of client is unable to assume much responsibility for himself and his affairs, and his involvement in any social work process that concerns his welfare can therefore be only marginal. However, this margin of participation, even though it may be limited in regard to the actual decisions that are broached and implemented, can influence practice, and this section will attempt to show the importance of trying to establish a professional relationship with clients functioning at this level, and the specific ways in which it can offer them direct help with their problems of social functioning and adjustment.

When considering the client role of the more handicapped grades of the retarded—that is, those within the moderate, severe, and profound ranges of retardation—it is useful to view their potential for forming a relationship with the social worker along a graduated continuum, with meaningful involvement decreasing as intellectual and adaptive deficits increase. At the bottom, the profoundly retarded (who usually have serious physical impairment as well) can relate only in terms of perceiving the outgoing overtures of the social worker, without proffering any significant response or feedback to indicate that these attempts at communication have registered. At the opposite pole the moderately retarded adolescent or adult who is also socially alert may be capable of a considerable degree of understanding about his social situation, with a corresponding potential for cooperation or resistance toward plans made on his behalf. An important function of the social worker therefore is to assess accurately the extent and kind of involvement each client is capable of, and to tailor the professional approach to suit the particular kind or level of client-role each can fill. This role will determine the nature and depth of the relationship which can be built up between the client and the social worker and indicate toward what aspects of functioning her efforts at help should be specifically directed. This statement may seem obvious, but there is still a tendency to assume that nonverbal individuals with very restricted or imperfect behavioral responses do not have the same emotional capacity or needs as normal individuals and are therefore incapable of forming meaningful relationships. McAndrew and Edgerton[11] have described a very strong and functional relationship between two adults with marked physical and mental impairment which refutes this limited viewpoint.

In the case of the more seriously handicapped, the major contribution will lie in the degree of genuine acceptance and concern she can *feel* toward the client and also be able to *convey* to him in spite of his limited capacity to communicate. In this regard it is helpful to realize that clients with severe intellectual deficits and marked organic impairment are functioning at a more *primitive* level of *adaptive* behavior and that, while their equipment for coding and communicating more complex intellectual clues may be extremely deficient, their capacity for emotional rapport may be quite high. Their extreme dependency, and the strong protective responses this calls forth in their family and other adults involved in their care, tend to strengthen a pattern of intense empathic communication, and it is on this level of intuitive emotional exchange that the social worker can convey her goodwill and concern for their happiness and well-being. This may be achieved by talking to them directly so that they can perceive the sounds of her voice even if the words have no meaning, or through a friendly gesture such as a physical caress or handshake. For the more perceptive, admiring some detail of the client's appearance (such as a new hair ribbon or tie), or joining in with whatever activity he is currently engaged in, is an easily appreciated way of conveying sympathy and concern. Exchanges of this sort provide the stimulus of another human contact to supplement the inevitably limited social experience of the seriously retarded, and the effort made to bridge this gulf of communication serves to remind the social worker of their essentially *human condition*, as well as underpinning their *social status*. This can be very helpful to the family in dispelling their fears that the retarded member is a socially unacceptable nonentity, and in fact many insightful parents or relatives intuitively try to establish the retarded individual in social terms. One elderly widowed lady, for example, who had been brought up in a small country town in eastern England during a period when good social manners were highly valued, always insisted that her fifty-three-year-old brain-injured son shake hands with the social worker and say good morning when the latter visited the home. On the occasion when Arthur muttered a perfunctory hullo instead of rising to his feet and abandoning his current preoccupation (fiddling with his record player), he was sharply reminded of his social obligations and told to stop what he was doing at once.

This recognition of a social bond between the client and himself makes it easier for the social worker to handle the retarded adult, if subsequently some action is needed involving the latter's direct care. This point was also illustrated by the case just cited in that the client's mother said she was not at all apprehensive about his eventual institutional placement because "he always got on so well with gentlemen" and would therefore enjoy being in a male unit and would not object to being escorted there by the social worker who was also a man.

As one moves up the scale of social responsiveness in clients, a greater range of communication techniques can be brought into play, and the scope of the relationship can be extended to afford the client a more active role. This is very important because the moderately retarded adult client often has considerable awareness about what is going on around him in both emotional and practical matters, and his understanding of impending decisions and their effect on him can make a good deal of difference to whether he

responds in a cooperative or obstructive way. Since the latter reaction creates a great deal of stress for the retarded individual himself and his family, as well as for the professionals involved, it is
an important function of casework to ensure that the retarded
client understand to the limits of his ability what is being done,
why, how it will affect him, and what he can personally do to make
it more acceptable for himself. The concept of self-determination
which is so germane to casework cannot be applied in its full extent to the dependent retarded type of client who is not able to
communicate with full understanding with normal people or fend
for himself, but the principle behind this practice should be respected, so that a limited degree of active involvement can be provided for and encouraged. This point is illustrated by an account of
how a quite severely retarded four-year-old boy was "persuaded"
into being placed in a foster home without any great fuss because
each step was explained to him when the final placement was made,
and the expectation conveyed to him that he would be able to make
this adjustment if he cooperated.[12]

If this emphasis on involving the client directly seems to be laboring a very obvious point, it is because there has been such a strong
tendency in the past to overlook the reactions of the poorly communicating retarded and to manipulate their environment for their
own good without purposively involving them in the process. Since
they are such easy victims of being manipulated, it is the more incumbent upon social workers to ensure that attention is paid to
their feelings and opinions, and that they themselves are made to
understand both the reason for events that closely affect them and
the fundamental good intentions that underlie them.

The techniques for creating and sustaining the sort of relationship that produces this assurance of goodwill vary a good deal and
must utilize a wider range of communication skills than those that
are applied in social work with clients who have a greater facility in
understanding, and expressing themselves in, verbal terms. This
necessity for employing nonverbal methods is not limited to work
with the retarded. Child welfare workers have long recognized
that the professional helping relationship for children must often
be expressed through gestures and actions which symbolize graphi-

cally the social worker's good intent rather than literally spelling it out in words. Today when there is a greater emphasis than previously on social work with this disadvantaged client—both child and adult—for whom verbal communication with a relative stranger is often culturally foreign, the need to develop other skills in communication is even stronger. The technique of acting out a benign role toward the client, which was mentioned earlier, applies very much to the moderately retarded client who can often interpret the social worker's intentions and attitudes from what she does to or for him when the spoken message does not get through.

For example, a very meaningful relationship was established with Joseph Griffiths, a moderately retarded man of forty-two, when he needed to go for a hospital checkup for persistent minor illnesses. Since his parents were elderly and in indifferent health and no other relatives were easily available to take him to the hospital, this was undertaken by the social worker attached to the sheltered workshop where Joseph was employed. He was told that because of his many bad colds the doctor who had recently examined him wanted him to see another doctor. The reason for this was tied in with his frequent absences from work and loss of time and earnings. To make what might have been a threatening experience more acceptable, the whereabouts of the hospital was explained to him in details he understood (such as its relative proximity to the local shopping center, and the bus route that served it), and he was warned that he would see sick people around. The normalcy of going to the hospital was reinforced by relating it to the fact that a staff member had been attending for treatment some months back. Probably because of this careful preparation and the feelings of security it engendered, when immediate in-patient treatment was recommended (following the diagnosis of acute anemia and a fear of cardiac complications associated with Down's syndrome), the social worker was able to persuade him to remain in the hospital while he went home to fetch his parents.

Although the social worker had been familiar with Joseph as part of the workshop staff, a significant relationship did not develop between them until this crisis precipitated the worker into an *obviously helping* role, which also represented an extension of family care. The client was dimly aware of this connection, which was consolidated when the social worker brought his parents to see him in the hospital. This piece of studied casework was instrumental in ensuring this quite limited man's cooperation in his medical treatment so that it could be maximally effective.

A final point needs to be made about the dependent retarded client. This is the absolute necessity of remembering that the retarded beyond school age is an adult, even if his social behavior does not always reflect this fact, and that he must always be ascribed the dignity and social recognition normally accorded to adult status. The old concept that the retarded dwell in a limbo of chronic childhood is an extremely misleading, and also self-perpetuating, myth, and is responsible for a pattern of interaction between the retarded adult and his social peers which supports the expectation that his understanding and behavior will be on a permanently childish level. This "institutionalizing of retardation" within normal social relationships can in fact maximize deficits (in the same way that custodial regimes do), and it is a vital function of the social worker to prevent this from happening.

In the case of Joseph Griffiths, just cited, the limited experience and powers of comprehension of the retarded client were catered to by the simple and frequently repeated explanations of what was happening, but this was done within the expectation that he could, and would, conduct himself like an adult in this new experience. This in fact is what happened when he agreed to immediate hospital admission instead of demanding to go home. His mature behavior had a reassuring effect on the hospital staff and counteracted any fears they may have had as to whether they would be able to handle this deviant patient in their normal regime; as a result he was treated with greater sympathy and understanding because of his demonstrable capacity for cooperation. The fact that he attended a sheltered workshop, which denoted a responsible adult status, and that the social worker was associated with this independent aspect of his life probably helped to fortify his more mature behavior. This provides an excellent illustration of how the caseworker's relationship with and approach to the dependent retarded client can not only support his more effective functioning but also elicit more understanding and cooperative treatment from other normal individuals with whom he has to interact in a significant way. The diminution of stress for the elderly and inevitably anxious parents, which was a consequence of their son's adjusting so well at the hospital, was the third beneficial outcome of the casework process. It provides a good note on which to end this chapter.

8 THE PROFESSIONAL RELATION-SHIP WITH THE MILDLY RETARDED CLIENT

IN OUR DISCUSSION of how the professional relationship can be used to help mildly retarded individuals we shall be concentrating on adolescents and young adults because these are the stages in life when most individuals without serious impairment are capable of forming independent relationships outside of their immediate family and can legitimately be expected to assume some responsibility for their own affairs. We place great emphasis on the relationship between the social worker and this group of nearly mature retarded clients on two counts. First, the question is still often raised as to what extent individuals with limited intelligence can benefit from casework help, and particularly whether they can appropriately utilize the professional relationship. Second, the experience of a professional relationship is often greatly needed by retarded clients to help them cope effectively with some of the social problems that their handicap imposes.

Skepticism about the effectiveness of casework with the retarded derives from several sources. One is the confusing discrepancy between the mental and chronological age, which endows the retarded client with an ambiguous status. When low mental age is expressed in serious maladaptive behavior, it raises the question of how much personal responsibility the client can be expected—or even permitted—to take in solving the problems he presents. Furthermore, social welfare provisions for the retarded have been traditionally tied to legal restrictions upon their rights and status as adult citizens, and this has reinforced the tendency toward their social, legal, and political belittlement. This fact has added to the social worker's dilemma by placing the retarded client in an authority-oriented context which does not entirely fit with the practice of social work that is based upon the principle of self-determination. A third reason has been the pervasive belief that limited intelligence hinders the capacity to communicate, which in turn is an obstacle to becoming involved in a meaningful relationship.

In this chapter we hope to explode some of these residual myths by showing that the mildly retarded are as capable of making full and appropriate use of the professional relationship as any other client group and that many of the social work techniques most helpful to them have equal relevance to clients with other types of social difficulties. In order to explore this aspect of casework more precisely we must look at some of the social characteristics generally associated with mild retardation which might require a special handling of the professional relationship. We shall then examine the sort of approach needed to offset these unusual features and the specific techniques by which this can be realized. None of these ideas are new. Social workers primarily engaged in work with the retarded have persistently maintained a dynamic approach toward their problems, and in the past few decades there has been a gradual evolution of more sophisticated thinking throughout the social work profession.[1] This chapter is in some respects a summation of these trends.

To better understand these shifts in attitude and to give them impetus, it is important to look closely at the type of individuals who are defined as retarded and who come to the attention of social workers on account of this disability. Except for a very small number who come from relatively secure backgrounds, the mildly retarded belong to the lower strata of society, often to the most poverty-stricken and socially deprived segment of our population. Within this environment many will have spent a precarious childhood with irregular and inconsistent care at home and a fitful and not very relevant educational experience in school. In addition they will have encountered in varying degree the vast web of social survival problems that afflict individuals and families at the bottom of the economic scale (low income, poor housing, unstable relationships, conflict with authority, etc.). Individuals with this sort of history will be found on the rolls of school social workers, child welfare workers, probation officers, family agencies, and public welfare departments, and though they may not all be officially designated as retarded, their poor social adjustment combined with their adverse circumstances will have resulted in the same type of problems as their officially retarded counterparts demonstrate.

Other mildly retarded clients will have had even more destructive experiences, such as involvement in court charges of parental neglect or in delinquent acts of their own, with the disturbing sequel of their being removed from home during their childhood.

A third category may be those born out of wedlock who were placed in foster care at birth and had inadequate substitute parental care which failed to stimulate development. After a progressive decline in intellectual functioning, these children end up with the label of retardation and probable commitment to a residential facility specializing in this handicap.

Because of the social pathology which has colored their environment from the earliest days, it is very difficult to determine how much the manifest problem of low functioning intelligence and its correlate of maladaptive behavior is innate (i.e., resides in some biological impairment) and how much has been created by the stunting social experiences they have been exposed to. The social worker who is confronted with a mildly retarded client must be able to appreciate this concept and realize that his problems rarely stem from his subnormal intelligence alone but are the result of this one identified factor in interaction with some additional social hazard, such as the environmental pressure of poverty and deprivation, the psychological difficulties of interpersonal relationships, or, at times, general economic dislocation which threatens his role as an independent wage earner. When a retarded adolescent or adult requires specific casework help (as opposed to the generalized help of specialized services discussed in Chapter 3), it is either because the social system to which he belongs does not meet his needs and so he becomes alienated from its main functioning patterns, or because he has personal problems which prevent him from satisfactorily fulfilling some of the more essential roles that are demanded of him. For example, the young retarded adult may get into employment difficulties because the economic system demands a higher level of adaptive skill than he can manage or because he relates poorly to fellow workers and superiors, which prevents him from holding down a job, even though he has the technical capacity for it.

A second important point is that mild retardation of societal origin inevitably contains some strong emotional components which derive from childhood experiences of psychological and material deprivation. These are often more responsible for the negative and self-destructive behavior that the mildly retarded adolescent or adult in trouble displays than is the subnormal intelligence alone. The latter merely complicates the total picture by adding to the difficulties which arise out of the unsolved emotional problems as well as influencing the way in which the client handles them. This situation is illustrated by the case of Kenneth Cripps, who had spent ten years in various kinds of residential care because of an extremely adverse home situation. At nineteen he was placed on parole in the care of his grandmother and received his discharge at twenty-one, having made a very good adjustment to living and working in the community. Shortly after the completion of this successful probationary period, he suddenly gave up his job, began to spend his money recklessly, kept late hours and bad company, and was eventually turned out of his relatives' house for consistently refusing to pay for his board and lodgings. Two psychological explanations seem to underlie this irrational behavior. One was the misguided belief, which he verbalized, that his long period in institutions and on parole was a protracted penance, paying for which gave him the right to a special form of freedom, which he interpreted as a bout of self-indulgence to compensate for the deprivation he had acutely suffered. The other explanation was that this was an attempt to restore the dependent family situation which he had never properly experienced in childhood and from which he had felt prematurely removed. By not fulfilling his adult social and financial obligations to his grandparents, he somehow hoped to retrieve the lost period of his childhood.

One or more of these social and emotional factors are invariably present when a retarded client is in difficulty. Therefore, the imputation that he may not be able to utilize normal casework process on the grounds of his poor intelligence is not valid when this factor is but one of the total configuration of problems and not the most crucial one. The social worker, therefore, must initially apply herself to sorting out the primary components of the client's overall problem and, while recognizing some of the limitations set by his lower intelligence, she must not let this be a major obstacle to intervention. Once the more complex components of emotional and social stress are perceived as the focal problem, the question of the client's capacity for relating to the social worker in the problem-solving process loses its significance. This may seem to be laboring an obvious point, but it is necessary to crack the stereotype which concentrates primarily on a circumscribed disability and overlooks the much wider range of normal human reactions and capabilities.

This brings us to the point previously mentioned, the alleged inability of the retarded client to communicate with the social worker in a meaningful way and the fear that this will impede his involvement in a cooperative effort to solve his problems. This belief is in general unfounded and reflects more upon the practice of social work, and a lack of skill in the practitioners, than on the clients, since it stems from the preconception that the best method of communication is verbal and that without this facility the normal processes of casework will be hampered. This limited view is wrong on two counts. First, it is not always true that mildly retarded clients cannot communicate verbally. In certain circumstances they can be quite articulate, as, for example, the youth of seventeen who, when reprimanded for cashing his pay check and spending some of it on coffee instead of handing it over to the warden of the hostel where he was living, turned the table on his supervising social worker by inviting her to put herself in his place and think what it was like to want a hot drink on a cold afternoon at the end of a hard week's work.

Granted that the slower thinking processes of the retarded client and his poor educational attainment may make it difficult for him to find the right way to say what he thinks or feels, this does not mean he cannot use a verbal method of communicating. Rather, it imposes upon the social worker the obligation to find fresh ways of opening up communication which will make him feel at ease with her so that he is not intimidated from trying out his possibly halting speech and limited vocabulary. This reflects back to the feeling aspects of the relationship: if the social worker has a genuine concern for the client as someone with common human needs whom she is asked to help, his intuition will pick this up and it will inevitably stimulate a reciprocal response. In cases where the client seems not to respond, it is important to be aware that he may be deliberately using his poor verbal facility as a means of self-protection because he feels too vulnerable to expose himself to an unfamiliar person. Since the social worker is usually encountered in a situation of stress that emphasizes his inadequacy—for example, when he has lost his job or been turned out of his lodgings or is before the court on a delinquency charge or is on parole from an institution—this attitude is easy to understand. Adolescents and young adults who have had a long history of insecurity, such as many changes of foster home placement, often resort to silence to protect themselves in strange situations. In one instance a quite competent girl of eighteen with an I.Q. in the 70s lost her job and was on the verge of being placed in an institution because her foster parents could not tolerate her excessively long periods of moody silence. When she was placed in a factory job (on a trial run that was not expected to succeed) where her silent application to the assembly line was an asset and no one bothered her to talk, she gradually emerged from her shell, developed into a fast and reliable worker, and then began to communicate with her fellow-employees and supervisor. Eventually she thawed with the social worker to the extent of admitting that she enjoyed her work and liked the people there. She also became more outgoing in her foster home so that they felt they could begin to understand her and keep her.

When given sensitive encouragement, many mildly retarded clients with inhibiting past experiences can express themselves with surprising poignancy and can often grasp quite subtle emotional nuances. Such an example is Alice Swan who, at the age of forty-eight, came to live with her brother and sister-in-law on parole from an institution where she had spent thirty years. The town where her family lived was quite a distance from the institution, which was in the depth of the country, and she felt very insecure in her new environment, did not like going out alone, and lacked the confidence to seek a job, although she had had an excellent record in the institution. When the social worker discussed with Alice her feelings about being on parole and her main difficulties, she gave a very insightful account of the fact that when she was in the institution she knew she could function well and that it seemed sensible to try to live on the outside. When she was away from the safe and familiar environment, however, she felt unable to follow through and mobilize her skills, even though she knew she had them. In her way she gave a very good description of the damaging effects of institutionalization and showed a rather tragic insight into the discrepancy between her legitimate aspirations and what she could actually realize. Her ability to express these complicated concepts gave the social worker an opening to explain the universality of these feelings and to suggest that, though the situation seemed to be overwhelmingly threatening, she felt from her experience with other women in a similar position that the client would eventually regain her lost confidence and skills and be able to adapt to this new sort of life.

Even when a client has apparently little ability to communicate on a verbal level, this is not an indication that he cannot or does not want to communicate; it merely means that some other method is more familiar or has more meaning to him. Retarded clients, like anyone else in a stressful or uncomfortable situation, want to feel that they are accepted, that someone has concern for them, and that help will be forthcoming with their present plight whatever it is. When speech is limited, the social worker may have to deduce feelings and wishes from rather minimal and unorthodox cues and also convey her good intentions by practical actions rather than in words. For example, the mildly retarded girl or young woman who is trying to make an independent life in the community and misses family or institutional living may derive a sense of support and acceptance from being taken to a meal by the social worker instead of having an office interview. Contrariwise, it may be supportive to an older client's self-esteem if she can entertain the social worker in her own home and display her social skills as hostess. This happened with a middle-aged woman who moved out of a residential hospital job to a rooming house, in order to have a place for her illegitimate boy of thirteen to visit. As she was a basically dependent woman who had never worked through her relationship with her own mother, this move represented a daring step fraught with emotional hazards. The ceremonial visit of the social worker for coffee helped to consolidate the new pattern of life she was assuming and underwrote her role as an independent adult who was trying to build her own home. This symbolic approach to important emotional issues has been habitually used by child welfare workers in working with deprived children who have to experience material comforts in order to understand the more general concern for their welfare, and more recently it has been extended to deprived adults who have grown up without having basic emotional needs adequately met.[2]

In another instance the social worker managed to keep a concerned relationship open with a very fearful, nonverbal boy of low intelligence who had been sent to a maximum security institution for some violent delinquent behavior. He came from a close-knit, though sociopathic, family, and separation from home at a distance that prohibited frequent visiting was very distressing to him. The social worker, who had supervised him at home and kept in touch with his family, wrote him regular letters and cards and sent small presents for the major holidays. These were not acknowledged, and he had no idea whether they had reached their destination until several years later when the boy returned home and made his way to the agency to find the gentlemen who had sent the "letters and ties." Although the boy's behavior continued to make him a serious problem, this case does show that even very limited clients in very unfavorable circumstances will respond to overtures of concern made in good faith.

The other point, which concerns the capacity of the retarded for involving themselves actively and responsibly in their own affairs, is intimately related to a pervasive characteristic of this client group— that is, their poor self-image and expectation of failure. The psychological processes that produce this defeatist attitude have been clearly described by Cobb[3] and Zigler[4] so we shall not elaborate except to say that the origin of such attitudes, while related in part to the faulty perceptual and adaptive equipment of the retarded, is also very strongly determined by their social experiences.

These have tended to be negative and unrewarding because of the low esteem generally accorded to individuals with inferior intellectual endowment and the abnormal treatment they are likely to receive from their normal counterparts.[5] Most people do not have a respectful attitude toward the mentally retarded adult, and the well-meant but overprotective infantilizing pattern of interaction that is foisted upon them by their peers does not build up a sense of mature self-worth. One unfortunate by-product of these attitudes is that the mildly retarded client, when in a difficult situation, may resort to regressive behavior and assume an infantile manipulative approach to the social worker, which is intended to secure his release from any adult obligations or responsibility on the grounds of his incapacity.

This poor self-image and the lack of personal dignity from which it derives are important factors in determining the pattern and quality of the casework relationship with the mildly retarded client. The first task in the treatment process must be to try to restore this damaged identity and to re-create for the client a sense of his human value and dignity. Included in this approach must be some explicit expectations about the client's responsibility for cooperating in the helping process to the best of his ability, and these expectations should be related to his normal social role as an adolescent or adult. When, for example, a mildly retarded boy (or girl) in the late teens persistently loses jobs and spends money recklessly so that he is unable to pay for the necessities of life, he has to be firmly confronted with the inappropriateness of this behavior for his age and its serious consequences. Such a redefinition of role and society's expectations must be followed with a more explicit discussion of what is involved in acting according to one's age, and the adult formula must be put into the normative context of what other people do. From this we do not imply that bestowing dignity and high expectations on an unstable retarded client will immediately modify his behavior, but it must be emphasized that endowing him with a devalued status and assuming that he does not have to be accountable for his actions encourages him to be childish and irresponsible.

In order to establish the retarded client on a more equal footing and build up his self-esteem, it is important to understand what perception he has of himself—his negative self-image and the compensatory one that he secretly aspires to. The image that the retarded cherish is usually brought into being to neutralize the unacceptable connotations of being treated as retarded and the associated stigma; and wherever it is feasible and compatible with reality this more acceptable identity should be reinforced. Goffman talks of the importance of "passing" for individuals with a socially stigmatizing disability,[6] and Edgerton describes this process as it relates specifically to retardation.[7] From the caseworker's angle it is vital to offer help in a form that will repair the marred identity and strengthen the client's impaired ego.

This leads into a very important issue: How can the social worker help the client to accept a realistic appraisal of his limitations without too much damage to his already frail self-esteem? To succeed in this very difficult task the social worker must come to terms with the notion that intellectual limitation is not a totally pervasive handicap, that it does not necessarily determine the entire pattern of a client's behavior or social functioning (though the by-products of feeling inferior may be a potent cause of maladjustment), and that it is only one aspect of the total individual that is functioning below par. This approach presupposes many other strengths and capabilities that can be mobilized to aid functioning. For example, a girl with a pleasant personality who is anxious to please and well motivated to learn may become a competent and valued worker in the sort of work she can master, and the satisfaction of doing a job well will add to her sense of competence. However, because they feel retardation to be such an undesirable handicap, many social workers are ill at ease when they have to discuss its reality aspects with retarded clients and how it impinges upon their day-to-day living. It does not, however, make it easier for the client if the social worker skirts the central issue. Instead, the problem will assume greater proportions and the client's anxiety will be sharpened if he feels that people are afraid to mention his shortcomings, of which he is usually all too aware. The experience of individuals—professional and lay—who have been intimately connected with the retarded indicates that once the taboo is lifted, and it is not felt to be an unmentionable disability, the retarded are very ready to talk about their problem.[8]

For this bold but essentially compassionate confrontation to be helpful, it is important to emphasize that the limitations in performance and achievement that are creating adjustment problems have to be dealt with as a *current reality* but that their existence in the here and now does not necessarily imply permanent dysfunction. This not only reinforces the concept of a growth continuum—in contrast to the sterile concept of the static intelligence quotient—but also puts limitation of functioning into a behavioral frame of reference rather than a disability context. How to interpret the limited functioning and potential of the retarded in terms that are both understandable and acceptable to them and their families and friends is an important function of the professional relationship. This can be illustrated by the case of Arnold Lewis, who had been admitted to a state school at the age of eighteen for difficult behavior in the home, including persistent enuresis. He was of borderline intelligence but had a very poor relationship with his mother, who had been deserted by the father and identified Arnold with his father's irresponsible behavior. He improved very quickly in this new environment away from the conflicts of home and was soon placed in the community on parole where he did well, eventually being discharged at the age of twenty-one. Two years later the supervising social worker was telephoned out of the blue by a young woman who said she had been married to Arnold for six months and had been rather anxious recently upon coming across an old letter from the social worker which referred to his having been in a hospital. She wondered whether this meant he had a health problem that she did not know about and was telephoning the social worker because Arnold had sometimes mentioned him.

This request required a very quick decision which would respect the confidential nature of the client relationship and at the same time give the wife enough information to prevent her from developing an overanxious attitude that might jeopardize the apparently stable marital situation. After making some rather generalized inquiries about the courtship and marriage and what contact the couple had with Arnold's two sisters (who had been closely involved with him and knew the social worker), the worker explained that Arnold had not settled down well after leaving school, and had been sent away for training. He also mentioned that the training establishment was for young people who had done poorly in school and that when Arnold left there the social worker had kept in touch with him because of his difficult relationship with his mother and the absence of a father. The wife realized that he was poor at reading and writing so this did not come as a shock, and since she knew his family she was also aware of some of the strains in interpersonal relationships and appreciated the need for social work supervision. She was moreover so relieved to find there was no serious health problem that these minor handicaps posed no real threat. She agreed to tell Arnold of this conversation with the social worker, and described with considerable pride how happily they were married and what Arnold was doing in the way of work and other social activities.

This explanation of the disability in dynamic behavioral terms satisfied, and was understandable to, this girl whereas the flat description of retardation and the legal status involved might have been highly threatening and would certainly have represented her husband in a light that did not truly reflect his current social capacity or his future potential. (He was a very handsome, normal-looking boy with many compensations that could be exploited once he developed self-confidence and a feeling that he mattered to someone.) This same approach is necessary when explaining the adjustment problems of the retarded to normal people with whom they will have significant dealings. To define a fourteen-year-old boy as retarded may prejudice foster parents against taking him into their home, but if he is described as doing poorly at school, slow at catching on, and needing rather more supervision than most boys of his age, he may be regarded as well within the cultural norm of the foster parents or as a challenge to their skills.

This way of looking at mild retardation (and the impaired adaptive behavior implied in the condition) gives it a developmental frame of reference and places it within the continuum of normal behavior. Such a perception of the disability has great significance for casework because it presupposes the possibility for change; and the dilemma of self-determination and its validity for the retarded client is at least partially resolved when he is credited with a potential for maturation and increasing responsibility. Again it must be stated that the special adaptive problems associated with mild retardation must be related to other manifestations of stress and pathology within the client's cultural group, and the social worker must realize that the retarded client and his delinquent or emotionally disturbed relative or neighbor (from whom he is technically distinguished by the fallible criterion of a few I.Q. points) require basically the same sort of therapeutic treatment to undo the accumulated damage of their past experiences and current environmental pressures. In this context the question of how to help the retarded client to develop a sense of social responsibility, which is implied in the idea of self-determination, so that he can grow into a more completely functioning social individual ceases to be specific to his handicap and becomes identified with that of the entire alienated and defeated subculture.

Given this reorientation, casework with the mildly retarded takes on an important new dimension—namely, a relearning emphasis which will enable intellectually, emotionally, and socially underdeveloped individuals to work through the negative social experiences that in the past have cut them off from self-fulfillment and a sense of social identification and accountability.[9] The concept of self-determination and the practical management tactics that spring from it can therefore be exploited as an invaluable part of this learning process, and its *regulated* use may become the means by which clients of limited social awareness and responsibility can begin to see themselves as belonging within a more satisfying social framework and functioning in a constructive rather than a self-defeating manner. The legal restrictions that can (and often do) impinge upon retarded clients, and the isolating and discriminating aspects of some of the provisions for their special care (for example, state school commitment for a delinquent or antisocial act which is punished differently in the case of offenders of normal intelligence), make it especially important that in the casework situation they are offered and exposed to, or even forced to resume, as much self-determination as they are capable of assuming. This is particularly true for retarded adults who have had long spells in institutional regimes, where initiative has not been encouraged and the patterns of their lives have been arranged for and imposed upon them with little or no involvement on their part, or even explanation as to why certain courses were followed. This sort of situation is typified by the case of John Knight, a seventeen-year-old boy who had had several different foster homes in his school phase. When the social worker was trying to unravel with him the events leading up to these moves, he replied with the succinct but not very revealing comment that "letters came." This boy was able to understand immediate cause and effect situations and later showed a capacity for cooperating in plans for another change in his life so that there was no reason for his not being told about these earlier moves.

This example indicates what must be the first and most elementary step by which the retarded client can become involved in confronting and coping with his own problems. It is the provision of a clear and unequivocal explanation about what is going to happen to the client, its effect on him in the present or very near future, and its longer-term implications, together with the reason for such a step, including the authority by which it is being done. For example, when placement in a residential treatment center or state school is arranged, this move should be related to the factual problems that have led up to it (poor school record, difficult behavior, stress in the family), to the admission procedures (psychological testing, interview with the psychiatrist, etc.) and to the length of stay envisaged. The institution's whereabouts, size, and mode of organization and functioning should also be described, and where there is legal commitment, this should be explained in simple functional terms and its limitations clarified. The long-term objective must also be pointed out and its benign intentions made clear, even though the client himself cannot appreciate it at this critical point. However, keeping the retarded client properly informed about arrangements which may have to be made on his behalf is a way of acknowledging his vital investment in the new plans, and though at this stage it may not be administratively feasible to give him the opportunity of sharing in the decisions made, his knowing about them from a reliable and authoritative source represents some involvement, however minimal, on his part. Further, this knowledge can be the basis for more active involvement at a later stage of treatment, such as plans for his return to the community. If he is aware of the principal factors that were responsible for the placement phase, he is likely to have a better understanding of the continuity of the whole process and therefore be motivated to cooperate. When placement (or any other major decision) is presented in arbitrary terms, it is liable to take on magical and malign omnipotence. The next stage of planning is likely to be perceived as an equally capricious reversal of previous bad fortune into good, and the client's contribution toward making the new step successful then tends to get submerged in this ambiguous confusion.

In other instances where the solution of the problem does not demand such a drastic step as residential placement, the retarded client can often be much more actively involved in different aspects of the problem-solving process and permitted a larger share in making the decisions for his welfare. However, the normal process of self-determination (which is generally taken for granted as a basic ingredient of the relationship with clients of normal intelligence) may have to be employed in a slightly different way with retarded clients. While the social worker must always uphold this *principle* in her attitude toward the retarded and in her overall plans for his well-being, it may be necessary to modify its *practical application*. In this there is a resemblance to the situation of an adolescent of normal intelligence—or any other client who is learning how to manage independence—in which the amount of responsibility for making his own decisions has to be gradually evoked and then consolidated by a series of experiences which increase in number and complexity as the client shows he is able to manage a greater depth and range of responsibility. Since the exercise of self-determination can provide a valuable learning experience, the practical utilization of this concept should be directed toward increasing the client's capacity for self-responsibility and gradually diminishing dependence upon other individuals or authority-based institutions for planning and arranging his or her life. A simple example of the partial use of self-determination can be found in planning for the employment of a

retarded individual when the social worker (or vocational rehabilitation counselor) canvasses that person's views on what he would
prefer to do and what he sees as feasible for his circumstances, and
from this data and her own knowledge of what is actually available
engages him in making a *realistic* choice. Holding the retarded
client to reality without depriving him of all scope for self-expression
or initiative may not be easy because his personal limitations and
the correspondingly restricted opportunities combine to produce
a range of alternatives that do not always coincide with the client's
aspirations. This is particularly true when there are strong elements
of fantasy (which may be an essential part of the system employed
by the retarded for denying the disability and its socially handicapping effects). Sometimes the client's aspirations are realistically at-
tuned to his own capacities but may not be immediately realizable
for some external economic reason.

Provided there is an open acknowledgment of the client's right
to express his preferences, however, and a serious attempt to meet
them, many retarded adolescents and adults will accept realistic
goals, as in the case of an eighteen-year-old boy who cherished a
great desire to work as delivery assistant to the driver of a truck
that delivered railroad supplies. When such a job was not available,
he agreed to work in a laundry (which was hot, dull, and had few
prospects) and then gave it up after a few months with the hope
of getting the job he had previously demanded. Since there was
still no opening in this line, he was persuaded to take another
factory job, with the promise that he would be considered for the
first truck job that became available. He was also helped to understand that his chances of getting placed as delivery assistant would
be much better if he were employed, because the company operating
the trucks was very selective and liked boys with steady employment records. This was acceptable to him as an interim measure
because he had confidence that he would eventually get an opening
on the trucks. This case illustrates how the opportunity for choice
and decision can be provided for the retarded in a context which
is realistic but also meets some of their aspirations. By contrast, the
very unrealistic plans of some retarded clients do not permit scope
for a viable choice and then the social worker's role is to protect

them from the inevitable frustrations of not being allowed to try the coveted job or of trying and failing. An example of this is a retarded adolescent girl who wants to take up nursing, is unaware of the academic demands, and does not have enough insight to appreciate that the responsibility involved would strain her limited powers of judgment and foresight. When the social worker has to assume this role of frustrating the retarded client, it is important to give a factual explanation of why this step will not work out and to allow the client full scope for expressing her objections to the social worker's point of view and her hostility toward the seeming unhelpfulness. Expressing a legitimate objection represents another facet of the self-determination concept in that the client, although not able to follow through on his own intentions, does not remain a passive recipient of services but is involved in the process even if only negatively by way of protest.

Because the mildly retarded are not skilled in abstracting generalizations from specific and concrete experiences, they tend not to learn from past experiences to avoid a similar (but not identical) occurrence. Therefore, in order to develop a retarded client's competence in making his own plans and decisions, the social worker may have to let him take a calculable risk or even try out a course of action that has a strong risk of failure. This sort of situation highlights one of the paradoxes in social work with the mentally retarded —the inevitable conflict between the two important social work tenets of permitting the client to decide himself how to cope with his problems, on the one hand, and on the other hand, trying to help clients solve their difficulties in a constructive way which will be a learning experience for future predicaments. This conflict, as evoked by the plight of the retarded, may partially explain why the profession has sanctioned a more protective pattern of service in regard to their problems, with greater emphasis on the use of authority than is applied to clients with so-called normal endowment.

This paradox, inherent in the relationship with the mildly retarded client, may be a source of confusion and anxiety to the worker who must constantly try to gauge when the client should be encouraged to try out his own often inadequate skill and capacity for making independent decisions with calculated risk of failure and when she should exercise a degree of inhibiting authority which exceeds that normally resorted to in casework. What is the element that can reconcile these conflicting components? The answer lies in a particular type of relationship that can be very usefully exploited for some retarded clients. This is the role-playing or *model* relationship mentioned in Chapter 7 in which the social worker takes on the role of a socially significant individual who is currently missing in the life of the retarded client (or was missing at significant developmental stages in the client's past) and is needed in the here and now to fulfill some important emotional or socializing function.[10] This can be described as a sort of artifact transference phenomenon in which the professional worker precipitates this type of relationship by discovering the essential individuals who are currently, or have been, absent from the collective social supportive system of the retarded client and stepping into the gap herself. Since the retarded client in trouble is almost invariably emotionally, intellectually, or socially underdeveloped, this type of significant relationship is likely to simulate that of a parent or nurturing older sibling figure who can help him in his current difficulties and also ideally provide the opportunity for learning the social skills and insights which should have been assimilated at an earlier stage. This type of relationship, with its socializing purpose and origins in learning theory, has been postulated for other client groups that share many of the problems of the retarded, particularly those that stem from a deprived upbringing and the persistence of deprivation in their current life pattern.[11] Generally it has been used with parents to help them carry out their responsibilities within the family, but the basic ingredients of this approach are equally relevant to the mildly retarded client, whether a parent, spouse, or single individual.

In this guise the social worker can legitimately combine the two tasks we have earlier described as being in opposition—permitting scope for risk-taking at the expense of failure and interposing authority when the destructive capacity of the retarded client has to be contained. Both are activities which concerned parent figures have to apply to their children when they reach the stage of practicing and testing out their ability to act independently, and it is a challenge to the professional insights and skills of the social worker to decide which of these two opposing tactics she should employ for individual cases in specific circumstances.

There are certain factors associated with each of these trends which are germane to the casework relationship with the mildly retarded client. The first is *availability in crisis,* which the client must feel he can count upon if he is to weather the possible failure of trial and error and learn something from it other than its destructive potential. Closely tied in with this is the often pervasive and deep-seated disinclination of the retarded client to trust anyone (particularly social workers and the authority world they signify)[12] and the equally strong reactive compulsion to test out in crisis. Should the social worker fail to come through with the necessary support at such times the client is confirmed in his strong suspicion that life is a dangerously unpredictable affair in which one cannot count on help; and the current emergent situation does not teach him anything about how to avoid similar mistakes in the future. An example of this is Keith Allen, who was in a residential catering job on parole from a state school. After a series of minor tiffs with his employers (which had been kept from the supervising social worker), he walked out of his job at an hour's notice, went to his parents' home hoping his mother would take him in and, when she refused, turned up at the social worker's office with little money, a suitcase, and no lodging for the night. As he had very strong feelings about his parents' rejection of him (which were of long standing and one of the factors responsible for his placement in the state school), it was extremely important for the social worker to be able to respond effectually to this SOS and all resources were mobilized to find him a suitable temporary placement to meet the immediate crisis of homelessness. The very stringent time factor (he eventually caught up with the social worker at 6 P.M.) put a limit on choices, and at one point a return to the state school for a few days seemed the only possible solution. This was unacceptable to Keith, who would have regarded it as a retrogressive step, and the social worker, recognizing this, went to great pains to find an alternative solution in a hostel for older men in a nearby community. Within the next three days intensive efforts were made to find him another residential job, and in a week he was reinstated in a stable living and working situation.

The dynamic factors in this situation of crisis were that Keith had tried out his family and, in his eyes, been let down by them in his hour of need; he then tested out the social worker and found her prepared to help him out of the predicament and in a way that was not punitive but understanding. Thus the easiest practical solution, returning him to the state school, was not immediately resorted to because it would have been regarded as a highly rejecting and punitive action. Furthermore, the whole incident served to sharpen reality testing in that Keith saw firsthand the risks of acting without forethought and the difficulty of finding an immediate solution. It also brought home to him the fact that much of the upset might have been averted if he had discussed his difficulties at work before they reached a critical phase. This boy, because of his unstable home background and his emotional reaction to parental rejection, tended to this pattern of flight under pressure, but the next time he found himself in a similar situation he tried to deal with it in a more foresighted way by contacting the social worker before taking precipitate action. Another important factor in the casework situation was that the parents were able to see that, when given help in a crisis, Keith could stabilize himself in a new situation. This reduced their anxiety and hostility toward his erratic behavior which they had feared would be reinforced if they allowed him to run home whenever he got into difficulties.

The second significant characteristic of this role-filling aspect of the professional relationship is the importance for the social worker sometimes to assume a controlling position which involves her in action that the client does not regard as in his interests. This point is illustrated by the case of Eric Cooper who lived alone with a mildly retarded widower father, who was totally unable to exercise any control over his son. As a result Eric was frequently out of work, went around with a near-delinquent peer group, got into debt, and eventually came to the probation officer's notice for running away from home and being found without visible means of support. When he returned home at the age of seventeen, after eight years in foster care following a neglect charge against his father, Eric had received a great deal of close support from the social worker supervising him, but these efforts were not sufficient to keep him stabilized when he was exposed to the feckless and sociopathic living habits of his father, who drank, and was out of work most of the time and in constant debt. Because of the boy's increasing maladjustment, the father was approached about placement in a state school but he refused to involve himself in this step which would incur his son's displeasure and also involve contact with the legal authorities (of whom he had reason to be somewhat chary). It was clear that Eric could not withstand the undermining and corrupting influence of his father, that he did not have the psychological and practical resources necessary to start a separate life of his own, and that he was obviously destined for serious trouble with the law if there was no outside intervention. Therefore, the social worker assumed the role that should have been the father's and himself petitioned for the boy to be committed to a state school on the grounds of his past bad behavior and present vulnerability to moral danger. Since Eric had maintained a very warm and supportive relationship with the social worker and had perceived him as a friend who could understand his difficulties and intervene between himself and his father when the latter became too difficult to cope with, this step demanded both courage and clear thinking from the social worker. It also required an ability to tolerate the boy's sense of being let down, plus the professional skill to be able to interpret to him the reason for this seemingly negative step and the fundamental concern for his ultimate well-being that had motivated it.

A final word needs to be said about this role-filling relationship and its simulation of the good parent figure. It must be utilized as a growth-producing relationship which provides the opportunity for the client to identify with a socially effective adult whose standards can be made clear, copied, and eventually internalized.[13] This sort of surrogate parent relationship should *not* be confused with a paternalistic one, which assumes a protective authority for the retarded client and maintains him in a dependent and infantilized role so that he cannot develop greater maturity and his own independently accepted standards of behavior. Since there has been a tendency in the past for services for the retarded to be dominated by this sort of kind but misguided approach, it is important that social workers today be aware of its basic inappropriateness and not try to perpetuate it.

So far we have been concentrating on the social attitudes and mode of interaction that enables the social worker to build up the retarded adult's sense of worth and ability to assume some responsibility for his life. Before leaving this topic, it may be useful to run briefly over the techniques and strategies by which these principles are put into practice. In many ways this represents the hard core of social work with the mildly retarded in that it involves translating the more abstract principles governing social work with this client group into simple, concrete terms. Perhaps the most important activity is reiterated explanation and clarification because only by this means can clients with limited powers of comprehension develop some perspective on how the bewildering events in their lives can be effectively reduced to order.

The first factor of the casework process that needs clarification is the identity and role of the social worker, the precise nature of her function toward the client, and, perhaps most important of all, the scope of her powers in relation to him. Because many of the contacts that the mildly retarded have with individuals outside of their own socioeconomic group tend to be in authority-oriented settings (such as the school, state institution, and law courts), there is a risk that the social worker is perceived primarily as an authority figure and that expectations of her function are based on this perception. It is therefore most important for the establishment and maintenance of the casework relationship that at the outset the client is helped to understand clearly what authority the social worker represents and the sort of help she can offer, including its limitations as well as its positive potential.[14] Generally speaking, the social worker's most telling role in the eyes of the retarded client is expressed in the tangible help she can provide toward easing the mechanics of living, such as helping him to find somewhere to live (if he is without a home of his own), steering him to the sort of work he can do, putting him in touch with individuals or groups where he can make friends.

For the retarded client the *primary* difficulties are invariably with the practical issues of daily living. Therefore this interpretation of concrete services has great meaning, and they should be ranged conspicuously in the forefront of the social worker's repertoire of assistance. Because of its practical and visible value, this concrete evidence of help forms the basis of a realistic trust in the social worker and creates a climate which often makes it possible for the client subsequently to bring up less tangible difficulties (such as feelings of inadequacy, lack of confidence in personal relationships, intrafamily tensions) and receive help with these more subtle problems of adjustment. Since many of the mildly retarded also have their fair share of emotional difficulties, it is most important to offer them an opportunity for expressing and working through some of these in a situation that they can understand and where they feel at ease.

This point leads into another aspect of the relationship which is concerned with the expression of emotions, particularly of negative feelings and attitudes. One of the features frequently reported about mildly retarded individuals is their tendency to discharge their emotional tensions in acting-out behavior rather than through more introspective verbal methods. The case of Keith Allen, described on page 194, illustrated this when he threw up his job without warning because of the despair and anger about the constant rejection and criticism that he felt he encountered in adult authority figures, as exemplified in the immediate work situation and in his parents at home. The destructive practical consequences of such behavior (in this case being homeless and workless) add considerably to the overall adjustment problems of the retarded and must therefore be a central concern of casework. Equally, the reasons underlying such a pattern of reaction must be understood by both client and worker so that the client can avoid a repetition of such behavior.

One of the legitimate functions of the casework relationship is to provide a safe and neutralized forum within which the client, whatever his personal qualities or problems, can be helped to an awareness of his strong and seemingly destructive emotions so that he will ultimately be helped to control them. For the mildly retarded client this problem may have an added dimension which the social worker must understand and cope with. This springs from the fact that many retarded clients have had long experience of having to repress their negative feelings in their developmental years. This is particularly true of those who have been in educational and institutional regimes where conformity was highly rewarded and the opportunity for becoming familiar with negative behavior and its origins was extremely limited. As a result of this sort of experience many clients tend to be unduly inhibited about overt expression of hostility, or alternatively, when this inhibition is lifted, they feel exposed to overwhelming emotions over which they have no control. When the retarded client ventures to express aggressive ideas to the social worker in the casework situation, this hostility may be accompanied by strong feelings of anxiety in case it is met with realistic retaliatory retribution or in fantasy terms if its destructive potential succeeds in destroying the worker. Permitting the client to test out this dangerous impulse may be very valuable in demonstrating that his negative side is neither unacceptable nor completely destructive, and it also implies a psychological equality with the social worker which is helpful in building a more self-respecting self-image.[15]

The pitfall, however, is that the client may interpret this permissiveness too broadly, discard his earlier repressive control devices, and react without discrimination to all adult figures as symbols of the authority that he first grew up to fear and then, via the social work relationship, learned to challenge. Therefore, while it is an important task of casework to convey acceptance of the client's negative feelings and to offer him safe scope for trying them out, this learning situation must also be tempered with a firm awareness of the difference between the casework situation and regular social intercourse, and the appropriateness of different behavior for each. Unless this is made very clear the client may find it hard to understand why it is entirely permissible for him to vent his anger and criticism on the social worker who has placed him in a suitable but demanding employment, when a similar reaction is not acceptable to his employer.

In dealing with the retarded client's hostility and resistance, it is well to bear in mind that these may really be an expression of fearfulness since the diminished capacity for understanding and the poorer social skills of the retarded make them subject to a chronic low-grade level of anxiety and vulnerability which is likely to flare up to a crisis point if practical difficulties occur in their day-to-day living. This latent anxiety can be assuaged to some extent by factual knowledge, and the social worker must ensure that her retarded client is equipped with a clear understanding of whatever plans are being devised for his welfare, both in small detail and in a broader perspective. This means breaking down a plan into segments that are familiar, showing the reason for each stage, how it interlocks with the next phase, and also managing the timing so that there is a minimum delay between broaching a plan and starting to implement it. For example, it is not helpful to discuss a prospective change in the current life situation of a retarded adolescent or young adult as an abstract concept. Instead, it should be presented as a concrete proposal that can be realized within a prescribed time. If the proposal can be described in detailed terms that are already familiar to the client, it will have more meaning for him. Thus timing is better related to seasons or events than to the passage of months or weeks. To tell a retarded eighteen-year-old girl that she will be going out on parole to work in a hospital after Christmas or in the summer will set up a more vivid train of anticipatory associations than saying she will go out on parole in January or June. The potentially fearful step of moving into a half-way house can be mitigated if the client is told where it is, how he will get to work from there, with whom he will be sharing his sleeping arrangements, where he will eat, where the local church or movie house is. Such details re-create a familiar world and enable the client to make a transition to his new situation via the familiar details of the old one which will be replicated. Underlying this is the same dynamic of permitting a child to take a familiar toy into the hospital, which takes the edge of separation from a familiar environment and reinforces a sense of continuity.

This may serve as a suitable note on which to end this chapter on the social work relationship with the mildly retarded independent client, because all the components of the professional relationship and the technique it subsumes are directed toward clarifying, underlining, and strengthening the social role and identity of the retarded client so that he can assume some responsibility for himself and his affairs and gradually become assimilated into the social fabric of his community as a competently functioning adult member. In the earlier chapters we discussed the three levels of contact that could be utilized to deal with the peculiar type of problem that the pervasive chronicity of retardation creates. These three levels of crisis-directed, supportive, and retainer contacts and the different patterns of help they demand also apply in some measure to the mildly retarded, and the professional relationship with this client group should derive its direction from any of these approaches as they seem appropriate. For example, difficulties in personal relationships or sudden loss of earning opportunity will create a critical situation demanding immediate and focused help of limited duration. However, the resolution of an emergent crisis may not result in the retarded client's immediately regaining his equilibrium and complete competence to manage on his own without supervision so that the supportive relationship may have to be provided for a longer period. And even when he seems adjusted to a satisfactory life pattern, the potential vulnerability associated with his handicap calls for the reassuring existence of the retainer relationship in the background. This triple approach provides maximum potential support at the same time that it gives maximum help and encouragement for the client to develop his own independent way of managing his life. In this way his deficits are realistically acknowledged; but more important, by the availability of help and also in keeping with the tenets of a dynamic social work approach, his assets and potential for self-realization are recognized and capitalized. This represents the successful functioning of a sound and progressive social welfare policy on behalf of a minority group that has many social liabilities but can be made to function well. We shall conclude with a case description that illustrates how this supportive service can also stimulate a retarded client to plan for and carry through a quite difficult change in her life.

Brenda Kemp, twenty-one years old, was within the higher range of mild retardation and the eldest of four children living at home with her widowed mother. She had an unhappy relationship with the mother, who resented the girl because she had been born illegitimately before her marriage to her late husband, and was ashamed of her poor school record and the necessity for special education. Because of this unsatisfactory situation at home, Brenda had been sent to a boarding school at thirteen, and on her return home at eighteen had been placed under the school's social worker for supervision and aftercare. She formed a good relationship with the social worker who attempted to develop a more understanding attitude between Brenda and her mother and also to help the girl form other satisfying relationships and interests to compensate for her mother's constant criticism. After three years of uneasy truce within the family, during which Brenda had proved herself very competent and conscientious at work, had made some good contacts with local youth groups, and had started to take classes to improve her reading and writing, she decided she could not tolerate living at home any longer and requested the social worker to find her work and somewhere to live in the country. As she had a warm contact with the boarding school, she asked whether she could go back there.

Since Brenda was of age and obviously determined on this course, the social worker contacted an agency in the area where the school was situated and asked for advice on the prospects of suitable employment and living accommodations. This preliminary action was explained to Brenda with the warning that it would not be easy and might take several months before anything came up. It was also suggested that she explain her intentions to her mother at this early stage and try to win her cooperation or at least approval. Although she would have preferred to leave home secretly without warning, Brenda was helped to see that this was an irresponsible action which would confirm her mother's poor opinion of her, and she agreed to speak to her mother as soon as a good opening occurred. When she had done this, she would telephone the social worker, who offered to visit Mrs. Kemp, clarify details of the plans under discussion, and if necessary interpret why the social worker was supporting Brenda's request. This arrangement was explained on the assumption that Mrs. Kemp would be concerned about new plans for Brenda and that, as her mother, she had a right to be reassured that the project was not harmful. Although Brenda feared a negative reaction and was skeptical about her mother's interest in her, she was in fact secretly pleased at the suggestion that her mother might be genuinely concerned.

Although the initial impact of the news brought a stormy reaction, Brenda was able to handle it fairly calmly, pointing to the realities of the situation rather than falling back on irrational recriminations (which had usually characterized the style of her interaction with her mother) and promising that the social worker would call very soon to explain things better. In addition to implicitly recognizing Mrs. Kemp's rights as a mother (even if a rather ambivalent one), this served to involve her in the plans and disposed of any resentful feelings she might have had about being pushed aside in favor of the social worker. Although in her more immature moments under stress Brenda did fall back on playing one adult figure against the other, the social worker resisted this manipulative behavior by showing herself as an impartial and concerned outsider who was primarily geared to the resolution of the current situation rather than taking sides over the emotional issues that emerged.

When an opening for hotel work occurred in the town near her old school, Brenda took time from work to go for an interview, was met at the other end by the social worker of the local agency and introduced to the hotel manager. As the job seemed well within her capacity and she liked the neighborhood, she said she would like to take it but would prefer to talk it over with the social worker in her home town to be sure. This was agreed to and she was given three days in which to decide and two weeks before starting.

In the interim period she was in frequent touch with the social worker about plans for her move, where to buy luggage, what extra clothes she should get, and so forth. Fortunately she had been encouraged to save when she first started to work so she had some savings to draw on for getting new things. This provided a good object lesson on the advantages of saving, as she came to realize. At the time of departure Mrs. Kemp rather surprisingly asked if she could accompany Brenda to the station and see her on to the train and at the last minute she produced a small traveling alarm clock as a farewell present and to make sure she got up in the mornings. This was a dig at Brenda's difficulty in this area, but it also expressed her mother's concern that this fault should not interfere with her job prospects. Brenda settled well in her new milieu, resumed some contacts with the staff of her old school, and formed a warm relationship with the social worker of the local agency who kept in friendly unofficial contact. She also kept in touch with her family at home, occasionally coming home for visits and having her mother and two of her younger siblings to visit her one Sunday. This case illustrates how a mildly retarded young woman was helped not only to plan an important change in her life in a purposeful and well-thought-out way, but also how to manage in a constructive fashion the quite taxing emotional components that were involved in her separation from her family and particularly her skeptical and ambivalent mother. This produced a double maturing of emotional capacity and practical planning skills.

9 SOME CONCEPTS OF GROUP WORK

A RECURRENT theme in this book is that the handicapping condition and status associated with mental retardation demand a total therapeutic milieu to compensate for the disability of the retarded individual and the stress it imposes upon his family. The components of this benign subsystem have been delineated in earlier chapters, starting with the public health approach needed to ensure the provision of actual services and continuing with an exploration of how organized social work, through its methods and specific techniques, can contribute to this totality of help for the retarded. In the four preceding chapters some of the basic components of social work have been discussed together with the casework method in particular. This chapter will deal with group work and its special contribution to work with the retarded.

In his paper "The Social Worker in the Group" [1] Schwartz advances the challenging idea that to divide social work into three methods is to create rigid and artificial divisions where none really exist and to hinder practice from being maximally effective. His alternative is to emphasize the functional aspect of social work, which "implies the existence of an organic whole, a dynamic system," and he defines the goal of social work in practice as mediating "the process through which the individual and his society reach out for each other through a mutual need for self-fulfillment." Within this conceptual framework, what has been identified as the group work method is redefined as the generic social work method practiced within a particular system; namely, the small-group system, to distinguish it from other systems of social work such as the one-to-one interview used in the casework method. This definition of what, for convenient brevity, we shall continue to term group work is especially appropriate for work with the mentally retarded because it emphasizes flexibility in the choice of help to be offered and makes it possible for this and other methods to be used interchangeably as the situation demands. The diversity and complex nature of the social problems associated with retardation render this approach essential. To quote Schwartz again, "the group is a system of relationships which, in its own unique way, represents a special case of the general relationship between individuals and their society." [2] For the mentally retarded and their families social group work serves just this purpose in providing them with an opportunity for testing out in this microcosmic unit the social attitudes, skills, and patterns of interaction that will enable them to fit into and participate in the wider organization of society at large. This type of *organized* help is invariably necessary to ensure that the retarded client group (which includes their families) achieves full social acceptance, because the social and psychological stigma attaching to retardation, and the difficult adjustment tasks it imposes, tend to inhibit or interfere with the social relationships that under normal circumstances —i.e., where there is no retardation—develop spontaneously.

This broad objective of helping the retarded and their families to realize their fullest potential for social interaction despite their handicapping circumstances applies in some degree to clients at all levels of social competence; and social group work in the retardation field can be divided into three separate patterns, the characteristics of which are determined by the varying needs of different types of clients. For the family or normal relatives of the retarded individual (whether he is a child or independent adult) the principal function of social group work is to establish communication between them and others who are experiencing a similar type of problem, and so reduce the social isolation which often accompanies their stressful situation. Through the group work process the disturbance to the family's overall social functioning, which has been created by the presence of a serious and chronic disability and is often exacerbated by the resultant social isolation, may be mitigated and reversed.

For retarded individuals themselves social group work is an equally valuable tool of rehabilitation and, though its scope may differ from that which is used with the families of the retarded, it has essentially the same goal of helping the retarded individuals to function more adequately and appropriately in a social context. Depending upon the level of social competence of the retarded individual (which also means his capacity for independent decision and action) group work activities assume differing forms, ranging from group counseling which utilizes verbal skills to participation in an organized program of recreational activity in which group involvement is implicit but not spelled out. For the mildly retarded client group, whose handicap stems primarily from social and cultural deprivation, group work is essentially an educative process which offers a testing ground where they can learn social behavior that is appropriate to their age, sex, and the cultural norms of the social group to which they belong. Group work should offer scope for decision-making in a relatively protected setting and for acquiring the confidence and skills in social interaction normally required in day-to-day living. For this category of the retarded it is a learning process which helps their near-normal social functioning.

For the moderately retarded, on the other hand, group work serves the purpose of providing a contrived social experience to simulate that of the normal peer group from which the moderately retarded are invariably excluded because of their conspicuous handicap and lack of social skills. Group work has an educative function also for these clients because it helps to develop social skills that will improve the scope and quality of their relationships within their family and among friends. In addition it complements this objective by providing organized social experiences to take the place of friendship and other informal social contacts that normal children and adults build up as part of their social and developmental patterns. Further, this organized activity serves the secondary but equally valuable end of providing recreation which compensates for the limited resources for amusement that the retarded individual has. The overall purpose of group work for the moderately or severely retarded individual, whose social life will always involve at least partial dependency, is to maintain his adjustment in a relatively stable situation in the community, usually in the home of immediate relatives.

GROUP WORK WITH THE FAMILIES OF THE RETARDED

Because of the social dysfunction inherent in retardation and the impact of this handicap upon the normal individuals associated with it, social work intervention, regardless of the method employed, is concerned primarily with helping the retarded individual or his relatives to function as well as possible in their normal social context. When there is a conspicuously retarded child or adult present, the ability of the family to maintain normal functioning is seriously threatened by a number of factors. These are the unfamiliar task of coping with the special needs of a retarded child; the sense of isolation that stems from having a defective member in the family; and the complex of emotional responses evoked by this situation which appear atypical, destructive, and unacceptable by both the personal standards and the cultural norms subscribed to by the family.

The principal focus of group work with families of the retarded should therefore be on the atypical features of their social situation, since this is the common denominator in their lives. This frame of reference identifies the basis of their many problems and opens the way for dealing with other more specific areas of difficulty, such as the distortion of roles within the family, problems of interpersonal relationships among the immediate and extended family system, the pattern of interaction with the wider social group, and the psychological reaction to the retarded person and his defect.

Group work with families may be provided in a variety of settings: those that are directly involved in the care of the child [3] such as special clinical facilities, day care centers, schools, recreational facilities, residential institutions; those that are geared to generic family problems such as a general psychiatric clinic or a family and children's agency,[4] and those concerned with other aspects of retardation than direct treatment, such as parent organizations.[5] The purpose of the setting will determine to some extent the detailed content of the group's operation; for example, group work associated with a service to the child will most likely take the form of counseling, whereas the group activities of a parent organization will have a greater orientation to community action. The bias of a group will also be affected by the stage of emotional and intellectual familiarity with retardation that the parents have reached, and this again will be at least partly determined by the type of facility that is offering the group counseling. Thus a parent's group held in an evaluation center is likely to be crisis-oriented because of the overriding necessity for the group to assimilate the hard facts of retardation and the inevitable shock that clinical confirmation imposes.

By contrast a counseling group that is run in association with a training program for the child has a different focus in that it is not primarily concerned with the critical phase just mentioned because the fact of the child's being accepted in a training regime implies that the family's situation has moved from one of initial shock to gradual adjustment to the chronic stresses created by retardation. A slightly different pattern in group counseling is needed for the families of older retarded individuals. This kind of help (which has not been much reported in literature) must be chiefly concerned with the chronic component of retardation, its main goal being to help families to understand and cope with the unusual and demanding task of maintaining a permanently disabled dependent adult. Parents find it extremely difficult to accept the adult status of a retarded son or daughter, and group counseling can serve an invaluable purpose by providing the opportunity for them to ventilate some of their practical problems and deeper nagging fears. This sort of group work is appropriately associated with an adult training facility[6] or it can be a useful adjunct developed by a parents' organization.[7]

From a consideration of the principal types of settings in which group work can be most effectively provided for the families of the retarded, we must now examine more carefully what aspects of retardation and its problems are particularly amenable to the group work approach and what are the special therapeutic ingredients that this particular method can bring to this disability. Mention has already been made of the emotional and social isolation that afflicts the family of a retarded child or adult. Closely associated with this major and pervasive difficulty is the atypical parental situation in which families find themselves on account of their child's handicap. This different experience occurs initially with the parents' reaction to the child's birth, which triggers a different set of emotions from those evoked by a normal newborn child. Second, it relates to the drastic revision of expectations for their family life which the child's chronic dependency necessitates. The third area of major stress is the ambiguous parent role that the child's deviance imposes upon them. Because of the child's markedly different characteristics, the parents face a threatening unfamiliarity in the tasks of parenthood, which raises doubts about specific management and care and may undermine their general confidence as parents. Fourth, the strong emotions that the advent of a retarded child evokes are liable to disrupt the normal patterns of family interaction in both the immediate and the wider circles of relatives. The disappointment, grief, guilt, and conflict of ideas about long-term care for the child often create disharmony within even a close-knit family, so that the emotional and practical support that is usually forthcoming from this nexus of relationships is not only absent but may in fact be turned into an added source of emotional stress for the nuclear family. This sort of psychological separation from the kinship group is another facet of social isolation which is particularly damaging to the susceptible parents who are coping with a retarded child.

Social group work counteracts these hazards in a variety of ways. Through membership in a group parents automatically come into contact with other families similarly placed, which is the first step toward abandoning their isolated position and starting to develop some meaningful communication with others. In the process of sharing the common problems of retardation they discover that the atypical situation of trying to raise a retarded child is not unique and, moreover, that for this *particular* group it is the *norm*. Within this frame of reference the ambiguous and conflict-ridden parent role becomes more acceptable, and the ambivalence toward the child and the confusion and doubts about management and planning are perceived as an integral part of this unusual but not unique situation.

Bearing in mind the special and overriding need that this client group has to find a common identity among themselves, we must now examine in greater detail the specific components of group work by which this objective can be achieved. These fall into eight main groups and will be discussed separately although their inter-relatedness will be obvious.

Criteria for selection of group membership. The basis on which members are selected for any group that is centered around problems and their solution is a vital index to its potential success, and for groups that involve the complex difficulties associated with retardation it is especially necessary to give careful thought to what types of problems will provide the best basis for meaningful group interaction. For the sort of group we are discussing, in which major emphasis is on the distortion in parental functioning and roles that occur as a by-product of the child's disability, the degree of defect and associated behavior he manifests must be one of the principal criteria for selection. If there is too great a disparity among the children in the level of functioning and the severity or complexity of the disability, the common ground of concern and interest which is essential for group identification will be lost and the parents will be confirmed in their conviction of being isolated in a unique and painful situation.

On the other hand, there is some advantage in selecting children who present a certain range in both disability and age because this heterogeneous quality heightens the *social* orientation of the group. A diversity in ages of three or four years permits a wider scope of advice to be exchanged between parents. Problems that one family may be trying to deal with in the present may be helped by the insights of parents who have coped with the same problems at an earlier stage in their child's development. Also, if the group contains families with children whose retardation is manifested in a variety of socially handicapping forms, this can be utilized to bring home to parents the fact that they are all dealing with a diversified disability which must be individually understood for each child. This makes demands on the skill of the social worker to be able to maintain the cohesiveness of the group while pointing up the differences in the types of disability, level of achievement, rate of progress, and idiosyncratic behavior of individual children. It is, however, a valuable function of a parent group because it not only helps each family to individualize its management of their child but also gives

them an insight and understanding with which to counter the stereotype of retardation that they so frequently come up against among
their relatives, friends, and other individuals and groups.

In considering what levels of disability can be effectively grouped
together it is important to bear in mind not only current levels of
handicap but also prognosis for social development because this will
affect the parents' attitudes and management. For example, in a
group for parents of profoundly retarded children it would be a
mistake to include a family who had a child with a serious degenerative condition—such as Tay-Sachs disease—in which the principal
problem was the gradual deterioration of physical and mental function and early death. For parents who face this particularly distressing type of problem, a group based on a single identified condition,
such as that described by Yates and Lederer,[8] will have more value
in that the pooling of experience, knowledge, and feelings has a
greater thrust because of its homogeneity and concentration of shared
experience. This I would term a *clinically* oriented group in which
the focus is *intensive* and narrowed, and simulates the *treatment*
situation rather than the *social interaction* one, with the contrived
arrangement of a group based on a single deviance as an intrinsic
component of treatment. By contrast, the socially oriented group
draws its strength from its diverse composition, which simulates
the variety of normal social experience and interchange encountered in real life.

Another point round which a parent group may be formed is an
area of service which is not primarily affected by the child's degree
of handicap. For example, a residential facility may utilize parent
groups to interpret its program to families of children on the waiting
list, and the grouping will be arranged according to prospective date
of admission rather than to the child's personal characteristics. Since
the content of discussion will be concerned with the emotional components of separation and the change in family life that will occur
when the retarded child is placed, the diversity of handicap is not so
important. A similar basis for a parent group is the formation of one
by a voluntary organization for the specific task of discussing plans
for obtaining improved services for the retarded.[9] The children of
such parents may cover a wide range of disability and needs, but this

will not necessarily interfere with group cohesiveness since it is not the individual children's defects that are the focus of concern but the lack of services common to them all. The purpose of such a group would not be to provide reciprocal support in problems of child management but rather to develop the parents' skills for handling the tasks of interpreting retardation to the community and soliciting its tolerance for this disability.

Structured organization of the group. Structure is another important factor in parent groups which influences, and is influenced by, the therapeutic objectives involved. For a group that operates in connection with a special clinical diagnostic facility, the principal goal may be to help families accept the findings of retardation and its long-term implications. In this context group work serves to neutralize the crisis that attends the discovery of retardation; and in order to cope with the highly charged emotions set off by the impact of the shock, the group structure needs to be tight, with a limited and prescribed number of parents involved and formal agreement on plans for meeting. Only if its members meet regularly and involve themselves fully in going through the common misery of understanding what it means to have a retarded child will the group develop basic solidarity and constancy. This contractual arrangement provides the setting in which chaotic emotional responses can be contained within the firmness of external reality; it also lays the foundations of psychological strengths and social solidarity which parents need in order to withstand the many frustrations and trials they will face in the future.

On the other hand a group which is primarily directed toward redefining parent roles rather than the resolution of emotional distress may profitably utilize a more informal structure which reinforces its social orientation. Such flexibility may be expressed through permitting new members to join at any point, by allowing visitors to come for occasional meetings, and by throwing it open to an assortment of interested family members. Open-ended group organization contains a varied range of therapeutic possibilities. For example, when the content of previous group activity has to be recapitulated in order to orient newcomers to the group's purpose and direction, the existing members may become aware of new facets to problems already discussed, and the repetitive aspect of this group exchange may help them to assimilate ideas that had at first seemed strange and unfamiliar. Reviewing the content of group discussion and interaction also accustoms group members to describing their situations and feelings to outsiders; this may make it easier for them to interpret their child's retardation and its social implications to other individuals outside of their own family or immediate circle of friends. Introducing outsiders to a group is also a very valuable way of neutralizing the sense of affect-charged secrecy associated with retardation, which is a factor that tends to alienate families with a retarded child from other individuals or groups who do not carry this highly stigmatized burden.

The therapeutic thrust of an open-ended group derives less from the content of group discussion (though this of course is very important) and more from the solidarity that is implicit in the members' sense of group identity and their readiness to permit other interested outsiders to participate. Further, the different approach to problems presented by newcomers can contribute to the existing group's dynamic movement by activating a significant new response. This was illustrated clearly by the mother of a severely retarded four-year-old boy with behavior problems, who entered a group of parents with moderately or severely retarded children some months after its inception. This new mother began to talk almost immediately after the session began, voicing the family's despair at their inability to toilet-train the child and their fears (grounded in reality) that he would never get into an educational program while this major social deficiency persisted. After some discussion about his condition, she recounted the cause of his chronic brain syndrome, which was the sequel to a very high fever from a severe measles' attack, and ended up by saying that he was a "very bad case" (implying much worse than the children of other parents present) and that toilet training was "a lost cause." The other more experienced parents, who had been dealing with behavior problems and their own feelings about them in the group for several sessions, and had developed both group solidarity and a sense of personal achievement in managing their own children, listened with great sympathy, and offered their own negative experiences to demonstrate that these setbacks were not irreversible. They directly challenged the attitude that training was of no avail, and when the new mother questioned the value of the child's damaged life (which threatened their own more hopeful concepts), they moved into more emotionally charged areas of discussion which previously had not emerged with such clarity. They talked about what constituted a valuable life for an individual, and to what extent such an evaluation reflected parental hopes rather than the child's own potential. This led several parents into confessing their pervasive disappointment about their child's handicap, and how they frequently found themselves wistfully comparing the reality of their situation with what it would have been if their child had been normal.

Size and time factors. The optimum *size* of a group will vary according to its therapeutic aims, but certain broad limits need to be defined. For an intensively focused group, between ten and twelve is probably a good number because this allows for close interaction but is not so small that the inevitable absences will destroy its viability. Sessions should be one or one-and-a-half hours in length for this minimum number to allow for group interaction to get under way and for each member to have the opportunity to contribute.

The *time span* over which a group should function and the *frequency* of meetings are other important components of group work treatment which will vary according to whether the treatment has an acute or more chronic focus. We have already mentioned the difference in the structure of groups that deal with crisis problems as opposed to those concerned with longer-term adjustment tasks; the time element between these two approaches is also different. A group dealing with the initial shock of retardation may need to meet more frequently and for a circumscribed period in order to absorb the severe onslaught of feelings that parent members may both experience themselves and inflict upon each other. Being able to rely upon the group at regular and frequent intervals over a guaranteed period — for example, once a week for three or six months — supports parents in this stressful period of adjustment. Against this, a parent group that has moved from this initial crisis point to the task of trying to delimit and build up their roles and functions as parents of a child with a permanent disability may do better with less frequently spaced meetings spread over a longer period.

Content of group focus. When inviting parents to join a group, it is essential to give them a clear explanation of the group's purpose which they can all understand. This in effect should be clarified as a recognition that having a retarded child creates certain unusual problems and that sharing them with other parents in the structured social group work situation may relieve tensions and suggest some ways of solving them. It is of utmost importance to establish an objective to which all parents subscribe because the sense of group identification that is so necessary for breaking into the social isolation experienced by so many parents depends on this. The creation of this common bond and goal can be initiated by inviting each member to describe briefly the outstanding characteristics of his child—age, sex, type of handicap, and level of functioning—and to name the problem that currently is causing the most stress and for which they would like help. This tactic promotes a sense of group involvement because it enables parents to see their own difficulties reflected in other families (which underlines their common character) and because the act of admitting to a problem implies a willingness to share experiences, even if painful. It also helps to bring into the open problems which parents inwardly regard as insignificant or inadmissible. The social worker can help to consolidate this sharing process by listing the problems and then asking the group which one they should tackle first. Their choice may express an affirmation of common concern or their view on priorities in regard to severity of problem.

Practical management issues. Most parents tend to cite specific management problems—such as feeding, toilet-training, poor sleep habits—as their main focus of concern to begin with, inasmuch as these interfere most conspicuously with the family's total functioning. Because this represents the greatest overt threat to their parental role, and because competent handling of the child improves his social functioning and status, it is very appropriate that group work with parents should be initially focused on these crucial practical issues. Further, when the group addresses itself to ways of dealing with the specific needs and problems that the retarded child presents, it develops a pattern of exchanging management experience which results in a reservoir of pooled knowledge and expertise upon which all members can draw and to which they all contribute. The management of their shared problems then becomes a rational and tested stratagem, in lieu of the trial-and-error method which many parents feel they are reduced to because of their ignorance. This exchange of proven expertise builds up confidence in the total task of being a parent, and when a member submits to the group a technique of management or attitude about which he or she has doubts because it is a departure from normal child-rearing practice, its acceptance by the rest of the group not only validates this specific method but also affirms the parents' confidence in their innate capacity to rise to the child's unusual demands. This type of interaction also redefines the role of every member as a parent with competence and expertise, and identifies an emerging body of applied knowledge which converts the previously confused situation of ignorance and unfamiliarity into one of recognizable order.

Moreover, a discussion of practical concerns almost invariably leads into less tangible topics, such as family attitudes toward the retarded child, the status he is given, the pattern of interaction between parents and other family members that develops as a result of his handicap. For example, when parents describe how they respond to the excessive demands of a retarded child or what disciplinary tactics they use, they may also reveal that he is given highly privileged treatment within the family at the expense of the normal children's needs and that these children in turn are reacting to this discrimination with resentment and disturbed behavior. Experience in parent counseling, both individual and in a group, indicates that the more emotionally toned topics tend to emerge in the context of a safer practical issue. This may reflect the fact that while parents are aware of the emotional problems surrounding their child's handicap, they find them too painful for immediate and direct confrontation but can accept them when they are related to practical management.

Because retardation is an emotionally invested handicap which carries implications of parental failure (in having produced a damaged child and in feeling inadequate to cope with its special needs), it is important for the group to be involved initially with an area of functioning that has some positive features, such as the management skills that parents have already developed out of their special experience. A discussion of the relatively neutral topics of practical management helps to establish a benign climate of unthreatened acceptance from which it is often possible for parents to move into the more painfully charged area of feelings, attitudes, and beliefs about retardation and their child.

If the discussion of management problems is geared to a very specific description of how the child functions and is handled by the family, this procedure can be one of the most illuminating revelations of attitudes and feelings. The social worker, by gently pressing for exact details, can utilize this concern with practical problems to bring the situation being described into vivid relief, which other parents in the group can visualize and identify with. The narrative presentation of behavior conveys the actual emotional content of a situation much more sharply than a straightforward description of feelings, and this underlying psychological component can be further highlighted by the social worker's interjecting comments on the feelings that the situation evoked, which may then be taken up by other group members. This may be a way of introducing a fresh emotional slant to a situation, not hitherto recognized by the parent involved. For example, the mother of a three-year-old girl with cerebral palsy was describing the child's reluctance to go to bed and how all the adults in turn lay down with her until she fell asleep. This tedious situation was claimed to be inevitable because of the child's tendency to go rigid and provoke a seizure if thwarted, and it was cited by the mother as an example of the *factual* problems that were created by the child's fairly severe neurological impairment. The social worker commented that this must be a very exasperating performance for everyone concerned and a great trial to the mother's patience. Other members of the group echoed this reaction, citing experiences of their own in which their child's handicap had created difficulties they resented. This enabled the mother to consider her own feelings instead of inhibiting them in the course of what was perceived as a necessary duty, and was the start of her examination of considerable negative feelings toward the child's handicap and the burden it imposed on her. With this help she gradually moved toward a recognition that these hidden hostile feelings were forcing her into a placating attitude toward the child which the latter sensed and exploited. This revelation of "bad" feelings was made tolerable because she received the group's sanction to have such feelings. Also, the more effective management tactics, which she had described in regard to other aspects of the child, were favorably commented on and suggestions were made as to how she could tackle this more difficult problem along similar lines.

Psychological issues. This book has dwelt on the point that to solve the stresses imposed by retardation social work help must weave constantly between the practical and the emotional elements that create a hard-core problem for parents or other relatives. As we have suggested, group work is particularly suited to this approach because it permits the easy transition from the obvious practical problems to the less easily accepted psychological issues. In the past two or three decades a good deal has been written about the emotional themes that parents with a retarded child present,[10] and group work has been emerging as a useful vehicle for helping to ventilate and resolve some of these pressures. The disappointment, resentment, fear for the future, and recurrent despair that are inevitable because of the insoluble nature of the problem all constitute part of the "normal psychological equipment" that parents of retarded children must assume when they face the task of recognizing their child's lifelong defect and its social implications. Such parents also frequently wonder whether they will be able to survive the overwhelming onslaught of feelings evoked by their tragic situation, whether they have the capacity to comprehend and meet the child's unusual needs, and whether they can remain intact as normal adults in spite of their apparently impaired capacity for healthy parenthood which the child's defect calls into overt question. Being able to share these disturbing emotional experiences with other adults similarly burdened produces a psychological bulwark which helps parents of a retarded child to withstand the tremendous self-doubts with which they are assailed.[11]

In addition to the resolution of individual tensions through sharing a common experience, the group process offers parents another sort of outlet for emotional pressures. This is in the communal mourning rite that is brought into unconscious play when parents discuss emotionally laden themes that appear recurrently in the group, usually expressed as described events. The principal happenings which parents evoke for this grieving ritual are the shock of discovering the child's abnormality (or the worse experience of living with a growing suspicion which no outsider will refute or confirm), the seemingly insensitive handling of the diagnostic revelation, the subsequently recapitulated birth trauma, the long haul of self-doubts and despair at the child's slow progress and the sustained intensive care required to produce even this. Other topics which emerge and re-emerge constantly as sources of distress and frustration are the saga of endless visits to specialized facilities for guidance or treatment, the persistent quest for accurate information on causation, and the underlying and eventually voiced question as to why it should happen to the family concerned. Solnit and Stark[12] say that this recurrent preoccupation with events relating to the defective child's birth and subsequent development is an intrinsic part of the mourning process, and it is essential for the family's adjustment that they be permitted to harp back constantly to the unassimilated shock events. When these bad experiences are shared in a group, they serve a valuable function of highlighting and projecting into external reality the negative aspects of retardation, and these negative features become the basis of the shared mourning process in that they are the outward smaller manifestations that represent the larger common tragedy in which all group members are involved. To continue the analogy of tragedy the group process bears a certain likeness to the chorus in classical drama which recounts, comments on, and makes acceptable painful and inevitable events. It is the structured pattern of the chorus and its corporate character that make it possible for the tragic events of the drama to be tolerated because the responsibility for communicating the horror involved falls on more than a single individual.

When emotionally charged material is first brought up in a parent group, it is almost invariably related to an aspect of retardation that is separate from the child and his family. The lack of services or poor quality of care provided (which are justifiable sources of anger) are often utilized as a "safe" medium through which the negative feelings engendered by the total retardation situation can be expressed with impunity. When parents feel able to express negative feelings more directly about the child's defect, they usually direct them toward the more general aspects of their plight, such as the disappointment at having a disabled child, the problems this creates, and its effect on other children. It is rare for the actual child and his handicap to be the butt of hostile or derogatory feelings.

This inhibition is probably a culturally reinforced safeguard which the group worker should respect because it contains a sound psychological truth—namely, that there is no helpful catharsis in expressing open hostility when the source of the negative feelings is insoluble and permanent and has to be lived with in practical ways each day. On this account some negative feelings are better left dormant than brought into consciousness, unless it is obvious that they are seriously affecting relationships and family functioning to an extent that the group cannot be unaware of them. For example, when the topic of overprotective care is discussed (which it frequently is), parents are usually very firm in justifying this attitude on the grounds of feeling extra protectiveness and responsibility because of the child's realistically disabling condition. Since this is a comfortable stance for parents which tunes in with their idea of the "good" parent role, it is better to acknowledge this as a socially appropriate attitude than to introduce the concept of ambivalence and forbidden unconscious death wishes expressed in excessive fear. To confront parents with the latter interpretation in a situation where it receives group validation is to institutionalize a socially unacceptable attitude. This may then interfere with the family's ability to relate to the retarded child in a normal way.

Gisela Konopka[13] has coined a useful term—"anonymity of insight"—to describe a type of group interaction which is appropriate to this sort of situation in which heavily laden emotional topics can be therapeutically handled without exposing them to the group's explicit recognition. This insight may be acquired by a group member privately through the group discussion and interaction, but it does not have to be verbalized in order to be validated and accepted. The following example of group interaction illustrates this concept.

It has special relevance to retardation because of the acute feelings of devalued self-image and social status that are associated with the disability. The topic for consideration was introduced by an intelligent black mother in her mid-forties whose fourth child was mongoloid. She felt the stigma of this acutely and on two occasions at least had expressed to the group her anger toward members of her family and neighbors who had reacted in a slighting manner toward her child. In the initial intake she had verbalized a strong sense of being discriminated against racially, and it was clear that an obviously defective child was a final seal on her poor self-image. On the occasion being described she presented to the group a dilemma concerning her normal sixteen-year-old daughter who was being compelled to do gym and dancing at school in her bare feet. The mother (Mrs. Pratt) strongly disapproved of this practice which she regarded as unhygienic and undignified, and she wondered whether she should take her daughter out of school rather than conform to this requirement. In tones of great disgust she described her deep-seated objections, saying that going barefoot was dirty, unsuitable for a school, and likely to breed and spread disease. The images evoked by her description were much stronger than the reality situation warranted and they conveyed a deep-seated conviction that dirt and disease in her children were very threatening and associated (at least unconsciously) with poverty-stricken, disease-ridden barefoot children in the rural south. A second Negro mother who had a much more secure self-image responded in a warmly reassuring way by saying that she did not see any harm in doing gym in bare feet, adding that in her childhood in Florida they often went without shoes and enjoyed it. A middle-class white father took up the thread by commenting that orthopedists today recommended walking barefoot for good posture, and the group as a whole chimed in with some equally cogent evidence that bare feet were not in themselves physically harmful or socially demeaning. In the face of this unanimous more positive interpretation Mrs. Pratt conceded with grudging relief that she had perhaps been oversensitive on the matter and decided against making an issue of it. This mother's sense of rejection because of her imagined racial inferiority was a major problem to her, and she found reassurance in being able to air her fears to the group and find that they understood and responded sympathetically to the emotional issues behind this seemingly practical problem. This conviction of being devalued had in many previous situations served to isolate her from other people, which in turn confirmed her sense of inferiority. This illustrates the hidden agenda in group interaction when feelings are sensed and responded to appropriately without having to be put into the more explicit but more threatening medium of words.

Role of the social worker. There are several features concerning the social worker's role that need to be carefully understood if she is to be maximally effective. Because of the baffling problems that retardation presents for parents, there is always the tendency for a parent group which is trying to work through its bewilderment to become unduly dependent on the group leader and to invest her with disproportionate expertise, to compensate for their own acutely perceived inadequacy. This attitude will demonstrate itself in a general inclination to place the social worker in a teaching role in which she will put her invaluable knowledge at the group's disposal and in this way pass on her skills intact to them. As Beck[14] has pointed out, this is a justifiable demand on the parents' part because they do lack experience and confidence in handling the unusual problems of their retarded child, and it is appropriate for the social worker to lend this authority that derives from her specialist knowledge and wider experience to the group in its early stages. However, it must be understood by the group that one of the chief functions is to develop its own skills and become a specialized parent group with its own competence. As the group becomes more relaxed and gains self-confidence, this knowledgeable role can gradually be transferred by drawing on the special qualities or areas of skill of its individual members. To give a very elementary example: One mother voiced her concern about toilet-training and appealed for specific advice on how to set up an effective schedule for her six-year-old boy who was disproportionately behind in this skill relative to his other capacities. The social worker invited another mother who had had similar difficulties earlier and had been helped by a training schedule set up by the public health nurse to describe the approach and techniques that she had found particularly helpful.

This education by peers carries a great deal of weight among the parents because it stems from the *firsthand* experience of someone in identical circumstances, in contrast to that of the professional worker whose counseling is based primarily on theoretical concepts reinforced by the *secondhand* experiences recounted by clients. The process is also valuable in that it helps to transfer expertise from the professional *out*sider to the parent *in*-group, thereby counteracting the tendency for group members to become overly dependent on the superior knowledge which they imagine professional workers to possess. The process of transferring expertise should start as soon as possible, and the social worker should keep it in play by constantly referring questions back to the group in general for their response or, when this is not forthcoming, by canvassing a particular parent because he or she is likely to have the answer. In a group attended by both parents this technique can have an additional use in highlighting the roles of parents that are specific to their sex. It may offer a good opportunity to point up the contribution of the father in raising the retarded child, which is often overlooked to the detriment of the child as well as the total family. An example of how the masculine viewpoint can be stressed to show the importance of another dimension in the care of the child occurred in a group which was attended by both parents, sometimes together and sometimes separately. In one session the mother described a disquieting habit her eight-year-old son (who had chronic brain syndrome with some autistic features) had developed of unscrewing all the electric light bulbs and throwing them downstairs. When corrected, he modified this activity by placing the bulbs in a row on the table. The group on the whole tended to regard this as not very satisfactory behavior and concurred with the mother's disapproval. A month later the father reported that the boy had become intensely preoccupied with unscrewing nuts and bolts, adding that he regarded this as a step forward because it showed he understood the proper use of a screwdriver and could manipulate it. The question of his unscrewing electric light bulbs was raised by another mother whose son was also indulging in this form of exploratory activity and she questioned whether it should not be stopped on grounds of potential danger. The father met this question by describing the various safety mech anisms that were built into sockets and assured the group that danger was minimal. This view had already been voiced by the husband of the second mother and its confirmation in the group by another male dispelled most of her doubts.

From specific points of actual management the much wider and more emotionally charged topic of social roles and identification based on sex can develop. In the case cited, the father was pointing out the value of his son's being involved with some minimal competence in a primarily masculine task. Another example which illustrates the concern and confusion families have about this area of development is the complaint raised by a mother that her four-year-old moderately retarded boy had become preoccupied with girls' activities, either imitating her household activities or playing with his sisters' dolls whom he liked to tuck up in his own bed. The social worker commented that this demonstrated rather creative play and suggested that the boy might be given a doll's bed for Christmas to play with on his own. This provoked the mother to confess her fear that this effeminate tendency would become crystallized unless it was stamped out early, since she had read that early learning patterns persist in retarded children for much longer and even permanently sometimes. The group questioned this premise, pointing out that most boys play with toys of either sex during the preschool phase, and the mother began to see that her fears might be springing from her own stereotyped perception of retardation rather than its reality. Her shift to a more normal attitude toward the child's behavior was supported by one of the fathers in the group who said he had been extremely attached to a large doll up to the age of going to school. This admission was a tacit but very strong means of emphasizing the child's essentially masculine sex role (since his model was a highly successful, normal adult man), and it expressed for the group the recognition that identification with the appropriate sex is of great importance to a retarded child's development. The unspoken fear that sexual deviance and retardation are closely associated was also implicitly dispelled by the admission of a normal adult male of similar behavior.

It has already been stated that for group work which is oriented primarily to assisting the social functioning and status of the whole family in which there is a retarded member, a major objective is improving the latter's behavior and social competence so that he can be more easily assimilated into the family pattern. It is therefore very important for the social worker to clarify general issues for the group which underlie the specific management problems they bring up. This helps to replace specific techniques for handling individual difficulties by general principles, which are connected to underlying attitudes and roles, and gives the family a wider perspective of understanding. For example, the specific problem of how to control an impulsive retarded child in the street without being stiflingly restrictive can be used to introduce the broader issue of how to balance the calculated risk-taking that is necessary to develop independence with the equally important protection against the hazards that may result from the child's limited comprehension. This topic provides a basis from which the group can move toward considering how parents view their retarded child, by what yardstick they assess his competence to deal with social situations, how comfortable they feel when he reaches the point of being past their immediate physical control, and the techniques they devise for maintaining proper care of him when he is past the baby stage. In one group a youngish mother repeatedly voiced her conflicted feelings about the increasing independence that her five-year-old girl was developing as a result of nursery school experience. While she realized this was very healthy growth, she was also apprehensive about her ability to control the child, particularly since a neighbor had commented that she was getting fresh. This mother, who verbalized very well, was able to relate the child's manifestation of greater competence to her own need to reassess her expectations for the child and to tailor her management to this higher level of functioning. This new phase in the parent-child relationship was rather dramatically symbolized in the report the mother brought to the group of how the child had recently locked herself into a room alone and how the mother had been able to convey sufficiently clear and authoritative instructions to the child which enabled her to climb on a chair, snap back the catch, and let herself out. This incident set a fresh level of control for the child.

A discussion of specific handling can also lead into the question of how parents can distinguish behavior or functioning that is directly attributable to the handicap from that which is normal and common to all children—for example, what is impaired comprehension and what is pure obstinacy. This is an important basic concept for parents to grasp since it produces a clearer and more circumscribed definition of the disability and sustains the notion that even though handicapped in some specific areas, the child possesses many normal features that must be recognized and fostered. The parent who can say with conviction to the group that her seven-year-old boy knows right from wrong in certain respects and needs to have this reinforced by appropriate discipline is in fact expressing expectations of social competence; this is much healthier than the defeatist attitude that the child's disability puts him beyond the scope of being trained to some degree of social responsiveness.

Resolution of intrafamily tensions. Another extremely valuable function of group work with parents is that it provides a testing ground in which the intrafamily tensions and strains created by a retarded child's presence may be worked through outside of the home so that there is less stress within the family. A parent group can serve this purpose by inviting teen-age siblings to attend some of the meetings to discuss the problems they encounter with the retarded child and the effect of these on their relationship with their parents. The teen-age sibling is a very significant member of a family which has a retarded child, and his or her problems should be recognized and dealt with. On the one hand the teen-ager can be a tremendous source of emotional and practical support to the parents as well as contributing much to the retarded child's happiness and growth. On the other hand, the presence of the retarded child— particularly if his handicap is conspicuous—produces many difficulties for the adolescent sibling. Fears that the retardation is of genetic origin may blur aspirations and plans for eventual marriage; the actual presence of the retarded child may deter the teen-age child from developing intimate relationships with peers; and there may be a residue of guilt about not wanting to take a larger share in the retarded child's care. Communication between parents and adolescent children is often difficult under normal circumstances and it is likely to be exacerbated when there is a serious common problem in the family which impinges on all members. Parent groups that offer the occasional opportunity for frank interchange on this vital and often painful topic may be very helpful in resolving conflicts between parents and their older normal children that center round the retarded child.

Such an example is a family of five in which the eldest son was in his first year at college and the youngest child was a mongoloid boy of school age. At the time of the group meeting the older boy was very concerned about modern therapeutic methods of handling the younger retarded boy and insisted on trying to superimpose his psychology textbook ideas on the disciplinary pattern that the parents were trying to evolve. The confusion which this conflicted dual control created for the child resulted in quite disturbed manipulative behavior at home and at school and led to his being suspended for constantly disrupting the class. This obvious evidence of the child's poor social adjustment (and its serious practical implications) was very threatening to the parents, and they began to doubt their capacity to handle this child at home and were considering placement. The three normal school-age children in the family were also adversely affected by the conflicts and reacted with difficult behavior. When the situation was first described to the group, one parent suggested that perhaps the son could be invited to the group to share his ideas and see whether a compromise could be worked out at home. This gesture achieved several things. First, it demonstrated to the troubled parents that they had sympathetic support from their peers whose judgment they respected because they too had retarded children to deal with. Second, it recognized that the college son, through his superior education, might have some insights that they could incorporate into their child-rearing methods. Third, it acknowledged this son's wish to offer some responsible (and as he thought specialized) help to the total family problem. And fourth it helped him to reconcile his impractical but theoretically sound ideas with those of his parents' generation because the group represented outsiders to whom he related as an equal adult. Lastly, the consensus of support that his parents received from group members reassured the young man about their competence to handle the problem and permitted him to realize that the burden of enlightened efficiency did not rest on him alone. This group involvement succeeded in converting the positive impulses of the two generations into a mutually supportive cooperative effort in lieu of the destructive situation which was developing in the family.

The intimate family group represents the paradigm from which all social relationships are drawn, whether these concern the subsequent phases of one individual's personal development or a whole family's interaction with the community beyond its confines. It is therefore important that its internal dynamics be helped to function as effectively as possible, and the use of group work to achieve this end is a valid purpose.

GROUP WORK WITH THE MENTALLY RETARDED CLIENT

The introduction to this chapter stated that the primary purpose of group work in the field of mental retardation is to break into the social isolation that frequently results from this disability and its stigmatized devaluing social connotation. We have discussed the potential isolation that parents of retarded children experience and must now explore how this same problem affects the retarded themselves. For them, social isolation is an equal handicap, but it is of a slightly different order in that it originates not only from the attitude and behavior of society toward the mentally retarded but also from the impaired social functioning that, in varying degrees, is inherently associated with their disability. Group work with this segment of the retarded client group must, therefore, deal simultaneously with the isolating social role ascribed to them by the dominant value system of society (and the negative self-image this creates) and with their own limited social competence that reinforces this rejection. This involves recreating and affirming a viable social role and developing social skills to support it. These skills may be lacking because of the innately poor adaptive capacity of the retarded individual (as in the case of the moderately and severely retarded) or because of limited opportunity to learn and develop this sort of expertise. The latter almost invariably relates to an environmental lack, as in the case of children growing up in a poverty area or in the equally depriving environment of large and impersonal institutional regimes.

Earlier in the book, we described the wide range of characteristics subsumed under the general heading of retardation and the necessity of utilizing a variety of approaches and techniques to meet the particular social needs that different groups of clients present. The primary function of social group work intervention should be to define the different social roles that individuals within different categories of retardation can assume, and to prescribe suitable tasks that will support these and develop the needed skills. The objectives sought will depend on the type of social interaction that the retarded can cope with. For the mildly retarded, the ultimate goal should be a satisfactory relationship with wife and children, relatives, employers, fellow-workers, friends, and more formal social groups—for example, a trade union or church group. Individuals with moderate and severe retardation have a more limited range of social interaction, but it is nonetheless an important feature of their social adjustment and they should be offered help in developing it. Clearly, group work will contain many different ingredients for these two principal client categories, but before considering these it is important to look briefly at the issues and problems the retarded share.

Broadly speaking, there are three factors which have a special significance for group work that are common to all the retarded, irrespective of their degree of incapacity or their social circumstances. The first is the actual social, psychological, and physiological characteristics which, in combination, make up the retardation syndrome. Second, there is the pattern of social behavior that the retarded tend to adopt in reaction to the way they are perceived and responded to by normal members of society whom they encounter. Third, there is the distorted and devalued self-image that gradually evolves from this negative feedback. These different facets of the retarded individual's social status and self-perception have been described with insight and clarity by a number of writers. For example, Cobb describes the retarded individual's self-perception in a general context;[15] Segal relates it to the crisis of approaching adulthood and the need for economic self-sufficiency;[16] Ferguson and Parnicky and Brown discuss the same problem in regard to institutionalized clients who are facing resettlement in the community.[17]

An understanding of these three elements is vital in group work with the retarded because they provide insight into the exact nature of the problems in social interaction that the retarded face, and from the diagnostic and treatment angles they indicate the specific type of help that can be offered by a group experience to a single individual or to a whole class of the retarded. To illustrate, if a mildly retarded adolescent boy has developed a self-image of infantilized incompetence through the overprotective handling of his family, group work must address itself to offering him a more positive role model on which he can base a more optimistic perception of himself and his social capacities. Likewise, when a group of retarded adults have been institutionalized for a substantial period of their lives, it is essential to appreciate the effect that this atypical living situation has had upon them, particularly in defining them as social deviants with expectations of lowered competence. These illustrations utilize psychological and sociological insights, but it is equally important to understand the physiological bases of impaired social behavior, and to differentiate clearly between those aspects which derive from adverse social experiences and those which stem from organic impairment, since both need to be taken into consideration when a group work program is being devised.

This means that group work, like the other two methods, must be able to assess the normal and specialized needs of the retarded and plan its programs accordingly. To weld these two related but sometimes opposing aims into a unified whole, we are borrowing a concept of group work from Gisela Konopka, who offers the following definition: "The group process is the net of psychological interaction that goes on in every group. The group *work* process means that a conscious helping force, the group worker, has entered this interplay of relationships." [18] If we envisage retarded clients as individuals whose social experience has been either distorted or impoverished by a negative interplay of psychological interaction, then group work becomes an essentially corrective process which provides them with a more benign pattern of psychological interaction through the conscious helping intervention of the group worker. For the moderately retarded, as we observed earlier, group work is a formalized process for furthering social development and skills which evolve from *normal* social interplay with normal adult and peer groups when there is no impairment to obstruct this learning. In this context, group work takes on a *restitutive* function in that it adds components to the retarded individual's social growth that his own innate deficiency cannot furnish. For the mildly retarded, its purpose veers in the direction of revamping social experiences and opportunities to give them greater scope for development, and for this range of client, group work can have a *remedial or preventive* function, depending on the age of the client group and their previous social experience.

With these broad objectives of group work outlined, we should briefly consider the type of retarded clients who can benefit from this process, the social situations for which group work can be most effective, and the particular form that this method should take. Because group work activity demands some perception of social behavior and some capacity for independent personal interaction, this method is inevitably limited to retarded individuals who can reach a certain level of social maturity in terms of both chronological age and mental ability. In general, this means the mildly (or educable) retarded, the moderately (or trainable) retarded, and *some* children or adults within the severe range whose social maturation is ahead of their functioning levels in other areas. In regard to age, the mildly retarded can participate in social work group activities from school age onward, but children with more severe defect are unlikely to be ready for this experience until later in their developmental span.

Social group work is a valuable form of intervention for a variety of social phases or situations which present problems in adjustment for the retarded. For children of any age, it offers an adjunct to the educational or training program, which will prepare them for a fuller and more satisfactory social role in their developing years and in adulthood.[19] In addition, group work can provide a stabilizing force to meet the crisis points which retarded children or adults encounter either as a function of normal maturational experience or because of some vital change in their social circumstances. Graduating from childhood to adolescence or from adolescence to adulthood are *developmental* crises, and moving into or out of a residential situation are *extraordinary social* change crises. Crisis theory postulates that extra help is needed to reinforce the coping mechanisms of an individual (or a social unit such as a family) when they are subjected to undue stress which may overstrain their normal adaptive resources. Since the social adjustment of the mentally retarded is at best precarious (inherent in the definition of retardation is impaired adaptive capacity), any serious change in social circumstances and the demands this imposes is potentially hazardous. If critical experiences are handled through the group work process, the client at risk can be helped by the support of his peers, and by gaining some insight into the implications of the stressful situation he may be able to weather it successfully. Another socially hazardous situation which group work may neutralize is that of the marginally adjusted retarded adult for whom this type of service may be a sustaining process which keeps him in touch with a wider circle of social experience than his working and family life can provide. For this sort of client, social group work does not differ much from that which serves other marginal individuals: for example, the elderly, the physically disabled, or individuals with chronic psychiatric disabilities. In this category of retarded adults are included the mildly retarded who are economically independent but inadequate in their social relationships,[20] but it also contains the more severely handicapped who are dependent on their family for support, who need sheltered industrial training, and require structured consistent help in their social life.[21]

Having outlined the broad scope and aims of group work for the mentally retarded as a whole, we must now consider by what techniques and specific tasks these objectives are achieved. If we grant that the retarded client's social behavior is the passport to acceptance by society at large, the first task of social group work must be to inculcate an appropriate perception of socially approved norms and teach the skills that are needed to perform in this way. Basic to this learning, however, is the client's perception of himself as a social being, and social group work must be initially directed toward reforming the distorted and devalued social image that most of the retarded entertain of themselves. That is, it must be concerned with the psychological components that motivate and fashion the behavioral responses of the retarded. It is fair to assume that most retarded individuals feel that they are social rejects or misfits, and until this attitude changes and they can find a status with which they can comfortably identify, they are not likely to develop any very meaningful social interactive skills. To ensure this, the externally oriented program aspect of group work through which performance skills are fostered must be combined with the psychologically oriented aspect of help which is geared to helping the client become aware of his social potential.[22] How these two separate but essentially related aspects of group work will be balanced in any one program will depend on the level of social adjustment of the clients being served. To clarify this point, we shall discuss the two major client groups separately, starting with the more severely handicapped.

For the moderately and severely retarded who have extremely limited verbal ability, these psychosocial learning components must be built into the structure and content of the program itself, and the process of educating the retarded to a perception of themselves as socially acceptable and successful beings has to evolve implicitly from the practical experiences provided by programming.[23] For example, the fact of belonging to an organization that meets regularly and has a clearly defined purpose invests the moderately and severely retarded client with a social identity by providing him with his own reference group that is not shared by his family or normal peers. From the actual group situation, he derives an opportunity for choice and self-direction because its activities are so organized as to be within the scope of his limited judgment and execution. In this respect, it is important to consult the client's own wishes about joining a group, and when the plan is proposed, he should be given a clear explanation of the activities he will be engaged in and their purpose. Since this situation offers one of the rare opportunities for the more severely handicapped client to exercise his right of choice and self-determination, it is very important to reinforce this principle, even though it goes no further than a concrete explanation of plans and a limited choice of alternatives. Aside from the ethical aspect, if the client is a reluctant participant, the group experience will be frustrating for him, the group worker, and his family alike; it must be realized therefore that while the family or the social worker may make arrangements for the client to join a group, only his cooperation can make the plan succeed.

In order to ensure that a program-centered group also operates as an organic interactive system rather than a mere collection of assembled individuals with only their stigmatizing handicap in common, the program must comprise activities that members actively enjoy. These should offer scope for successful achievement which is visible to the retarded themselves and to their normal counterparts, and should give individual members the opportunity for taking some personal responsibility for the group's success. Moderately and severely retarded individuals are often credited with a much lower capacity for social observation and interaction than they are in fact capable of, and it is an important function of group work to recognize and exploit these hidden skills through program development. The social involvement which starts over practical issues invariably deepens into a less tangible psychological cohesiveness which can then be utilized either implicity or explicitly to build up an awareness of emotional relationships and social roles. An illustration of this sort of group cohesiveness and identity was provided by a Training Center for young unemployable adult men around the annual Christmas party. The social worker attached to the Center suggested that three conspicuously retarded boys with physical handicaps, who were normally homebound, be invited to attend the party. The Center boys were informed of this plan ahead of time and asked to make a special effort to help the visitors feel welcome because they had very little opportunity for pleasure outside of their homes. As a result of this approach, the Center boys were extremely helpful with maneuvering the wheelchairs, saw that the visitors were in a good position for the entertainment, and kept them well supplied with food. Of much greater significance was the fact that the following day the more articulate members discussed the sad plight of the visitors with the staff and commented on their own much more favorable situation because they were able-bodied and could do so much more. This experience indicated that the group recognized its own identity which was based on competence in certain areas, e.g., work and productivity. Because of this positive self-image, members felt comfortable in evaluating their own deficits vis-à-vis those of other individuals with even greater handicap.

Group work with the more conspicuously retarded must, however, also try to ensure that they achieve some *active* acceptance within the normal social system to which they belong. *Active* acceptance implies more than a positive attitude of mind; it means that the retarded have an opportunity to be purposefully involved in some activity with normal individuals on a basis of equality. This may be achieved by linking up a specialized group, catering primarily to the retarded, with a normal group around certain activities that demand the sort of social skills at which the retarded are most adept. An example of this is a recreation club run by a formal parent group for adolescent boys and young men, which includes in its program a basketball team composed of retarded members and their normal teen-age brothers. An arrangement of this kind is very valuable in giving the team the boost of more skillful players and providing an opportunity for the retarded members to learn from their normal peers. By affording a dimension of normalcy it raises the standards and status of the entire outfit, as well as demonstrating the common interests and skills shared by normal and retarded youths. This helps the latter to identify with the aspirations and achievements of their peers and is an important factor in creating a sense of socially belonging for the more seriously retarded.

With mildly retarded clients, social group work has the same goal of absorbing them into normal society, but in practice it has many different features from those we have been discussing in relation to the more seriously retarded. One important factor is that the higher intelligence of the mildly retarded and their closer proximity to normality make them more sharply aware of their social isolation and of how their own shortcoming contributes to this. Therefore, social group work must deal more explicitly with this problem of their marred social identity and the social experiences that have interfered with satisfactory development in this area. Although we talk of the mildly retarded as a single category to distinguish them from the retarded with other grades of impairment, it is important to recognize that their social development may have been affected by a varied range of experiences, leading to different sets of problems. The principal one affecting the mildly retarded is whether they have grown up attending special facilities in the normal community or have been separated from society at large by long-term commitment to residential care. The pattern of services for the retarded has relied heavily upon residential care until quite recently; therefore, there are today many mildly retarded adolescents and adults who have spent a large part of their lives in an institution and now face massive problems of social adjustment in the community outside.

The remainder of this chapter will concentrate on how social group work can help this category of clients, because the original circumstance of their being placed in residential care implies a difficulty in social adjustment (either of their own making or through their family's inadequacy) and their subsequent experience of growing up in large-scale congregate care will have created many others. Besides, although this particular living situation contains many atypical characteristics, nevertheless the overall social experiences of the institutionalized retarded crystallize the essential social inadequacy, rejection, and isolation that most mildly retarded individuals experience in some degree at some point in their lives. Before moving into a detailed discussion of group work with the retarded in institutional settings, it will be helpful to examine briefly the differences in their social experience from those encountered by the mildly retarded living in the community. Concepts of social group work with the latter have been admirably formulated by other writers, and the reader is referred to these sources for a more detailed discussion of the method's use in this context.[24]

Clients in both community and institutional settings have one major problem in common—alienation; but with the former, it is isolation *within* the normal community and with the latter isolation *from* it. The by-products of these two situations are a different set of psychosocial adjustment problems. The retarded individual in the community is often a marginal character in that he is not obviously disabled and entitled to the special provision and consideration that goes with the recognized sick role; but he is also without the skill or social bearing to be totally accepted as a normal individual. The result is an ambiguous identity and loneliness and a curtailed scope for developing social competence. By contrast, the mildly retarded individual in a residential setting belongs to a social subgroup that within its own geographical and cultural confines is intact and offers a good deal of companionship and interaction, though the quality of this interaction has many warped aspects which will be touched on later. The result of the first client's situation—isolation within the community—is confusion and conflict about roles and personal identity, whereas the latter have the sense of being separated from normality. For example, the mildly retarded living outside are constantly exposed to reality testing in their daily intercourse with normal members of the community; for their counterparts living in an institution, this is missing and consequently the demands of normal social life are an *imagined source of anxiety*, heavily fraught with fantasy, rather than an *actually experienced trauma*. The reverse is also true in that institutional residents are deprived of positive feedback from successful interaction with normal individuals, except in artificially structured situations.

The idiosyncratic character of institutional life in general and its effect on social behavior have been described fully from a multiplicity of angles.[25] Here we are concerned only with those aspects which foster a particular pattern of social behavior that is different from, and inappropriate to, living in the normal community. The chief of these is the hierarchical social structure with the resident at the bottom of a finely graduated scale. This pattern of social organization places a distance between him and the "normal" individuals in his environment (i.e., the staff), and it overemphasizes conformity to the mores of the major system (the institution) and its subsystems (the ward or building) as the index of good social adjustment. The resultant type of interaction leaves almost no scope for the legitimate and overt expression of disturbing emotions (especially hostility), which not only hampers correct psychological and social growth but also produces distorted substitute expressions of negative feeling. The submissive relationship with authority figures which this setting reinforces—in fact demands for sheer survival—becomes introjected as the model for relationships with all individuals who are not peers. Further, the infantilizing effect of this subordinate relationship tends to encourage primitive and regressed behavior among peers, such as acute sibling rivalry for attention, passionate jealousy of peer group friendships, and, because of prohibition on heterosexual attachments, a distorted perception of relationships with the opposite sex.

To counteract the atypical life style which prevails in institutional settings, group work must utilize a variety of approaches according to specific needs at a given time. One of its functions is to offer an opportunity for the limited but legitimate expression of emotions that are generally discouraged (or inhibited) in an institutional setting.[26] The second is to create a formal structure within which residents can learn and practice more realistic and dynamic patterns of interaction with peers and authority figures. The third is to involve them in the actual activities and the appropriate associated social behavior that they will encounter in the normal community. This combination process will embrace components from group therapy, group counseling, education, and programming, but its unifying goal will be to provide the model for more normal social interaction with which the retarded can identify. There are various ways in which this can be achieved. First, it is important to establish clear criteria by which residents are selected for group membership. These should reflect recognized levels of social expectation and competence of a realistic kind. Aside from the value of homogeneity to group functioning, this realistic selection is essential because institution populations usually encompass a wide range of deficit, which makes it difficult for the mildly retarded to form a valid self-concept of themselves. For the same reason, chronological criteria should also be realistic to avoid too wide an age span. This point needs stressing because the disparity between mental and chronological age and differing levels of social maturation sometimes blur the importance of underlining this as a realistic index of social status and role.

These factors of social status and achievement can be embodied in the activities and topics around which the group is organized. Since work and economic independence are highly valued as indicators of social competence and future freedom, training and eventual employment are significant issues for individuals in late adolescence and adulthood, which lend themselves well to group discussion. Further, they imply eventual return to the community and are therefore a valuable starting point for introducing many other associated social hazards such as relationships with superiors and peers, making friends, explaining the unusual circumstances of living in an institution, and so on. Similar themes will crop up for mildly retarded children who are identified with special educational or residential

programs but have to face meeting their peers in a recreational setting; for example, when a normal facility hosts a small group of retarded school-age children who share common facilities and activities, or when they are invited to a community agency, as in the case
of four or five boys from a state school who joined the Scout troop
in the nearby town. Retarded individuals often regard their disability as a total one, and for those who have been institutionalized,
it has a very strong association with personal worthlessness, which is
felt to have provoked this step, or with parental failure or rejection.
If group work through the discussion and activity it provides can
recreate a new image that substitutes the concept of *inadequate functioning* for *personal inadequacy*, this helps to partialize the deficit
and introduces the possibility of remedying the defective aspects.

After selecting criteria, another important factor is the goal, which
should be explicitly formulated and clearly explained to members
when they are invited to join, and repeated at the initial meeting and
at subsequent intervals. It will help to remove potential confusion
and also convey the idea that the goals are common to the entire
group if the task of reformulating them from time to time is delegated to a member, rather than always being done by the group
leader. Because the retarded are slower in comprehending new facts
and because the communication system within institutions is usually
very poor, this task of conveying accurate factual information cannot be too strongly emphasized. It is an invaluable function of group
work to provide an opportunity in which plain facts concerning
events are made available in a context that permits the retarded individuals to digest them slowly and question the reasons behind them
and the implications for themselves. This is well illustrated by
Gelman in his description of a short-term group project for orienting
new residents to the institution immediately after admission.[27] It has
equal relevance to the opposite situation when the retarded are moving out to a new and strange situation. In both cases, the group offers
a reality testing ground where fears and fantasies and sheer miscon-
ceptions can be aired and corrected by accurate information.[28]

The duration of the group project should be carefully thought out
and regular attendance made a firm condition of membership, and
from time to time it is helpful for the groups to attempt to evaluate

whether the goals decided upon are being achieved and how useful the experience is. This voluntary commitment to join, attend, participate, and assess the merits of the experience is an extremely therapeutic aspect of group work because it imposes a clearly defined social responsibility upon the members and establishes the expectation that they are capable of doing this. In view of the submissive role of the mildly retarded adolescents and adult residents, this experience gives them a rare opportunity for taking part in some decisions on their own initiative.

The purpose of the group will significantly affect the role of the leader and how he interacts with the members. If the focus is educational, with emphasis on learning new social roles and patterns of interaction, an important function of the leader is to demonstrate that it is possible for the group members to relate to him on a nonauthoritarian basis, despite the fact that he is a member of the establishment. When the group has a more psychological bias and is geared primarily to dealing with emotional and personal adjustment problems, the transference process will place the group leader in a different role and he will be less likely to symbolize the idea of cooperation between authority figure and clients, as in the first instance. Rather, he will be seen as a representative of the establishment through whom the group works out its negative transference by making him the butt of their hostility.

The ventilation of negative feelings toward the institution (and the social events that originally led up to this experience) is an inevitable and legitimate function of a social group. Because it offers a rare opportunity for this exercise, however, it is necessary to guard against the danger of the group's becoming exclusively preoccupied with this aspect. Aside from its being unprofitable to concentrate solely on negative features, there is a more complex and subtle consideration which cuts into the very sensitive area of personal identity. For many institutionalized individuals, the institution may be the only consistent stable environment they have known, and despite its many shortcomings, it inevitably represents the security inherent in familiar surroundings. It is therefore invested with some positive affect, even if this is buried beneath seething negative feelings. A wholesale condemnation of the institution is therefore tantamount to condemning the resident's whole pattern of life and his accumulated identifications. It can induce a serious rejection of themselves as "good" persons through their identification with a "bad" place of origin. If the social group work experience becomes invested with positive feelings in contrast to the negative valences of the institution, there may be a split in psychological allegiance which fortifies ambivalences and conflicts. To avoid this, the group leader needs to partialize this reaction and try to separate the negative features from the positive, building on the latter. The cleavage that we have mentioned may be prevented by having a member of the building staff as co-leader of the group to demonstrate the link between these two seemingly divergent social situations.

The expression of hostility needs careful handling on another account. Because it is generally discouraged in the normal day-to-day regime of the institution, it will be regarded as a novel but suspect activity to begin with. Once attempted it may appear in disproportionate strength, which will be either emotionally threatening or, if acted upon outside the safe confines of the group, socially disruptive, with disastrous results for the client. The group must therefore serve as a medium which teaches when the expression of strong feelings is justified, appropriate, or desirable and when the prevailing norms of society will not tolerate it. This defining of limits helps to build up the idea of differentiated behavioral responses that may not have been fostered by the traditional mores of the congregate life in the buildings, where responses tend to be polarized between meek conformity or explosive defiance.

The actual content of group work programming should be carefully balanced between task-oriented projects and discussion, with equal time allotted to each activity unless there are strong reasons for concentrating more heavily on one aspect. The mildly retarded tend to be concrete in their thinking, and institutional experience does not in general encourage skillful verbal interchange; therefore, this aspect of group work is probably most effectively introduced around the practical activities. When a group is involved in discussing and planning its practical activities, this exercise inevitably compels an exchange of opinion and ideas which unobtrusively loosens up verbal skills. If the plans are successful, they provide a concrete feedback that discussion and planning are effective ways of dealing with problems and situations. At the point where the group is comfortable in this simpler task of talking about factual matters, it can then be safely steered toward less tangible topics such as feelings. This dual practical-psychological approach has been embodied in a group of four or five mildly retarded young dating couples who meet weekly for the purpose of learning some social adeptness in dealing with situations that they will encounter in the normal community, particularly those involving the opposite sex.* One week the group plans a practical activity (of a pleasurable nature) and the following week they carry it out. This alternating pattern also allows for a review of past plans, whether they came up to expectations, how they went wrong, what could have been done better; and inevitably more emotionally charged topics seep into the discussion. For example, does the group stand out as being different from the normal people it mixes with, how does it cope with taunts or derogatory remarks if any are overheard, what feelings of humiliation and rage do these evoke, and how can such a painful experience be dealt with on an individual or group basis? If a member indulges in conspicuously antisocial conduct which is likely to threaten the good social image the group is striving for, this becomes a matter for serious group discussion. Here the leader can and must play an unobtrusively active role by helping the group to analyze the reasons for the defaulting member's conduct, by invoking the corporate support of the group to help him contain this behavior next time, by suggesting practical ways by which this help can be given, and by resorting to temporary suspension only when these other remedial measures have failed. This process is an extremely vital learning situation because it passes the responsibility from the authority figure of the leader to the peer group, and helps them to a tolerant attitude toward substandard behavior, which is based on the objective process of analysis, and develops the idea of mutual reciprocal self-help. At the same time such an emotionally charged situation as group sanctions must be skillfully guided by the leader, to ensure that the group process does

---

* The author is indebted to Miss Patricia Buros, Vocational Rehabilitation Department and Mr. Michael Pratt, Social Service Department of the Walter E. Ferneld State School for this material.

not degenerate into scapegoating or psychological lynching, both of which are possible with unsophisticated and fundamentally insecure groups.

Exchanging ideas and feelings in a formalized ongoing context is not culturally familiar to most mildly retarded individuals so that frank ventilation of strong feelings or areas of great sensitivity can be very threatening. This is also related to a very important factor regarding group work in an institution; namely, the supreme importance of establishing the concept of complete confidentiality and of convincing members that this will be maintained. The pattern of interaction within the residential units does not reinforce this idea because both the physical environment and the management practices discourage privacy, and residents often work out their frustration and hostility by exploiting each other's vulnerable areas. It is therefore essential to impress upon the group that it can only function effectively if members maintain a more mature and responsible way of relating to each other and that its continued existence depends on this.

Inevitably, group work sessions will be used to work out patterns of personal relationships, particularly those most closely connected with the balance between peers and authority figures and the need to gain approval and attention from the latter. Many of the mildly retarded have been institutionalized as a consequence of seriously depriving experiences and therefore have an extraordinarily high craving for attention, which cannot be adequately met by the low staffing ratio that prevails in most residential institutions. The much smaller number in the group offers a better chance of being heard but also sharpens competition so that the leader must be constantly alert to which members consistently try to dominate proceedings and must try to maintain equilibrium within the interactive pattern by actively involving the more submissive ones. This can be quite difficult because the retarded are prone to resort to silence as a defense when they feel inadequate or threatened, and to keep up the group momentum there is a temptation to let the more dominant members carry the situation. When the inactive members cannot be involved by verbal interchange, it may be necessary to convey their importance within the group by nonverbal methods; for example, allotting practical tasks to the less articulate members or reshuffling seating positions. Such physical restructuring breaks into the possessive relationships that tend to form in the buildings and may convey the idea that relationships and roles can also be more flexible.

Group discussion serves another valuable purpose in that it can correct the atypical communication patterns that are encouraged by the amorphous social structure within the residential units. Here the residents develop an idiosyncratic style of speech and manner of response that would be conspicuous in the normal community. For example, they resort to silence when they feel threatened, fall back on giggling to mask the embarrassment of not fully comprehending what is being said to them, and express pervasive hostility to both the staff and each other, which is often disproportionate to the provoking incident.

A helpful way of handling emotionally charged topics that crop up in the course of group discussion is to universalize the experience. If the feelings under discussion can be related to those of normal individuals whom they respect, this can be reassuring. For example, if the group leader admits to having had qualms about starting his first job or compares admission to an institution to being inducted into the Army, this brings the emotions being discussed into a normal frame of reference and loosens their exclusive connection with being retarded. In the same way, it is also helpful to invite former residents who are now living in the community to talk to the group about their early experiences and the feelings they had when they started a new job and lived outside. This technique not only sheds light on the practical aspects of problems and how they can be solved but also demonstrates that such goals are feasible instead of being a pipe dream. Further, it invests the authority of knowledge in a peer rather than in a professional and by inference it endows the group members with a similar potential for, and expectation of, success.

A final point must be broached before concluding the chapter, because it has administrative significance as well as being controversial. This point is whether it is more advantageous to the retarded to integrate them into a normal group work facility or to provide a separate organization in which the type of activities and their pace will be geared to the level of social competence of retarded children or adults. This question crops up in regard to both casework and community organization, but it impinges particularly upon group work because this method most directly confronts the retarded individual's impaired performance and its effect on group interaction. There is considerable conflict of opinion on which is the better practice. A recent five-year study from St. Louis[29] indicates that educable children of varying mental and chronological age can be effectively assimilated into normal facilities, and other evidence suggests that the retarded are accepted if they do not seriously impede agency activities. By contrast, the consensus of experience from the Jewish Community Centers[30] suggests that it is more helpful to admit the retarded to a generic agency where they share some generalized activities with all members but where the bulk of their programming is specially tailored to their atypical needs.[31] Proponents of both viewpoints are, however, in full agreement that a very careful diagnostic intake is essential to the successful placement of the retarded into normal group work facilities (whether on an integrated or partially separate basis), that a precise evaluation of the retarded client's skills in a variety of functioning areas is needed, and that certain characteristics are fairly reliable predictors of successful integration. The point is also reiterated that the assessment should focus initially on what the retarded child or adult has in common with his normal peers and should concentrate on his assets; only after this positive picture has been established should the defective aspects be scrutinized to see what compensatory help they require.

This echoes one of the dominant themes of this book—namely, the emphasis away from pathology toward strengths—and before concluding we must sound another repetitive note, that is the equal importance of assessing the sociological factors that affect the adjustment of the mentally retarded. In regard to our immediate topic, namely, the feasibility of assimilating the retarded into normal social group work facilities, it is important to evaluate the sociological makeup and psychological climate of both the entire agency into which the retarded will be inducted and the specific group to which individuals will be assigned. This is necessary in order to assess whether the normal group can absorb a single atypical member or a cluster without detriment to its own viability or to the integrity of the retarded. This assessment extends the diagnostic process beyond the agency's confines into the community from which it draws its members in order to determine the prevailing attitudes toward deviances in general and retardation in particular.

With these diagnostic findings in mind, a final but very vital task is to secure the prior consensus of a representative segment of the agency's membership to the proposal to introduce this new and initially suspect element. This should be done by giving certain members in leadership roles the responsibility of interpreting the philosophy behind this move, the realities about the behavior of retarded individuals, and the expectations that the experience will be mutually satisfactory if there is cooperation. If the normal group membership is not at least partially prepared, the incoming retarded members may be treated with open hostility, silently ostracized or, perhaps most frustrating, given token acceptance in the shape of overcompensatory politeness, which successfully precludes any interaction on a meaningful level of equality. Since such interaction is the fundamental goal of social work in all three methods, this response in a group work facility would represent signal failure of the helping process. On the other hand, genuine acceptance by a group of normal peers (even at a partial level) can be a therapeutic and ego-strengthening experience for both the retarded individual and those who are closely concerned with his welfare.

10 COMMUNITY ORGANIZATION IN THE FIELD OF MENTAL RETARDATION

THIS BOOK has consistently emphasized the point that to combat the complex and multiple problems of the mentally retarded it is necessary to integrate all three social work methods into a common body of knowledge and practice which allows them to be utilized interchangeably as and when the client's particular needs demand. Casework and group work have already been discussed within this frame of reference, and this final chapter will round out the picture by examining the ways in which the third method, community organization, can be utilized in relation to this disabling condition and its social ramifications.

Community organization is a difficult topic to discuss at this particular phase of its development because both the theory and the practice are in a state of evolutionary flux which makes them subject to frequent redefinition as well as constantly expanding their boundaries.[1] The method assumes an additional complexity when applied to mental retardation and the social needs it creates because on first sight this handicap does not fit very well into the type of issues with which community organization has been traditionally concerned. A closer analysis, however, shows otherwise, as this chapter will demonstrate. The first point to be understood about mental retardation is that it is not a problem area round which it is possible to mobilize the interests and resources of a total geographical community since the incidence of *identified* retardation is necessarily limited to a minority of individuals and families. On the other hand, two other aspects must also be considered. One is that the acute and obvious problems of retardation are not encapsulated in the affected individual but have broader implications which, if neglected, will lead to other more diffuse problems that will adversely affect the larger community. For example, the family that is burdened with the care of a severely retarded child or adult without any outside help is liable to find its psychological and social stability undermined by the pressures, with individual members developing personal adjustment problems that over time will affect their social functioning and even require society's intervention. If a mother breaks down, she may need treatment in a mental hospital, the retarded individual will require surrogate care, any normal children in the family will have to be provided for, and so on. A second type of retarded maladjustment that will impinge adversely upon the community relates to individuals in the mild category of handicap. If educational, vocational, and social services are not available to help them develop some stability and competence for meeting the demands of adult life, they are liable to succumb to social hazards and drift into chronic unemployment, minor delinquency, marital and family conflicts, and incompetent parenthood. From a third angle mental retardation, by its close association with the pervasive problem of poverty, becomes allied to the crucial social issue of our times.[2]

Mental retardation can therefore be described as a discrete and circumscribed problem when it relates to individual malfunctioning of children and adults with the more severe range of impairment; as a broad general one when it relates to secondary effects of retardation upon normal individuals; and as a highly relevant one when it is associated with poverty. These three different dimensions will utilize various facets of the community organization process, thus demonstrating that mental retardation in fact lends itself very well to the multidimensional patterns and the flexible use of theory, methods, and roles that community organization demands today.[3]

In order to maintain clarity in this potentially confusing situation we shall start by delineating in some detail the objectives that community organization should address itself to on behalf of the retarded and their families; the tasks that must be performed to achieve these goals; the practice, theory, and methods utilized; and the resources needed. By taking this approach to what is a very broad theme it should be possible to keep a sharp focus on the specific issues deriving from retardation and on the various components of community organization practice which relate to the different aspects of the problem. In this book the term "community organization" is used to denote the type and range of activities directed primarily toward the development of services for the retarded that are currently lacking. This relatively narrow focus makes it an essential part of the integrated methods approach in that the tasks and processes to be described are on a scale which allows the method to be used within the same operational frame of reference as casework and group work. The large-scale planning aspects of community organization, which are a task unto themselves, and the broader social action approach, which is directed at the widespread latent social problems underlying the manifestation of retardation, will not be dealt with, although their relevance will be noted. Our approach will encompass the preventive as well as rehabilitative aspects, but both will be at the level of providing restitutive services for the identified problem rather than attacking its more remote causation.

In common with the two other methods the overall goal of community organization is to diminish obstacles to social development and functioning that the disabling condition of retardation imposes upon both the retarded themselves and their families. The explicit role of community organization is in developing the practical services that will neutralize or compensate for the social inadequacies inherent in this handicap. Unless such practical alleviative services are available for the entire *subgroup* of the mentally retarded, the efforts of casework and group work that are concerned primarily with the coping capacity of *individual clients* will be greatly diminished. The first objective, therefore, of the social worker who is exercising her community organization mandate for the retarded is to set about ensuring, within her prescribed operational area, as wide a provision as possible of all the services that a retarded individual of any age and capacity might require to overcome his handicap. The second, equally important, objective is to mobilize and set up services addressed to the more general social problems and pressures that have been identified as potential causes of retarded development—namely, material poverty and its psychological by-products that are inimical to family life, emotional growth, and the socializing process that together form the basis of healthy maturation in physical, emotional, and intellectual areas. A third objective must be to help the normal community to an understanding of retardation, its social etiology and manifestations, so that, in addition to formalized services, the community will develop an informal system of interaction with the retarded and their families which will break into their isolation and strengthen their scope for normal involvement in the community. This goal is intimately bound up with the first objective of establishing services, in that the community must have a sympathetic understanding of needs before it will allocate resources; equally, the provision of services builds up the social competence of the retarded and improves their status. The chronic nature of retardation means that it cannot be defined as a problem which ad hoc action tasks will solve; therefore, the broader one of helping the community to accommodate its attitudes to the long-term disability is equally necessary.

Here it may be helpful to consider the distinction made by Warren[4] between the different purposes of community action. These are (1) task accomplishment—i.e., a relatively circumscribed and visible goal, such as mobilizing a community to set up a small residential facility for semidependent retarded adults, and (2) the development or strengthening of horizontal patterns of communication around community affairs. In the field of retardation these distinctly defined goals have pertinence on two grounds. In regard to providing rehabilitation services for the retarded who have been identified as needing help, it is clear that the establishment of one service, or even a group of services, will not meet the overall problem adequately because within the chronicity of their handicap the needs of the retarded constantly change and expand with age, alteration of personal circumstances, and change in societal trends. Therefore, to ensure an ongoing development of services to keep pace with these changing needs, it is essential that the ad hoc community organization task also result in a better understanding of retardation and strengthen patterns of communication between the concerned segments of the community that can be brought into effective operation when subsequent action is needed.

The second objective listed previously—the prevention or arrest of retarded development by attacking the social hazards known to contribute to its incidence—has almost greater relevance to this broader purpose of strengthening horizontal patterns of communication. First, the preventive thrust against retardation in the poverty group involves a much larger client population: (1) the mildly retarded who represent 75 to 90 percent of the total retarded population and are clustered at the lower end of the socioeconomic scale; and (2) the population-at-risk, which in effect may be a large segment of the children in a poverty area together with women of child-bearing age, who are highly susceptible to health problems in pregnancy and the possibility of a damaged child. When retardation is defined as a potential as well as an actual danger, the pervasiveness of the problem and its enmeshment with many others indicate that its solution will involve a massive reorganization of the social environment and the social system. The community organizer, therefore, not only must develop or establish a particular needed service for her specialized retarded client group but in so doing must also help to form an action group that can address itself to the next service required, as well as to other needs of other groups within the community that are not being met. In this way the community organization or action that is primarily designed to meet the narrower needs of the mentally retarded can be used as a fulcrum for developing services for a broader deprived client group. It is important to remember this because when a worker is confronted with the massive and pervasive problems of poverty there is a tendency to feel that only by tackling the causes on a broad front—which, in effect, means the total ills of the poverty group—can any impact be made. In fact, the reverse is true in that most effective results are achieved by concentrating on a defined target which is within encompassable bounds while understanding its relevance to other problem areas and being ready to exploit this when the occasion is ripe. This point will be illustrated when we discuss work in the poverty area more fully.

To revert to the task of developing services specifically for the retarded client group, we can separate this broad activity into three main areas:

1. Planning for new services. This occurs at federal, state, and city levels and represents the main thrust by which the *continuum of care* is implemented. New planning is in general heavily supported

by public funding, either in toto or on a matching basis with a voluntary body.

2. Strengthening or seeding services in existing service agencies by (a) developing an extension of services in agencies already serving the retarded—e.g., adding a day hospital for profoundly retarded or multiply handicapped individuals to a residential institution; (b) stimulating the active participation of generic agencies which have not been appreciably involved with this client group—e.g., adding a residential unit for profoundly retarded or multiply handicapped children to a pediatric hospital or ward. This second activity is part of the total planning operation of a community, and some funds earmarked for the retarded should be made available for these "strengthening" or "initiating" projects.

3. Mobilizing concerned voluntary organizations to participate in planning and implementation of services. This applies particularly to the organized parent groups.

These three areas of operation correspond with the community organization frame of reference formulated by Gurin and Perlman[5] according to which the *organizational context* is the main factor that determines the pattern of methodology of the community organization process. This formulation contains three principal areas of organizational context—the voluntary associations, the professional agencies rendering service, and the bodies that plan and allocate resources. The relevance of these three components to the problem-area of mental retardation varies according to the type of social problem presented. This is related to the degree and nature of the client's disability, its manifestations and its origins, as well as to the environmental circumstances. To understand these points more clearly it is helpful to look at the client population to which the community organization will be directed and define its outstanding characteristics. In the previous chapters on casework and group work an attempt was made to distinguish between different client groups in the retardation field on the basis of socioclinical status and degree of functional impairment. A similar dichotomy in clientele may be postulated in regard to community organization, but here the distinction is based primarily on sociological factors. This definition of separate client targets is important because in some instances the needs of the two groups are different, demanding varying emphases in service. This will become clearer as we define and describe the target populations. To preserve some continuity of presentation, we shall base our client division on the different types of tasks delineated earlier; namely, the provision of remedial services specifically aimed at the mentally retarded and the mobilization of a wider spectrum of preventive services. This division cannot be clear-cut since the two types of provision must be seen as interlocking and mutually complementary and clients from both categories will require both.

The first and most easily identified client population comprises those individuals who are handicapped by retardation to a marked degree from an early age. In clinical terms, this almost invariably means impairment to the central nervous system involving considerable residual disability, which will need to be compensated for on a lifelong basis. For this client group, community organization must provide the network of medical, educational, and social services that will meet this long-term social deficit. This more conspicuously handicapped group of retarded is spread throughout all social classes and, with the exception of those who combine organic impairment with adverse socioeconomic conditions, the social problems that are encountered by their families are the result of their retardation and not its cause.

The other category of clients who are involved in the social by-products of retardation belong to families in the lowest economic strata of society, and for them this disability is just one of many other accidents of their existence and not necessarily the most serious. Although this group is mainly made up of the mildly retarded, it includes individuals with a more serious degree of defect. It may be distinguished from the first client group in that the social problems peculiar to retardation occur against a backdrop of more variegated and pervasive social pressures; services for the specialized disability must, therefore, form part of a much wider social provision. The pattern of community organization is significantly influenced by this environmental component, and for this reason we shall analyze the needs and services required by each client group separately. This division is, however, mainly an expediency, and it must not be taken to mean that the two groups do not share many common problems and concerns. This point will be clarified when the role of parent groups is discussed later.

Generally speaking, for the more socially secure middle-class* group, retardation is an unpredicted event that brings in its train considerable psychological strains of adjustment, with great and justifiable anxiety about how to cope with this unexpected and tragic blow, and how to meet the retarded child's unusual needs. For this group, effective help must take the form of services that will make it possible to assimilate the retarded child without a major disruption of family life. Implicit in this are two main goals: one is to foster the development and social functioning of the retarded individual to the maximal level so that his deficits impinge as little as possible on his family; the other is to preserve the social viability of the family as a whole. Although this second objective is not always immediately obvious, it is, in fact, a vital and integral part of services for the retarded because of their dependency on family and relatives for survival.[6] Both these functions of services are based on the concept of social role, and their ultimate aim should be to furnish an appropriate social role for the retarded and to sustain the normal members of the family in theirs. In more specific terms, the retarded child should be provided with the same pattern of services as his normal counterpart— ongoing medical care as needed, with specialist advice on peculiar health problems he may have; formal schooling or its equivalent; recreational resources; vocational training, employment, or occupation in adulthood.

Such a consistent pattern of help for the retarded member in itself offers considerable support to the family; beyond this, assistance may be needed in the shape of help in the home to free parents to meet the needs of their other children, temporary residential care to provide a break, counseling round management and emotional problems centering on the retarded child. Services should also be designed to meet phasic role changes. For example, parents do not normally expect to continue the protective nurturing role after their children are grown up, and when this necessity is imposed upon them by a dependent retarded adult offspring, there must be help to mitigate

* Throughout this chapter the term middle class is used very loosely to mean families or individuals with incomes above the prescribed poverty level.

the inevitable strain involved. At all points in the family's life cycle, residential care should be available for the retarded to replace their efforts when the family can no longer provide for him.[7]

The second client group with which the community organizer will be concerned are children and families whose social maladjustment stems principally from serious material and cultural deprivation. These present a very different social and clinical picture from the first client group, and they add another important dimension to community organization in that children of normal potential must be included in this target population as well as individuals who demonstrate identifiable retardation.[8] This segment of society lives on or near the poverty line, and the overt retardation is one aspect of a reactive process to the complex of social problems which beset their lives, the lives of their immediate families, and those of their cultural group. This client category requires broad social welfare provisions, starting with an adequate income to reduce material impoverishment and including comprehensive medical and education services, an improved physical environment, and a network of psychosocial remedial services to repair the fragmented personal and family relationships that are a by-product of poverty. The goal of such services is the alleviation and long-term prevention of many other disabling conditions besides retardation. For example, the maternal and infant care service is directly connected with reducing the incidence of mental defect by averting health hazards in pregnancy which are thought to have a positive correlation with neurological impairment,[9] but its scope is much wider for it also impinges upon other risks of childbirth and childhood. This service is of special concern to the community organizer because it not only is a measure that may prevent organic impairment but is also a source of casefinding for children with recognizable damage (such as cerebral lesions) and for others who do not bear these obvious earmarks but who are a population-at-risk—for example, babies born to large substandard families or young unmarried mothers who start off with adequate biological endowment but whose subsequent experience may be so adverse as to stultify development.[10] In dealing with the problems of mental retardation in the poverty client group, community organization must be involved with identifying these vulnerable children at all phases of their lives and developing services which will intervene before retardation has become a habitual response pattern. The comprehensive services that can render this preventive assistance include medical and social care in the prenatal and postnatal periods, day care, homemaker services, nursery school, parent education, counseling, and plain casework help with the multiple problems that are often found in families of children-at-risk. When these resources are not adequate for the child's needs, foster care can also be invoked as a therapeutic measure.[11]

This cluster of hidden vulnerable children, who must be salvaged through appropriate intervention and social provision, merge into the more clearly defined client group of mildly retarded whose disability is often the result of not intervening in the type of socially traumatic circumstances just cited. For these clients—children and adults—it is important to provide services that will arrest the retarding process and help them to function optimally in the present and future. Such services must center on a precise assessment of their deficits so that remedial help can be provided for specific areas of dysfunction. This will encourage a reversion toward normal, with a greater possibility of eventual assimilation of this client group into the social interstices of the normal community to which they belong. For this sort of help, resources should be obtained from both specialized and generic facilities.[12]

We have placed special emphasis on the sociological differences between the two client populations because this factor inevitably exerts an influence on how community organization addresses itself to their several social problems and needs. It is also important to take a brief look at the individual attributes associated with the different categories of retarded, because they too must be taken into account in planning services—particularly as this affects long-term programs and continuity in care. The two features of mental retardation that are important to consider in regard to long-term planning are the chronic nature of the disability, on the one hand, and, on the other, the concealed potential for progress and development, which is often latent within the chronic frame of reference.

We shall deal with chronicity first because this characteristic always colors thinking about retardation and, if its subtleties are not

properly understood, it is likely to have a very negative and distorting effect on the shape and goals of service. Long-term custodial
protective care for the mildly retarded, based on the misconception
of a static level of intellectual and social impairment, is an example
of this. It should be obvious that chronicity of handicap is closely
related to severity and that the concept cannot be applied in the same
way to the mildly retarded as to those with more severe impairment
of organic origin. For the latter, chronicity is equated with some
measure of irreversibility, permanent disablement, and partial or total
dependency throughout life. Continuity in care for this group involves provision of a complex mesh of services that will further
development in the formative years and be available (but not necessarily utilized) to meet all social contingencies that may occur at
subsequent points in the life cycle. The actual services any one individual may require and *when* will vary with his social circumstances,
so it is essential to have a flexible pattern. For example, a moderately
retarded adult in middle age may need residential care when his
parents die. If, however, other family members can offer him a home,
the primary need may be for a daytime facility to provide him with
some occupation and to share the load of responsibility for his
care.

For the mildly retarded at the top of the scale of social competence, chronicity has an entirely different meaning. Since the bulk
of the mildly retarded graduate successfully into normal adult life,
chronicity is not related to *disability* but to *vulnerability to stress;*
for their adjustment can at any time be undermined if the pressures
of life become excessive. A mildly retarded man or woman may be
successful in work (provided there is no economic recession) and
do well in marriage, but if this results in a large number of children
at too frequent intervals, the demanding task of maintaining the
family may progressively overtax the father's earning capacity and
the mother's resources for organization. This lowered threshold of
vulnerability to social pressures requires that services be available to
support the family in its critical phases and also over a longer period.
For the client with this type of marginal impairment, the continuum
of care is not a permanent structure of essential specialized services
but rather a network of assistance which will prevent his total col-

...hen social pressures disturb the rather precarious equilibrium achieved.

...other feature of retardation—the developmental potential—... mentioned in regard to planning services because it has been ... overlooked in the past as chronicity has been stressed. It ...ry important bearing on planning, because the capacity of ...individuals is very closely related to the quality and quan-...ervices available for them. Therefore, as better services are ..., the functioning of the retarded individual *at any level* is ...improve and this in turn will stimulate a demand for services ...r complexity and range. This progression upward is a func-...only of the retarded individual's personal response to better ...ed services but also of the expanded social roles and expec-...at the latter impose. To cite a very simple example: in-...medical knowledge has ensured that children with Down's ...will probably survive well into middle age, which auto-...creates a greater demand for services for them in adult-h... ...rther, since psychology and rehabilitation techniques have reveal... that the retarded within this range of functioning have a capacity to learn simple repetitive tasks quite efficiently, these services must encompass industrial training and long-term sheltered employment facilities to match these more recently developed social skills.[13] This in turn leads to requests for residential accommodation in the community since it is not considered appropriate to institutionalize someone who is successfully engaged in partially productive activity. This hypothetical example illustrates how a newly perceived social status can influence service provision, and it points up the necessity for social workers who are engaged in organizing community resources to keep abreast of significant changes in scientific knowledge about retardation and to understand how these will affect the social status of the retarded and enlarge their scope for social activity and involvement.

This chapter has concentrated thus far on the special features associated with mental retardation that must be taken into consideration when organizing services for the mentally retarded. We should now take a brief look at some of the characteristics of the service trends that prevail today since these will have a radical influence upon plans. One is the shift in focus from long-term segregated custodial care in an institutional setting to a diversified pattern of resources within the normal community. A second is the growing expectation that training and rehabilitation must be geared to a much wider range of deficit and lower levels of competence. Both these points relate to the remedial aspect of services. A third essential consideration in planning services is preventive, and relates to the increasing emphasis on retardation as a developmental process that is closely associated with sociocultural deprivation and is thus amenable to intervention if identified in time. These points all contain some significant implications for planning. The movement from intramural to extramural services means that resources and personnel will be spread over a much wider geographical area instead of being concentrated in one spot; this will involve, at least initially, a greater expenditure of money and professional resources. Recruitment and training of personnel with a greater repertoire of professional skills will be needed to implement the more diverse patterns of service that will be necessary when a large number of retarded individuals live in the community. A similar broad scope of expertise will be required to meet the needs of clients within these lower ranges of functioning. If these clients are to remain in the community in adulthood and childhood, services to meet wider needs than training or employment will also have to be developed. By the same token, if the majority of the mentally retarded are to be returned to the community from institutional placement (or to be retained at home instead of being placed away), there must be an expansion in general social service provision for the increased population who will be utilizing medical care, schooling, housing, and so on. Lastly, if we accept the correlation between stringent and chronic poverty and mental retardation, there needs to be a device routinely built into the antipoverty services for detecting potentially retarded children, plus services to meet their problems when identified. These broad considerations must underlie the planning of specific services and are propounded here as general guidelines from which we can proceed to explore how the objectives inherent in community organization for the retarded can be achieved and what specific professional skills will be utilized.

A first step in this process is to locate the forces within the community that can be most readily motivated to initiate and develop services for the retarded in their midst—in other words, those who have the most acute concern for this social problem. The most obvious group is the formally organized association of parents with children who have been identified as retarded or suffering from some other related handicap such as cerebral palsy, severe emotional disturbance, or organic learning disabilities.[14] This invaluable community resource happens also to correspond with the first client group that we have delineated, and the leverage it exerts will be determined in some measure by the social cohesiveness of the community and its socioeconomic character. That is to say, this group will wield most effective power in a predominantly middle-class community where the need for good public facilities is strongly felt because parents cannot afford private services and will not silently tolerate services that are inadequate in quantity or quality. Because mental retardation of the more conspicuous type runs through all social classes, this parent force will have the greatest strength if it can be organized to include different strata of society within its prescribed geographical orbit. One important task of the community organizer might be to help redefine the geographical boundaries of this functional community to include a broader socioeconomic representation. This will be elaborated later in the chapter when involvement with the parent groups is discussed in greater detail.

A second potentially vital source of support should be families from poor neighborhoods who are likely to include retardation among their many other social problems. Unlike the formal association of parents we have just described, these families are at present rarely organized to deal with this specific problem, but in these communities there is a growing political sophistication about social problems. Residents are developing techniques for corporate protest about wider social issues, e.g., better neighborhood schools, rights of welfare recipients, day care for children of working mothers, better housing. Many such families have a retarded child, and specialized care for him is of equal concern with these more general needs.

A third strong source of support is likely to be professional workers who are involved with the mentally retarded and whose own professional contribution is being constantly hampered by the shortage of ancillary or continuative services. For example, physicians who deal with the retarded in outpatient clinics, or public health nurses who visit retarded children at home, or teachers of special classes encounter extreme frustration when they cannot direct the family to other services the child may need besides those they are providing. A hypothetical illustration of this is a hyperactive four-year-old child who is badly in need of structured training, whose social development will deteriorate without this professional help, and whose family is being seriously disrupted by his current behavior. This type of case, which occurs all too frequently, may impinge upon a number of professionals in the community—the general practitioner or pediatrician who is being consulted by the overburdened mother, the child guidance clinic which is dealing with a sibling who manifests a behavioral reaction to the family stress, the personnel officer of a business or factory who is concerned with the father's anxious preoccupation with this taxing family problem and his resultant poor productivity at work. The degree of active interest among such professional groups will vary according to their proximity to the focal problem—that is to say, the physician who is treating the overt health problems of a vulnerable mother will have a strong incentive to cooperate in developing services for the retarded because the connection between this handicap and the health problem he is dealing with is immediately visible. On the outer rim of this circle of potentially involved citizens is the business executive concerned with productivity or the trade union representative concerned with the worker's welfare. In such situations, an important role of community organization is to point up the effect of a lack of services for a retarded child or adult upon his entire family and upon the other members of the community with whom they are vitally connected.

A fourth group can be termed the "good Samaritan" element in the community—organizations whose philosophical and ethical stance imply concern for the problems of their neighbors. In this category are the church groups of different denominations, political parties (particularly those committed to social equity and change), and social groups which add a benevolent ingredient to their usual activities—e.g., JAYCEES, Rotarians. This last group will probably have the least personal investment in the problem of mental retardation; but it almost always includes individuals and cliques who are important in the power structure, the business element which is an important source of employment, and can therefore be an effective instrument for fund raising, publicity, and the other complex apparatus of public relations necessary for developing services.

After identifying the motive forces in the community, which can be harnessed to the operation of establishing services for the retarded, the next task is to review the actual local resources that can be immediately tapped for this purpose. These fall roughly into two broad categories—manpower, which is essential for developing and maintaining programs, and material resources, which are necessary for providing the environment and equipment in which the program can function. We shall deal with manpower first because it represents a generating force which can be utilized to set material resources in motion. For example, it may be strategic to appoint a teacher qualified to handle retarded children to a preschool program for normal children so that she can both demonstrate the appropriateness of including children in the overall program and also form the spearhead of additional financial support by providing content for a grant application.

The first major resource which should be plumbed is the network of health, education, and social agencies that are primarily geared to serving the needs of normal individuals in the community but almost always have a tangential connection with mental retardation, as clients with this aspect of disability fall within their service area. For example, general medical services, family and children's agencies, public health nursing, and day care are all likely to receive requests at one time or another to service a retarded child or adult.[15] A second important group of agencies are those that deal with another handicapped clientele which shares some of the problems and characteristics of the retarded. For example, a sheltered workshop facility, originally designed for clients with psychiatric or physical disabilities, might be able to absorb certain retarded individuals whose overall social functioning and performance tallied with the norm of that facility. Besides the direct services offered by generic social and welfare agencies, another important asset is the available professional personnel in the community—those in the various disciplines who have expertise in the special problems associated with retardation, and the way their skills can be exploited to expand existing services or develop new ones. Because workers in most of the professional disciplines are unfamiliar with the social manifestations of retardation, it is important to ensure that a proper balance is kept between the manpower resources with the skills needed to understand this disability and the material resources that make a program feasible. This consideration should be among the first criteria in establishing priorities for setting up new services.

We must now consider what skills and knowledge the community organizer needs to deal with this formidable array of tasks. First, there is the paramount need for an accurate analysis of the community in which services have to be developed. This should include an assessment of its social and economic composition and its pattern of social interaction, particularly the extent to which relationships are close-knit and face to face. Related to this is the important factor of social and geographical mobility and the changes these introduce; for the less competent retarded, continuity of formal and informal social relationships is vital to their satisfactory social adjustment. A high turnover of industrial enterprises and employment, alteration of the physical terrain of a community because of urban renewal and housing developments, and a constantly shifting population impose upon the retarded the difficult adjustments of getting used to new types of work, employers and workmates, or new neighbors who do not understand their special problems. The social restlessness of a constantly shifting community also generates anxieties that can be expressed in hostility to such socially deviant individuals as the retarded. Another ingredient of the community that must be assessed accurately is the prevailing social attitudes toward social disability and social welfare provision in general, and specifically toward a conspicuous handicap such as retardation. It is also important to judge whether the norms for social behavior in a given community are essentially stable but flexible enough to tolerate the atypical. Because the retarded start off with a built-in, and sometimes permanent, deviance, it is important that the social fabric into which they are being integrated should be basically stable and support their normal aspects. This assessment is derived in the main from the social diagnosis model which is concerned with the client and his environment. In the community organization context, the subject of this diagnostic exercise is not the family and its collaterals but the community and its constituent parts; but the vital factor for both is the interaction between these parts, particularly in regard to how this facilitates the maximum development of the retarded and assists his adjustment within the normal community's frame of reference.

After analyzing the social profile of the community, the next step in organizing services for this handicapped group is to develop a cooperative working relationship with the subsystems in the community which offer the strongest potential source of help. These have already been defined as the interested families who have a first-hand investment in getting service and the professional agencies which are either already engaged in dealing with the problems of retardation or might be co-opted to do so. Behind these two heavily engaged segments of the community are the lay groups, which have a less direct interest but are nevertheless important elements in planning, developing, and sustaining services.

Parent groups must play a vital role in community organization. Indeed, over the last two decades they have provided the greatest thrust for new services in the field of retardation and allied handicaps. Through the activities of their national and local groups, they have pressed for legislative support for more services, for the establishment of pilot services for categories of the retarded who had not been previously helped, and for educating the professional and lay public to both the *needs* and *rights* of mentally retarded individuals and their families.[16] Within any community, therefore, the local Association for Retarded Children (ARC) should be a focal point for the community organizer, and if the parents have not yet organized themselves into such a body, one of the first tasks would be to help them to form one, either separately or by joining with parents of children with common disabilities such as brain damage or cerebral palsy.

Earlier we mentioned that as the principal consumer of services the parent groups are one of the major client targets. However, because of the considerable power they have developed over the years, the parent groups must be seen as an important resource for the professional worker and in the context of trying to organize services they do not function in the client role. Instead the relationship between them and the professional engaged in community organization must be essentially *cooperative* and *reciprocal* and based on the recognition that both parties have a body of expert knowledge to bring to the common cause. An analysis of these areas of expertise is necessary for effective community organization practice. Starting with the parent group, we can see that they have many assets and skills not easily accessible to the professional worker. The firsthand experience of the emotional and practical problems of having a retarded child can provide invaluable information and insights on the type of services most urgently needed. This direct involvement of the consumer has great relevance to some of the burning issues of social work today—particularly the increasing skepticism as to whether delivery of services, in kind or quantity, really meets clients' needs as they perceive them.[17] In regard to retardation, this may be specially pertinent because of some divergence between the views of the professional social worker and the parent on what services are most beneficial—for example, the relative advantages of institutionalizing a child or keeping him at home, and the sort of service that is most supportive to the latter choice. In addition, the parent groups will have a wide variety of contacts in their community through their employment and social affiliations which can be exploited to enlist sympathetic support for the problems of retardation. This personal, informal relationship to community systems and structures is different from that of the professional worker, and it can be a very useful tool for gauging the mood of the community (either of certain sections or in its entirety) toward the innovations that will be necessary for setting up or extending services for the retarded. Insights of this sort can augment the diagnostic acumen of the professional worker.

Parents who belong to the higher economic strata bring another very valuable ingredient to the community organization mixture: a personal link with the dominant power structure and firsthand knowledge on how to manipulate political influence in order to secure support for improved services. For example, these parents are likely to have contacts among the major employers and with groups that influence public opinion. Such resources can be helpful both for developing a longer-term program of services and for establishing more localized specific help. For example, they may be able to influence a chamber of commerce to employ retarded adults, or on a smaller scale, they may be able to provide introductions to sympathetic real estate firms which can assist in finding appropriate premises for a new facility, such as a small group residence.

The professional worker's expertise is equally important in this joint enterprise. We can conceptualize this cooperative parent-worker effort as one in which the parent provides some of the raw materials of planning, while the worker contributes the technical knowledge on how these resources can be maximally utilized. These two areas of skill are complementary and interdependent in that the more intensely subjective concern of the parent (which gives the impetus to the activity) is linked to the more objective professional viewpoint, which adds breadth and perspective. The objective component serves also to correct biases in planning that may result from the strong vested interest of the parents. The specific areas in which the professional can interject a wider view are several. First, professional knowledge about retardation in its different developmental phases will introduce the concept of the *vertical continuum* so that planning does not concentrate exclusively on a felt need of the moment but looks backward to services that should precede the one immediately desired and ahead to those that will inevitably occur later. This professional insight will be derived from knowledge about human growth and behavior and the social roles that emerge at different stages of maturation. The *horizontal continuum* must also be introduced into planning and the social worker has responsibility for emphasizing a wider spectrum of simultaneous needs for the retarded than may have been immediately apparent to their families. A third, and even more vital, facet which needs to be introduced into the thinking of organized parent groups is the fact that retardation cuts across class barriers and that the planning of services must also be addressed to the needs of children and families whose problem has social rather than biological origins. An understanding of these three factors is essential since a valid allocation of priorities must rest on an informed awareness of *total* need and on a long-term perception of goals. By providing this broader perspective the social worker helps to bridge the sociocultural dichotomy between the two client categories and their relative ignorance of each other's problems and needs. The other significant contribution is the knowledge about the generic agencies in the community and the potential each has for developing a service for the retarded. Associated with this is information on the types of funding bodies which, though not specifically geared to retardation, can encompass some of its aspects so as to be a useful financial resource. Both these areas of expertise stem from the worker's broad understanding of retardation in all its ramifications, which makes it possible to perceive aspects that are common to other problem areas. For example, a demonstration research project on the most effective method of imparting sex education and contraceptive advice is as relevant to mildly retarded girls who have spent their adolescence in an institution as to more mature women of normal intelligence who are not in touch with community agencies that handle this social health problem. Funding could therefore be provided from budgets earmarked for mental retardation or for antipoverty programs or public health.

We have discussed the professional expertise which the community organization worker brings to her joint effort with the organized parent groups. It is now relevant to look at the roles that are inherent in this professional relationship. In general, the professional worker should serve in a *consultative* role with the formal parents' organization at the planning stage, should be marginally involved in decision-making, and wherever feasible should leave the implementation of plans to parents, for a number of reasons.

One reason, already mentioned, is that parents as consumers have a powerful interest and motivation and carry weight in their community. There is, besides, the important psychological fact that depending on their own efforts, rather than on professional intervention, helps to diminish the sense of defeat and impotence that often results from having a retarded child. The establishment of effective services for their own and other children, by investing the parents with compensatory effectiveness in another area, reaffirms their competent parental role. We have already stressed the importance of meeting this particular need in group work and casework situations; community organization offers even greater scope because it involves a practical commitment of time and effort, produces the feedback of a tangible result, and does, in fact, significantly alter the situation of both child and family. Since the seemingly irremediable characteristics of retardation are the most difficult aspects of the disability, this component of significant change is an important therapeutic factor. It also illustrates one of the fundamental concepts of this book, that the problem of retardation is resolved not by ameliorative measures aimed at the basic disability of the individual but by manipulating the environment to better accommodate the defective social functioning.

The relationship of the community organizer to the parents of retarded children who live in poverty areas must involve many of these approaches and techniques, but some of the emphasis will be different. For one thing, many families of mildly retarded children may not perceive this minor deviance as a major social problem on which to focus their energies, since the children's development and behavior will not seem very different from that of their normal peers. Likewise, the families which contain a more seriously impaired member, while realizing the gravity of the condition and the problem it gives rise to, often tend to accept the disability as a chronic and insoluble health problem because of the associated physical handicap that is often present. This attitude may be due to their lack of knowledge about the range of services for this level of disability, so that they envisage no alternatives except to carry the burden of the child or resort to institutional placement. This client group will be less concerned with planning services on a long-term basis than in securing ad hoc solutions to the immediate pressing problems that the handicap imposes, and their orientation thus involves a different technique of community organization. As we have already mentioned, the social requirements of this client group far transcend the limited area of needs covered by retardation, so the latter will be ascribed a different priority than in the middle-class community. For the poverty group, the community organization social worker often has to stimulate an awareness of the special needs of the conspicuously retarded child, of his potential for improved development if services are provided, and of his right to this opportunity. It also means redefining his role in terms of partially successful development instead of invalidism, and it means sustaining the family in staying with treatment or services that will foster this. For mildly retarded children, the reverse situation obtains in that their families and other significant contacts within their environment may have to be helped to realize that some of their needs differ from those of their normal peers and may require a specialized service: for example, a period of vocational rehabilitation after school in lieu of immediately starting employment.

In communities dominated by poverty, parents of retarded children are less likely to be formally organized because there are too many other demands on their time, energy, and material resources. Therefore, one important task of community organization is to bring interested families together round their common problems on a regular basis. This action can either serve as an informal parents' organization or be the means of starting a group locally and it might be initiated through a group to discuss managing handicapped children, which could be set up in a variety of generic or specialized services with which most families have ongoing contact. For example, parents of school-age children could be organized round the special class for educable or trainable children within their local school system, while for preschool children the public health nursing service and the clinical facilities in the maternal and infant care services are areas in which parents of conspicuously handicapped babies might be brought together. The same applies to the public child welfare services in that AFDC and day care programs inevitably include families with a retarded child who could probably be interested in meeting to discuss their specific problems of retardation, since it has been shown that group work with ADC mothers has been helpful in dealing with other problems.[18] As the major problems surrounding retardation are the lack of services, such a group could be the beginning of a social action committee; the case (or process) described on pages 274–77 illustrates this.

These three professional service contexts, which cover different types and phases of children's normal needs, are a useful base of operation for the community organizer where she can establish contact with the client group, alert them to the existing specialized services that are available for their children, and stimulate their interest in trying to procure others that they need. In this sort of situation she will be functioning within the broker and advocate roles, but these may develop into the activist role if she succeeds in getting the families of the retarded mobilized.[19] The first of these roles lies in her task of interpreting to the families what further services they and their children are entitled to and indicating where they may be located. To illustrate, a poor family may be unaware of a specialized diagnostic facility that serves their area but is located elsewhere—for example, a diagnostic clinic in a teaching hospital or in a residential institution—or they may not realize that a local family and children's agency could provide guidance on management and planning for a retarded child's life. The advocacy element is introduced when it is necessary to co-opt the services of a generic agency that is not initially receptive to accepting a retarded child, even though the child is legally entitled to the service—for example, a preschool nursery or day care program for normal children supported by public funds. In such situations, the social worker may need to become actively involved with the agency in question, to interpret the needs of child and family for service, the ability of the child to benefit from such a program, and, in the final resort, his inalienable right to be served. If the families can be encouraged or guided to take a part themselves and co-opt other forces in their neighborhood to help obtain the service required, she is being an activist. Although the community organizer will be focusing directly on the needs of the retarded child in the first instance, it is important to keep a broader perspective which can relate to the similar unmet needs of the other members of the client-system she is helping, whether a single family or a group of families. For example, if an exploration of playground facilities for retarded children shows that this resource is lacking for all children, action must encompass this total deficiency as it affects everyone. In this way the defined handicap of retardation can become an effective lever for generally expanding services in poor communities on a wider scale than originally conceived. To illustrate, if a plan is put into action to set up pre-school programs for all children with developmental lags of a prescribed age—say two and a half or three years—as a preventative and early therapeutic measure, a case-finding mechanism has to be developed to catch the target population. This in itself brings the family of the retarded into the public eye while the actual service for the identified child-at-risk links the family to a helping system on a regular and potentially intimate basis which offers an opportunity for them to raise other problems. Further, by providing a service for a segment of the child population, demand for wider coverage is stimulated—i.e., for younger children or for those without any overt problem. This is an extended perception of all children's rights.

Although we have stressed the importance of the broker and advocate roles for the client group from poor communities because of their lesser familiarity with the social service structure outside of their immediate experience, community organization should involve this group in other stances also, particularly in organizing their own indigenous resources to pressure for or develop services. The therapeutic value of procuring services by their own concerted effort has even greater significance for this category of families of the retarded than for their socially more secure counterparts because the entire life style of the poverty group (as well as the occurrence of retardation) builds into a sense of impotence and defeat, which needs the counteracting force of planning and implementing a tangible service. Another salient factor that should influence community organization on behalf of the retarded is the need for a fusing of the resources of client parents from both the socially defined categories we have described. Because of its middle-class origins, the organized parent group (the NARC and its branches) has been primarily concerned with the problems of the more conspicuously handicapped minority segment of the total retarded population. This has meant a preoccupation with organic defects and services to compensate for the resulting residual impairment, and until recently relatively little attention has been focused on milder forms of the handicap and their association with large-scale social issues. Any preventive measures have been concentrated on medical rather than on social etiology, and even the connection between biological retardation among children of low socioeconomic status and social problems had not, until recently, been highlighted by the parents' group.[20] The common objective of these socially divergent groups needs to be recognized and a concerted effort made to mobilize the cooperative resources of each. This consists of pressuring the power structure that controls the planning of, and resources for, more and better services to combat retardation. Their separate and valuable contributions are the different tactics each group has developed for making these demands known and bringing pressure to back them up. In addition to the financial resources and the educational and social skills that are easily turned to political lobbying, the organized parent group frequently has contacts in the power structure who can be personally canvassed for their support for services for the retarded. These parents, at the higher echelons of their organization, are extremely powerful and competent advocates of their own cause. They are, however, numerically small because moderate, severe, and profound retardation accounts for less than 25 percent of the retarded population. Therefore, the cogent claims they press pertain to only a small minority.

The exact opposite applies to the client group from the poverty areas, first, because upward of 75 percent of the identified retarded population belong to this stratum of society, and second, because their problems and demands for service relate to a much wider spectrum and involve many more individuals. Furthermore, although this group has lacked sophistication in pressuring for support by legal and recognized formal channels, over the past four or five years it has been developing the powerful techniques of protest and confrontation around other problems. Two outstanding examples are the Welfare Rights Movement and the parents' demands to be more involved in the organization of schools and educational programs. These proven techniques and skills can be easily transferred to the cause of mental retardation, but within the overall picture of needs presented in the poverty areas, this disability still remains a relatively minor claim. Therefore, an indispensable task of community organization on behalf of the retarded should be to help these two minorities to join forces. Even when they do not share a common geographical community, some machinery should be set up for representatives of both to meet on the common grounds of their shared concern. One such device would be to include on the Board of the local ARC a number of *family* representatives from the poor neighborhoods who could present the viewpoint of this group of clients, as well as making a contribution to planning services from their knowledge of the poor community and its different needs and special resources. Alternatively, a specialized service facility could be the appropriate seeding locale; in areas, for example, where education for all but the mildly retarded is in the hands of the Association for Retarded Children, the different training facilities would offer this opening. The families of poorer children could be encouraged to join specific groups and eventually move into planning the educational curriculum. This measure could be set in motion by funding scholarships for children from poor families from OEO funds, which would involve more families from the poorer areas, at the same time as providing the financial support needed to build up the ARC programs. The current situation of preschool education and training for the retarded illustrates the fragmentation of service that occurs, because these two economically divergent client groups have different sources of help. Many local ARCs have set up facilities for this age group, but their limited funding can rarely provide a facility that covers all expressed needs, let alone the latent need, and the cost prohibits poor families from utilizing the service. On the other hand, Operation Headstart, which provides for preschool children in the poverty areas, does not include children with identified retardation below the mild range, although there is great need for such a service for moderately and severely retarded children from families who are living under difficult conditions of overcrowding, poor housing, and inadequate income.

To illustrate that cooperation is feasible between parent groups from different social strata, we shall describe a modest but very effective community organization project which developed out of an urgent need to provide a facility for severely handicapped children from the poverty group. The operation was initiated in an all-black public housing project in a southern city by the mother of a severely retarded child on a very long waiting list for the local state institution. When she expressed dismay at this delay (of at least five years), the institution staff suggested she look for a community resource to help her with the child's management at home in the interim period. The mother took this suggestion to the public health nurse of the well-baby clinic situated in the housing project, who in turn sought out other families with a seriously handicapped preschool child. These mothers were invited to a biweekly group at which they discussed the problems of their handicapped children and how they could obtain day care services. Their next step was to consult the state office of the Association for Retarded Children as to whether any program was available, and if not, how one could be initiated. With this agency's backing a daily morning program was planned to be held in the recreation hall of the housing project, with staff provided from the local Office of Economic Opportunity Youth Corps. These young helpers received three weeks training in mental retardation in one of the local ARC training centers for preschool and school-age children. Subsequently, the space in the housing project proved to be inconvenient, so a local church volunteered the loan of its hall, which was in the neighborhood. Transportation of the children was undertaken by the antipoverty agency and an extra component was added in the shape of a caretaker cook, paid from this agency's funds, who cooked a daily hot meal. Welfare foods were utilized for this, and the parents contributed 50¢ a week to make up the balance. The mothers continued to meet as a group to discuss their common difficulties. Children who progressed beyond the center's scope were admitted to Head Start (the center included severe physical as well as mental handicap) and eventually, if suitable, to special education classes. A clinic in the city hospital which specialized in birth defects and other developmental anomalies evaluated the children initially and subsequently provided ongoing medical surveillance.

This example represents a microcosm of community organization for one category of the retarded in that it involves the cooperative effort of many important community elements and demonstrates most of the important methodological principles. The impetus came from a concerned parent who needed a service urgently, and her immediate contact was a professional worker in a generic agency, which was both visible and accessible to the client. Through the record systems of the housing project (which noted serious health problems in a family's record) and of the well-baby clinic (which had a close contact with the city hospital where most poor mothers went for maternity care and delivery), a fairly reliable case-finding mechanism was tapped, and through the city housing department the basic ingredient of accommodation was made available. The state and city chapters of the Association for Retarded Children were brought in to discuss planning and provide consultation and practical training on the management of retarded young children. Since this particular client group was from a poverty area, the institutionalized services to deal with economic need (the Office of Economic Opportunity and the Department of Welfare) were co-opted, and a major voluntary lay resource of the community—the local church—added a significant contribution in the shape of better accommodation and by sponsoring the center for OEO assistance. The operation embodies most of the important principles which should govern community organization on behalf of the mentally retarded or in fact any other minority group which has an obviously defining handicap. These are as follows:

1. The expressed request of an individual client (i.e., the felt need) to initiate action by the professional (i.e., the public health nurse of the well-baby clinic).

2. The felt need of an individual client transformed into a general need of this total subcommunity (i.e., the group of parents with handicapped children).

3. Systematic identification of submerged need by case-finding (i.e., searching the records of the housing authority for reference to defect in tenants and the birth records of babies in the city hospital).

4. Ensuring client participation from the start by organizing the interested mothers into a group and sustaining this involvement after the project had been launched by continuing the

group meetings and having the mothers make a small contribution to the lunch.

5. Making the initial contact with the state chapter of the ARC which operated as the *fixed point of referral* for the community and through its close contacts with the Departments of Health and Education was the best informed on what existing services—if any—were available.

6. Utilizing *professional* and *voluntary* segments of the community (i.e., the Housing Authority, OEO, the city hospital, the local church, and the Association for Retarded Children).

7. Utilizing *generic* and *specialized* resources (e.g., the Housing Authority, the Public Health Nursing Service, the city hospital, ARC, and OEO).

8. Utilizing resources from *several* professional disciplines (e.g., public health nursing, medicine, education, social work).

9. Developing a community resource as an alternative to an institutional one.

10. Articulating this particular segment of service with other services (e.g., using the special clinical unit at the city hospital to evaluate children and follow up on their health status; referring suitable children for the next stage of education).

11. Utilizing the integrated method approach by combining group work and community organization.

We have talked about the different elements in a given community whose support and concern need to be mobilized if services for the retarded are to be developed—starting from the sharply focused consumer group of families of the retarded, moving outward to the professional individuals and agencies who are directly or indirectly concerned with providing services for the retarded or their families, and encompassing eventually the entire lay population. The lay population includes formal elements, such as voluntary planning bodies to which the community has delegated responsibility for developing services, and informal elements which are not necessarily involved in planning but are integral to its success for many reasons.

Because of their vital stake in the problem of retardation, much of our discussion so far has been concentrated upon the formally organized parents' group and its relationship with the community organizer. We have already suggested that, through their strong identification with sectors of the community that are not *professionally* concerned with retardation, the parent groups have valuable contacts with individuals and bodies who wield influence. In general these are the *informal* elements of the lay community who can and must be roused to an awareness of retardation and how they can help. Wherever feasible this area of organization should be delegated to the parents' groups initially with the social worker serving in the consultative role that has been mentioned already on page 268. This allocation of tasks does not imply an abrogation of professional responsibility in this area but a less visibly active involvement. That is, the professional worker must remain constantly available for active consultation to the nonprofessional (in this instance the parents') group and be ready to discuss with them the outcome of their efforts, and when this is not satisfactory, to help analyze the source of obstruction and devise different tactical approaches.

The social worker's more active involvement is with the *formal* segments of the lay community, specifically the planning bodies (which usually include some professional members), and with the professional groups themselves. This division of labor ensures that the nonprofessional parent group and its allies and the professional social worker apply their efforts and skills where their insights and contacts carry greatest weight.

Our next and last step in this book is to discuss how the professional worker relates to and mobilizes the concern of the formal segments of the lay community involved in planning and the professional groups who are likely to be involved in implementing some of these plans through service to the retarded. In her relationship with organizations that plan health and welfare services the social worker must have a greater awareness of the political components in this situation and adopt a more aggressive role than that assumed toward parents and fellow-professionals. Any extension of welfare services being planned in today's society will be subject to limited resources and the claims of many competing groups, each offering cogent grounds for priority. The professional sponsoring the claims of the mentally retarded, who have a generally low priority in the value system, will have to be vigorous in pressing her case and sophisticated about where to find powerful lobbying groups. In this she may call upon the informal supportive forces that we have assigned to the parents' bailiwick or upon certain concerned individuals or groups from the professional community. However, the effectiveness of such vocal and voting support will to a large extent be influenced by her own expert knowledge about mental retardation, the problems it gives rise to, the broader ramifications of these (as noted on page 252) and the sort of services required to neutralize them. At a subsequent stage when it has been decided to develop a service for this handicapped sector of the community, other features of her expertise will be necessary to guide the actual planners in how they develop their project, whether it is a single facility catering to one particular age group or category of handicap or a broader spectrum of services. The professional insights and knowledge discussed earlier on pages 267–68 will be applicable to both these aspects of service planning—that is, sponsoring its support and implementing it.

Finally we come to the part played by the community organizer in relation to her professional colleagues in the health and welfare fields and the equally strong need to convince them of the role that they can play and their capacity for doing so. Basic to this task is the assumption that wherever feasible the retarded (and this fiat applies to all handicaps) should be served in facilities that serve the community at large.[21] This assumption has both a factual and philosophical rationale. The factual reason for including the retarded in a generic facility is that many of their needs are universal and do not require specialized treatment. The second point is that even a specialized need is rarely all-encompassing, and with careful diagnosis it can be related to a particular aspect of the problem or clinical condition. To give a simple illustration: a retarded child with educable potential does not always need a special clinic to evaluate and plan for his needs. He may be handled just as efficiently in a general pediatric department with consultation from a special education resource, or in a school diagnostic clinic with referral to a hospital for any additional medical problem—e.g. motor handicap or seizures. A third reason for preferring generic services is that the specialized service will have greater stability if it is soundly anchored in a generic agency that has a wider sphere of vested interest to sustain it than the relatively limited area of mental retardation. A fourth reason is that the latter are usually situated near the community to which the family belongs and are therefore more visible, more accessible, and more likely to be utilized.

This point leads into the philosophical basis for setting up generic services. By serving the retarded along with other community members an implicit assumption is made of their common needs and common rights. When services are provided at a distance and in a specialized setting, the effect is to isolate the retarded and their families spatially: they have to make a journey to a special place instead of going round the corner with everyone else. In social role terms, they are defined as a specialized subgroup. Allied with this role prescription is the fact that when services are located at a distance they are less subject to scrutiny because the community feels no responsibility for them. This lack of direct involvement on the part of the immediate communities which support and utilize specialized services is probably one reason why large-scale institutional care for the retarded has been permitted to deteriorate. Their prevailing climate of alienation and depersonalization is due, at least in part, to their geographical and psychological distance from normal society. Susser has emphasized this point very cogently when he advocates day care facilities for severely handicapped children and adults within the community and suggests that if mothers, relatives, or friends can drop in on a facility casually, without warning, this not only serves as an informal system of surveillance but also demonstrates to the staff that outsiders are concerned with and interested in their efforts.[22]

Another negative aspect to assigning the retarded to clearly demarcated specialized services is that this defines them in terms of their deficit (which is the basis for specialized care) and creates a psychological predisposition in the family and the professionals concerned to perpetuate this handicapped status via a continuum of specialized care which does not obviously lend itself to reevaluation. Services for the retarded should always be structured to encourage a reversal toward the norm, and this is more easily fostered in a setting where normal functioning is the model. This concept is well illustrated in a short-term residential center for dependent neglected normal children awaiting foster home placement. Included in this facility is a small unit for twenty-five ambulant but severely and moderately retarded children between birth and five years of age. Although they have their own quarters and program, the more socially competent children mix with their normal peers in play activities, and where the child continues to show improvement, his involvement in normal activities is gradually increased until he can become fully assimilated into the program. At this juncture, a review of long-term plans for him takes place.

If special programs for the retarded are to be set up in generic agencies (as the preferable alternative to segregated special services), the community organizer must be prepared to invest a great deal of time and professional help in getting them established. Her tasks will fall mainly into three parts: education of the total agency about retardation, ongoing consultation with the staff on how to handle the more unfamiliar aspects of behavior associated with the disability, and steering the agency to financial resources that might be tapped to fund the expansion of current programs to include retarded clients.

Education about retardation as a social phenomenon must include agency personnel, the governing board, and indirectly the other client consumers. The last-named are particularly important in group programs where the retarded segment will be large and regularly visible and might evoke adverse comment. For example, children attending a daily preschool program will be much more obtrusive than the odd child and parent who come to a vocational rehabilitation center or orthopedic clinic, and parents, if not enlightened about their needs and the purpose of including them, might raise objections. This educational thrust should start with an interpretation of the social needs of the child and his family, particularly the benefit they both derive from being accepted and assimilated into normal community life. From this should stem some information on the child's social functioning capacities, with particular initial emphasis on those that are common to his peers, and finally his atypical features should be described in terms of their effect on his social performance. The way this orientation is handled with different groups will vary according to their sophistication about social problems and social deviance, but it is important that the factual information be salted with some insight into the emotional factors that surround retardation, especially the complex attitudes of fear and revulsion (and the accompanying ashamed denial) that retardation often evokes initially. The principal purpose of providing accurate information on retardation to generic agencies is to change the stereotype that still lingers in regard to this group and to offer some insight into the irrational emotional responses that individuals with this handicap evoke.

The second task is really an extension of this first basic one and consists of providing ongoing consultation to the agency which is accepting the retarded either as individuals or in a group until the staff have become more familiar with their special characteristics and feel confident in handling their problems. This consultation should include assistance from a variety of sources. For example, if a generic day care center accepts a retarded child or group of children, its personnel may require regular consultation with a professional teacher in special education to reinforce their own skills. If there is a social worker, he or she may appreciate an initial orientation on the particular problems that a family with retardation faces, as well as information about specialized facilities that might be needed—for example, temporary residential care if the mother is ill or expecting another baby. Consultation, therefore, should resemble a concentric circle in which the community organization social worker provides the initial guidance herself and then delegates this task to other disciplines or agencies as the circumstances demand. This important activity of spreading information and guidance on how to meet the needs of the retarded within a generic agency's frame of reference can be extended in another way by regularly bringing together the generic agencies that serve the retarded so that they can pool knowledge and offer mutual support in the innovative tasks they are engaged in. This procedure can also be utilized to set up a chain of help, as in Chicago[23] where park recreational programs that cater specially to the retarded refer families and clients to other appropriate agencies for help with other problems reported by parents or observed. These "specialized" parks have also been used by other parks as a referral source for retarded applicants. This is another means of reducing the isolation of the retarded client group in that their inclusion in normal programs begins to be seen as a socially positive activity which receives some professional consensus. In this respect, it is important that the nonspecialized agencies should view themselves as a skilled resource rather than a last resort dumping ground, because this will help to explode the prevalent myth that only specialized facilities can cater to the retarded and that service without this special component can only be a second best. The utilization of generic agencies introduces an important planning component; namely, that the resources of these helping systems must be carefully balanced with the needs of the retarded in any community in respect to how many retarded clients any given agency can absorb effectively and what degree of handicap and age range should be contained in this figure. It is also necessary to calculate what professional time and skills are available for consultation from the specialized services to bolster the generic agencies, because this will determine how many of the latter can be co-opted at any one phase of planning to participate in programs for the retarded.

The broader educational orientation of the community at large about the facts of retardation is an important feature of community organization for several reasons. First, there is a good deal of confusion and ignorance about the origins of this handicap, which leads to anxiety-invoking fantasies in place of objective judgment when the claims of the retarded for services are being considered. The historical association of mental affliction with such socially taboo topics as witchcraft and sexual excess perpetuates a *malevolent stereotype*, which is sometimes inadvertently reinforced by the more bizarre aspects of some retarded behavior. The extent to which the retarded can be rehabilitated and function as useful citizens is also not widely realized. More important, because this has been given even less attention than the points just cited, it is not generally appreciated that without adequate stimulation and training the retarded will regress to a level of functioning below their innate capacities. There is also still only a limited understanding of the close connection between the well-being of a retarded individual and his family's psychological health and social stability, and this point needs to be repeatedly emphasized. Finally, the traditional pattern of segregated intramural care has fostered a skeptical attitude toward the effectiveness or desirability of community provision for the retarded. Less frequently voiced but just as potent is the doubt as to the desirability of having a substantial number of conspicuously impaired individuals in the community at large, making overt demands on its normal members in both their formal and informal roles. The physician may have to include them in his practice or the social worker may be faced with the hard fact that the sometimes insoluble problems of this client group cannot be shipped off elsewhere with a clear professional conscience, and both these professional representatives of the normal community may find the retarded living next door, either with their own families or in a group residence.

This brings us to a final aspect of the role and skills that social work should bring to the organization of community resources to help the development and social adjustment of the mentally retarded. The fundamental and recurring theme of this whole book has been societal responsibility for individuals with this handicap, and this last chapter has been concerned with how to achieve a balance between the contribution that professional services make and that which comes from the lay element in the community at large. The social worker and the social agency together represent institutionalized continuity of care, while the lay members of the community (the neighbors, the church, the Association for Retarded Children) provide personal continuity. Put another way, the social agency embodies the community's formally established responsibility for the retarded individual; and when, as until recently, this formal service took the form of segregated residential care, the delegated responsibility was almost total. Now that there is a growing emphasis on community services, this investment of responsibility in a formal professional structure becomes less absolute and comprehensive, and one of the social worker's new and very vital tasks is to assist in transferring some of this responsibility back to the normal community of lay individuals where it used to reside. This involves providing the insights already outlined—the psychological insight concerning personal attitudes toward the retarded; the sociological insights into their changing role in society; the philosophical insight into society's obligation to this particular segment of its handicapped members; and last but most important, the insight into the great therapeutic potential that lies in the concern of society at large as much as in professional services. This benign partnership is well illustrated in Edgerton's study[24] of the adjustment of mildly retarded adults in the community after long periods of institutionalization, because the vital ingredient to their adjustment—the long-term consistently supportive benefactor role—was shared between professional and lay people. In some cases, the social worker who had supervised the client during his trial period in the community continued to maintain an informal but available supportive role and in others it was provided by nonprofessional day-to-day contacts such as an understanding employer, a fellow worker, a neighbor, or a family with whom the individual had previously had a significant relationship. Within this network of informal community resources, the marginally functioning individuals managed to maintain themselves with reasonable competence and, as the title of the book indicates, without obtruding their inadequacies upon the notice of most of their fellow beings.

NOTES

Chapter 1: THE SOCIOCLINICAL NATURE OF MENTAL RETARDATION

1. Leonard Krasner and Leonard P. Ullman, eds., *Research in Behavior Modification—New Developments and Implications* (New York, Holt, Rinehart & Winston, 1967).
2. Rick Heber, *A Manual on Terminology and Classification in Mental Retardation*, Monograph Supplement to the *American Journal of Mental Deficiency*, 2nd ed., 1961.
3. Lewis Anthony Dexter, "A social theory of mental deficiency," *American Journal of Mental Deficiency*, Vol. 62, No. 5 (March, 1958).
4. Herbert Goldstein, "Social and occupational adjustment," in Harvey A. Stevens and Rick Heber, eds., *Mental Retardation: A Review of Research* (Chicago, University of Chicago Press, 1964).
5. A. D. B. Clarke, *Recent Advances in the Study of Subnormality* (London, National Association of Mental Health, 1966), pp. 14–21.
6. Lewis B. Holmes, Hugo W. Moser, Thorlakur S. Halldorsson, Cornelia Mack, Shyam S. Pant, and Benjamin Matzilevich, *Mental Retardation: An Atlas of Diseases with Associated Physical Abnormalities* (New York, Macmillan, *in press*).
7. *Ibid.*, and Stevens and Heber, *Mental Retardation: A Review of Research*, Chaps. 9–12.
8. Heber, *A Manual on Terminology and Classification in Mental Retardation*, pp. 7–52.
9. *Diagnostic and Statistical Manual of Mental Disorders*, 2nd ed. (American Psychiatric Association, 1968).
10. Hilda Knobloch and Benjamin Pasamanick, "Complications of pregnancy and mental deficiency," in Peter Bowman, ed., *Mental Retardation: Proceedings of the First International Medical Conference at Portland, Maine* (New York, Grune and Stratton, 1962); and *idem*, "Environmental factors affecting human development before and after birth," *Pediatrics*, 26 (August, 1960), 210–18.
11. Rodger L. Hurley, *Poverty and Mental Retardation: A Causal Re-*

lationship (State of New Jersey, Department of Institutions and Agencies, Division of Mental Retardation and Planning and Implementation Project, 1968); and Hilda Knobloch, Benjamin Pasamanick, and Abraham M. Lilienfeld, "Socio-economic status and some precursors of neuropsychiatric disorder," *American Journal of Orthopsychiatry*, 26, No. 3 (July, 1956).

12. Herbert G. Birch, "The problem of brain damage in children," in Herbert G. Birch, ed., *Brain Damage in Children: The Biological and Social Aspects* (Baltimore, Williams and Wilkins, 1964); and Benjamin Pasamanick and Abraham M. Lilienfeld, "Association of maternal and fetal factors with development of mental deficiency: I. Abnormalities in the prenatal and paranatal periods," *Journal of the American Public Health Association*, 159, No. 3 (September, 1955).

13. Jane Mercer, "Who is normal? Two perspectives on mild mental retardation," in E. G. Jaco, ed., *Patients, Physicians and Illnesses*, 2nd ed. (New York, The Free Press, 1969).

14. Ann M. Clarke and A. D. B. Clarke, "The abilities and trainability of imbeciles," Chap. 13 in *Mental Deficiency: The Changing Outlook*, rev. ed. (New York, The Free Press, 1965).

15. Stewart E. Perry, "Notes for a sociology of prevention in mental retardation," in Irving Philips, ed., *Prevention and Treatment of Mental Retardation* (New York, Basic Books, 1966): and *idem*, "Some theoretic problems of mental deficiency and their action implications," *Psychiatry: The Journal for the Study of Interpersonal Processes*, 17, No. 1 (February, 1954).

Chapter 2: THE HISTORICAL BACKGROUND TO SERVICES FOR THE MENTALLY RETARDED

1. Gregory Zilboorg, *A History of Medical Psychology* in collaboration with George W. Henry, M.D. (New York, Norton, 1941).

2. Stanley Powell Davies, *The Mentally Retarded in Society* (New York, Columbia University Press, 1959).

3. Leo Kanner, *A History of the Care and Study of the Mentally Retarded* (Springfield, Ill., Charles C. Thomas, 1964).

4. Jean-Marc-Gaspard Itard, *The Wild Boy of Aveyron*, trans. by George and Muriel Humphry (New York, The Century Company, 1932); and Richard M. Silberstein and Helen Irwin, "Jean-Marc-Gaspard Itard and the Savage of Aveyron: An unsolved diagnostic problem in child psychiatry," *Journal of the Academy of Child Psychiatry*, I, No. 2 (April, 1962), 314–22.

5. Mabel E. Talbot, *Edouard Seguin: A Study of an Educational Approach to the Treatment of Mentally Defective Children* (New

York, Bureau of Publications, Teachers College, Columbia University, 1964).

6. Kanner, *A History of the Care and Study of the Mentally Retarded.*
7. Olive Bowtell, "The historical background," in Margaret Adams, ed., *The Mentally Subnormal: The Social Casework Approach* (London, William Heinemann Medical Books, 1960; New York, Free Press, 1965).
8. George Brown, "Obituary Address on Dr. Hervey Wilbur," *Proceedings of the Association of Medical Officers of American Institutions for Idiotic and Feebleminded Persons*, Nos. 1–10, p. 291.
9. Davies, *The Mentally Retarded in Society*; and Kanner, *A History of the Care and Study of the Mentally Retarded*, pp. 42 and 62–68.
10. Samuel Gridley Howe, "On the training of idiots," *American Journal of Insanity*, VIII, No. 2 (October, 1851).
11. *Proceedings of the Association of Medical Officers of American Institutions for Idiotic and Feebleminded Persons*, Nos. 1–10 (1876–1885.
12. *Ibid.*, Nos. 11–19 (1888), pp. 65–67.
13. Gunnar Dybwad, "Changing patterns of residential care for the mentally retarded: A challenge to architecture," *Proceedings of the First Congress of the International Association for the Scientific Study of Mental Deficiency, Montpellier, France, 1967* (England, Michael Jackson Publishing Co., Ltd., 1968).
14. G. A. Doren in *Proceedings of the Association of Medical Officers of American Institutions for Idiotic and Feebleminded Persons*, Nos. 1–10 (1878), p. 103.
15. I. N. Kerlin, in *ibid*, Nos. 11–19 (1888), p. 166.
16. J. Stewart, in *ibid.*, Nos. 1–10 (1882), p. 236 and Nos. 11–19 (1888), pp. 54–56.
17. Helen Leland Witmer, *Social Work—An Analysis of a Social Institution* (New York, Farrar and Rinehart, 1942).
18. Harry L. Lurie, ed., *Encyclopedia of Social Work*, Fifteenth Issue (New York, National Association of Social Workers, 1965), pp. 103 and 250.
19. Kanner, *A History of the Care and Study of the Mentally Retarded.*
20. Robert H. Haskell, "The American movement in mental deficiency: An apostrophe to the memory of a noble American," *American Journal of Mental Deficiency*, XLIX, No. 3 (January, 1945).
21. Van Wyck Brooks, *The Flowering of New England* (New York, Dutton, 1936).
22. J. A. Stewart, in *Proceedings of the Association of Medical Officers of American Institutions for Idotic and Feebleminded Persons*, Nos. 1–10 (1882).

23. William Rhinelander Stewart, *The Philanthropic Work of Mrs. Josephine Shaw Lowell* (New York, Macmillan, 1911).
24. Hervey Wilbur, in *Proceedings of the Association of Medical Officers of American Institutions for Idotic and Feebleminded Persons*, Nos. 1–10 (1878 and 1880), pp. 97–98 and 275.
25. G. A. Doren, in *ibid.*, Nos. 1–10 (1878), p. 103.
26. Isaac Kerlin, in *ibid.*, Nos. 11–19 (1888), p. 166.
27. J. C. Carson, in *ibid.*, Nos. 1–10 (1885), pp. 364–67; (1891), p. 377.
28. J. Stewart, in *ibid*, Nos. 11–19 (1892).
29. J. C. Carson, in *ibid.*, Nos. 1–10 (1880), p. 165.
30. H. H. Goddard, *The Kallikak Family: A Study in the Heredity of Feeblemindedness* (New York, Macmillan, 1912), Chap. IV.
31. Charlotte Steinbach, "Feebleminded children in a great city," *Journal of Psycho-Asthenics*, XXV (1920–1921).
32. *Proceedings of the Association of Medical Officers of American Institutions for Idiotic and Feebleminded Persons*, Nos. 1–10 (1879), p. 168.
33. Davies, *The Mentally Retarded in Society*, Chaps. V–VII.
34. Joseph P. Byers, "A state plan for the care of the feebleminded," *Journal of Psycho-Asthenics*, XXI, Nos. 1 and 2 (September–December, 1916), p. 36
35. Walter E. Fernald, "Thirty years progress in the care of the feebleminded," *Journal of Psycho-Asthenics*, XXIX (1923–24).
36. Samuel Gridley Howe, *Report to Inquire into the Conditions of Idiots of the Commonwealth of Massachusetts*, No. 51, February 28, 1848.
37. Wolf Wolfensberger, "The origin and nature of our institutional models," in Robert B. Kugel and Wolf Wolfensberger, eds., *Changing Patterns in Residential Services for the Mentally Retarded*, President's Committee on Mental Retardation, January, 1969, Chap. 5, pp. 100–7.
38. Reverend Karl Schwarz, "Nature's corrective principle in social evolution," *Journal of Psycho-Asthenics*, XIII, Nos. 1, 2, 3, 4 (September and December, 1908, and March, June, 1909).
39. *Royal Commission on the Poor Laws and Unemployment*, Vol. III, *The Minority Report* (London, Wyman and Sons, 1909).
40. Max Weber, *The Protestant Ethic and the Rise of Capitalism*, trans. by Talcott Parsons (New York, Scribner, 1958).
41. Helen MacMurchy, "Relationship of feeblemindedness to other social problems," *Journal of Psycho-Asthenics*, XXI, Nos. 1 and 2 (1916).
42. Isaac Kerlin, in *Proceedings of the Association of Medical Officers of American Institutions for Idiotic and Feebleminded Persons*, Nos. 1–10 (1879), pp. 150–62.

43. Kanner, *A History of the Care and Study of the Mentally Retarded*, p. 115.
44. Walter E. Fernald, "An outpatient clinic in connection with a state institution for the feebleminded," *Journal of Psycho-Asthenics*, XXV (1920–1921), 81–89.
45. Walter E. Fernald, "A state program for the care of the mentally defective," *Mental Hygiene*, III, no. 4 (October, 1919), 566–74.
46. George Kline, "Accomplishments and immediate aims in Massachusetts in community care of the feebleminded," *Journal of Psycho-Asthenics*, XXIX (1923–1924).
47. Walter E. Fernald, "The inauguration of a state-wide public school mental clinic in Massachusetts," *Journal of Psycho-Asthenics*, XXVII (1921–1922).
48. O. H. Cobb, "Parole of mental defectives," *Journal of Psycho-Asthenics*, XXVIII (1922–1923).
49. V. V. Anderson, "A study of the careers of 321 feebleminded persons who have been to special classes and are now out in the community," *Journal of Psycho-Asthenics*, XXVII (June, 1921–1922); and Schassa G. Rowe, "A study of one hundred and fifty ex-pupils of special classes in Boston," *Journal of Psycho-Asthenics*, XXVIII (June, 1922–1923).
50. Earl W. Fuller, "Extra-institutional care of mental defectives," *Journal of Psycho-Asthenics*, XXVI (1921).
51. Florentine Hackbusch, "The Organisation of clinics and extra-institutional supervision," *Journal of Psycho-Asthenics*, XXX (1924–1925).
52. Franklin W. Bock, "Mothers and children's preventatorium," *Journal of Psycho-Asthenics*, XV, Nos. 3 and 4 (1911).
53. C. H. Henninger, "The feebleminded outside of the institution and their relationship to society," *Journal of Psycho-Asthenics*, XVI, No. 4 (June, 1912).
54. Mabel Matthews, "Parole of the feebleminded," *Journal of Psycho-Asthenics*, XXVIII (1922–1923); and Alice Raymond, "Observations on the placement and supervision of mental defectives in the community," *Journal of Psycho-Asthenics*, XXVIII (1922–1923).
55. Charles Bernstein, "Rehabilitation of the mentally defective," *Journal of Psycho-Asthenics*, XXIV (1919–1920).
56. Inez F. Stebbins, "The institution in relation to community supervision," *Journal of Psycho-Asthenics*, XXX (1924–1925).
57. Charles L. Vaux, "Family care of mental defectives," *Journal of Psycho-Asthenics*, XL (1934–1935).
58. Walter E. Fernald, "Thirty years progress in the care of the feebleminded," *Journal of Psycho-Asthenics*, XXIX (1923–1924); Thomas

H. Haines, "Community service of the state institutions for the mentally defective," *Journal of Psycho-Asthenics,* XXVIII (1922); George Kline, "Accomplishments and immediate aims in Massachusetts in community care of the feebleminded," *Journal of Psycho-Asthenics,* XXIX (1923–1924); and Frankwood E. Williams, "Essential elements in any plan for community supervision of trained mentally defective persons," *Journal of Psycho-Asthenics,* XXIX (1923–1924).

59. *A Proposed Program for National Action to Combat Mental Retardation,* The President's Panel on Mental Retardation (Washington, D.C., U.S. Government Printing Office, 1962).

60. Mabel Ann Matthews, "Some effects of the depression on social work with the feebleminded," *Journal of Psycho-Asthenics,* XXXIX (1933–1934).

61. "History of Children's Bureau activities in behalf of mentally retarded children," in *Historical Perspectives on Mental Retardation During the Decade 1954–1964* (U.S. Department of Health, Education and Welfare, Social and Rehabilitation Services, Children's Bureau, No. 426, 1964).

62. Alan H. Sampson, "Developing and maintaining good relations with parents of mentally deficient children," *American Journal of Mental Deficiency,* XII, No. 2 (October, 1947).

63. Samuel Kaminsky, Personal Communication.

64. *Decade of Decision.* An evaluation report prepared by the National Association for Retarded Children, for the 1960 White House Conference on Children and Youth (New York, NARC).

65. Robert M. Segal, *Mental Retardation and Social Action* (Springfield, Ill., Charles C. Thomas, 1970).

66. *A Proposed Program for National Action to Combat Mental Retardation.*

67. Mervyn Susser, *Community Psychiatry: Epidemiologic and Social Themes* (New York, Random House, 1968).

68. Stewart E. Perry, "Notes for a sociology of prevention in mental retardation," in Irving Phillips, ed., *Prevention and Treatment of Mental Retardation* (New York, Basic Books, 1966).

Chapter 3: SOCIAL WORK PERSPECTIVES ON MENTAL RETARDATION

1. Mary Richmond, *Social Diagnosis* (New York, Russell Sage Foundation, 1917; reprinted Free Press, 1965), pp. 434–35 and 441–48.

2. Gordon Hamilton, "What the private social agency can do in the

supervision of the feebleminded," *Journal of Psycho-Asthenics*, XXIV (1924).

3. Stanley Powell Davies, *Social Control of the Mentally Deficient* (New York, Thomas Y. Crowell, 1930).

4. Marjorie Wallace Lenz, "Where does the program for the feeble-minded fail to meet the needs of the court?" *Journal of Psycho-Asthenics*, XLIV (1938–1939); Elizabeth Robinson, "The New York State program for the care of mental defectives. Where the program fails to meet the needs of the family agency," *Journal of Psycho-Asthenics*, XLIV (1938–1939); and V. Elise Seyfarth, "The way in which the New York State program for the care of the mentally defective person fails to meet the needs of the children's agency," *Journal of Psycho-Asthenics*, XLIV (1938–1939).

5. Walter A. Friedlander, *Introduction to Social Welfare*, 3rd ed. (Englewood Cliffs, N.J., Prentice-Hall, 1968).

6. *Ibid.*; and Helen Leland Witmer, *Social Work. An Analysis of a Social Institution* (New York, Farrar & Rinehart, 1942), Chaps. VII and VIII.

7. Virginia Robinson, *A Changing Psychology in Social Work* (University of North Carolina Press, 1932).

8. Witmer, *Social Work. An Analysis of a Social Institution*.

9. William Rhinelander Stewart, *The Philanthropic Work of Mrs. Josephine Shaw Lowell* (New York, Macmillan, 1911), p. 267.

10. Jane Addams, *20 Years at Hull House* (New York, Macmillan, 1911).

11. *Public Health Concepts in Social Work Education* (U.S. Department of Health, Education and Welfare, Council on Social Work Education, 1962).

12. Rodger A. Hurley, *Poverty and Mental Retardation: A Causal Relationship* (State of New Jersey, Department of Institutions and Agencies, Division of Mental Retardation, Planning and Implementation Project, Trenton, April, 1968).

13. Walter I. Trattner, "Homer Folks and the Public Health Movement," *Social Service Review*, XL, No. 4 (December, 1966).

14. Lydia Rapoport, "The concept of prevention in social work," *Social Work*, 6, No. 1 (January, 1961); and Milton Wittman, "Preventive social work: A goal for practice and education," *Social Work*, 6, No. 1 (January, 1961).

15. Harold M. Skeels and Harold B. Dye, "A study of the effects of differential stimulation on mentally retarded children," in *Proceedings and Addresses of the American Association on Mental Deficiency*, XLIV, No. 1 (1939).

16. Sally Provence and Rose C. Lipton, *Infants in Institutions* (New York, International Universities Press, 1962).

17. Alfred Kahn, "Planning services for children," in *Organization of Services That Will Best Meet the Needs of Children* (New York, Arden House Conference, 1965); and *idem*, "Social services as social utilities," in *Urban Development—Its Implications for Social Welfare*, Proceedings of the XIIIth International Conference of Social Work, Washington, D.C., 1966.

18. Charles Bernstein, "Rehabilitation of the mentally defective," *Journal of Psycho-Asthenics*, XXIV (1919–1920).

19. Charles Vaux, "Family Care," *Journal of Psycho-Asthenics*, XLI (1935–1936).

Chapter 4: THE APPLICATION OF THE THREE SOCIAL WORK METHODS

1. Margaret E. Adams and Ralph W. Colvin, "The deprivation hypothesis: Its application to mentally retarded children and their needs," *Child Welfare*, XLVIII, No. 3 (March, 1969); and Marlin Roll, "A study of young retarded children," in *Social Work Practice* (New York, Columbia University Press, 1962).

2. Herbert G. Birch, "The problem of brain damage in children," in Herbert G. Birch, ed., *Brain Damage in Children: The Biological and Social Aspects* (Baltimore, Williams and Wilkins, 1964).

3. Pauline C. Cohen, "The impact of the handicapped child on the family," *Social Casework*, XLIII, No. 3 (March, 1962); and Philip Roos, "Psychological counseling with parents of retarded children," *Mental Retardation*, 1, No. 6 (December, 1963).

4. Howard R. Kelman, "Social work and mental retardation, challenge or failure?" *Social Work*, 3, No. 3 (July, 1958).

5. Bess Dana, "Health, Medical Care and Responsibility," paper presented at the National Association of Social Workers' Symposium on Social Work Knowledge and Practice, May, 1965.

6. Carol H. Meyer, "Casework in a changing society," in *Social Work Practice* (New York, Columbia University Press, 1966).

7. Hugo W. Moser, Robert E. Flynn, Margaret E. Adams, and Murray Sidman, "Mental subnormality," in Sidney Gellis and Benjamin Kagan, eds., *Current Pediatric Therapy* (Philadelphia, W. B. Saunders, 1970).

8. "A preliminary statement on social work services for children in their own homes," *Child Welfare League of America Standards*, 1968.

9. Helen Harris Perlman, "Social work method: A review of the past decade," *Social Work*, 10, No. 4 (October, 1965).

10. Bernard Farber and D. B. Ryckman, "Effects of a severely mentally

retarded child on family relationships," *Mental Retardation Abstracts*, Division of Mental Retardation, Rehabilitation Services Administration, 2, No. 1 (March, 1965); and Wolf Wolfensberger and Richard A. Kurtz, *Management of the Family of the Mentally Retarded* (Chicago, Follett Educational Corporation, 1968).

11. Margaret E. Adams, "Study of the health and welfare network that serves the retarded in seven U.S. cities," unpublished material obtained as part of the Coordinated Program in Foster Care carried out by the Research Center of the Child Welfare League of America, 1968.

Chapter 5: SOME CONCEPTS OF CASEWORK

1. Carol H. Meyer, "Casework in a changing society," *Social Work Practice* (New York, Columbia University Press, 1966).
2. Helen Harris Perlman, *Social Casework: A Problem-Solving Process* (Chicago: University of Chicago Press, 1957), p. 7.
3. Bertha C. Reynolds, "Can social casework be interpreted to a community as a basic approach to human problems?" *The Family*, 13 (February, 1933), 336–42.
4. Werner W. Boehm, "The social work curriculum study and its implications for family casework," in Cora Kasius, ed., *Social Casework in the Fifties, Selected Articles, 1951–1960* (New York, Family Service Association of America, 1962).
5. Herbert H. Apthekar, *Dynamics of Casework and Counselling* (Boston, Houghton Mifflin, 1953).
6. Renee Portray, "The Impact of the Mentally Retarded Child upon the Family," paper presented at the XIIIth International Conference of Social Work, Washington, D.C., 1966.
7. Sylvia Schild, "Counselling with parents of retarded children living at home," *Social Work*, 9, No. 1 (January, 1964).
8. Walter Ehlers, *Mothers of Retarded Children; How They Feel; Where They Can Find Help* (Springfield, Ill., Charles C. Thomas, 1966).
9. Albert J. Solnit and Mary H. Stark, "Mourning and the birth of a defective child," *Psycho-analytical Study of the Child*, XVI (1961), 523–37.
10. Arthur Mandelbaum and Mary Ella Wheeler, "The Meaning of a defective child to parents," *Social Casework*, XLI, No. 7 (July, 1960).
11. Alexander Hersh, "Casework with parents of retarded children," *Social Work*, 6, No. 2 (June, 1961); and Ada Kozier, "Casework with parents of children born with severe brain defects," *Social Casework*, XLIII, No. 1 (January, 1962).

12. Solnit and Stark, "Mourning and the birth of a defective child."
13. Mandelbaum and Wheeler, "The meaning of a defective child to parents."
14. Simon Olshansky, "Chronic sorrow: a response to having a mentally defective child," *Social Casework*, XLIII, No. 4 (April, 1962).
15. Howard R. Kelman, "Some problems in casework with parents of mentally retarded children," *American Journal of Mental Deficiency*, 61, No. 3 (January, 1957).
16. Juanita Dalton and Helene Epstein, "Counseling parents of mildly retarded children," *Social Casework*, XLIV, No. 9 (November, 1963).
17. Lydia Rapoport, "The state of crisis: Some theoretical considerations," in Howard Parad, ed., *Crisis Intervention: Selected Readings* (New York, Family Service Association of America, 1965); and *idem*, "Crisis-oriented short-term casework," *Social Service Review*, 41, No. 1 (March, 1967).
18. Rodger T. Hurley, *Poverty and Mental Retardation: A Causal Relationship* (State of New Jersey, Department of Institutions and Agencies, Division of Mental Retardation, Planning and Implementation Project, Trenton, 1968).

Chapter 6: THE SOCIAL EVALUATION AND ITS SIGNIFICANCE FOR MENTAL RETARDATION

1. Mary Richmond, *Social Diagnosis* (New York, Russell Sage Foundation, 1917; reprinted Free Press, 1965).
2. *Stress in Families with a Mentally Handicapped Child*, Report of a working party set up by the National Society for Mentally Handicapped Children (London, 1967), pp. 24–25.
3. Mary Richmond, *What is Social Casework? An Introductory Description* (New York, Russell Sage Foundation, 1922).
4. Richmond, *Social Diagnosis*, p. 360.
5. J. Tizard and J. C. Grad, *The Mentally Handicapped and Their Families* (New York, Oxford University Press, 1961).
6. Gerhardt Saenger, *The Adjustment of Severely Retarded Adults in the Community*, New York State Interdepartmental Health Resources Board, 1958; and Katherine Spencer, "The place of socio-cultural study in casework," in *Socio-Cultural Elements in Casework*, Prepared by the New York Cultural Project—A Working Committee associated with the Council on Social Work Education (New York, 1955).
7. G. H. Zuk, R. L. Miller, J. B. Bartram, and F. Kling, "Maternal acceptance of retarded children: A questionnaire study of attitudes

and religious background," *Child Development,* 32 (1961), 525–40.

8. Robert B. Kugel and Wolf Wolfensberger, *Changing Patterns in Residential Services for the Mentally Retarded,* President's Committee on Mental Retardation, January, 1969, Chap. 5, pp. 68–83.

9. Michael Begab, *The Mentally Retarded Child: A Guide to Services of Social Agencies,* Chap. 3 "The families of the mentally retarded" (U.S. Department of Health, Education, and Welfare, Welfare Administration, Children's Bureau, 1963); Bernard Farber, *Effects of a Severely Mentally Retarded Child on Family Integration,* Monograph, Society for Research in Child Development (Antioch Press, 1959); and Wolf Wolfensberger and Richard A. Kurtz, eds., *Management of the Family of the Mentally Retarded* (Chicago, Follett Education Corporation, 1968).

10. Erving Goffman, *Stigma: Notes on the Management of Spoiled Identity* (Englewood Cliffs, N.J., Prentice-Hall, 1963).

11. Bernard Farber and David B. Ryckman, "Effects of severely mentally retarded children on family relationships," *Mental Retardation Abstracts* II, 1–17 (Washington, D.C., Division of Mental Retardation, Rehabilitation Services Administration, 1965).

12. Margaret E. Adams, "Siblings of the retarded: Their problems and treatment," *Child Welfare,* XLVI, No. 6 (June, 1967).

13. Shirley C. Hellenbrand, "Client value orientations: Implications for diagnosis and treatment," *Social Casework,* XLII, No. 4 (April, 1961).

14. Jane Mercer, "Sociological perspectives on mental retardation," paper delivered at the Inaugural Peabody-National Institute of Mental Health Conference on Socio-Cultural Aspects of Mental Retardation, Nashville, Tennessee, June, 1968.

Chapter 7: THE PROFESSIONAL RELATIONSHIP WITH THE DEPENDENT CLIENT AND HIS FAMILY

1. Florence Hollis, *Casework: A Psychosocial Therapy* (New York, Random House, 1964).

2. Helen Harris Perlman, *Social Casework: A Problem-Solving Process* (Chicago, University of Chicago Press, 1957).

3. Lawrence Goodman, "The social worker's role in clinics for the retarded," *Child Welfare,* XLIV, No. 4 (April, 1965).

4. Imogene V. Smith and Dorothy Loeb, "The stable extended family as a model in treatment of atypical children," *Social Work,* 10, No. 3 (July, 1965).

5. Elliot Studt, "Organizing resources for more effective practice," in *Trends in Social Work Practice and Knowledge* (New York, National Association of Social Workers, 1965).

6. Hollis, *Casework: A Psychosocial Therapy*.
7. F. E. Waldron, "The meaning of the word 'social' in psychiatric social work," *British Journal of Psychiatric Social Work*, No. 3 (November, 1949).
8. Elizabeth E. Irvine, "Transference and reality in the casework relationship," *British Journal of Psychiatric Social Work*, III, No. 4 (1956).
9. Annette Garrett, "Worker-client relationship," in Howard Parad, ed., *Ego-Psychology and Dynamic Casework* (New York, Family Service Association of America, 1958).
10. Noel Timms, *Psychiatric Social Work in Great Britain (1939–1962)* (London, Routledge and Kegan Paul, 1964), pp. 254–55.
11. Craig McAndrew and Robert Edgerton, "On the possibility of friendship," *American Journal of Mental Deficiency*, 70, No. 4 (January, 1966).
12. Miriam Mednick, "Casework service to the mental retardate and his parents," *Casework Papers* (New York, Family Service Association of America, 1957).

Chapter 8: THE PROFESSIONAL RELATIONSHIP WITH THE MILDLY RETARDED CLIENT

1. Margaret Adams, ed., *The Mentally Subnormal: The Social Casework Approach* (London, William Heinemann Medical Books, 1960; New York, Free Press, 1965), Chaps. IV and VI; *idem*, "Social work with mental defectives II," *Case Conference*, 4, No. 1 (May, 1957); Hester Crutcher, "Social work with the mental defective," *Journal of Psycho-Asthenics*, XXXVIII (1932); and Lawrence Shulman, "A Game-model theory of interpersonal strategies," *Social Work*, 3, No. 3 (July, 1968).
2. Dorcas D. Bowles, "Making casework relevant to black people: Approaches, techniques, theoretical implications," *Child Welfare*, XLVIII, No. 8 (October, 1969).
3. Henry V. Cobb, "The attitude of the retarded person toward himself," in *Stress of Families of the Mentally Handicapped* (Brussels, International League of Societies for the Mentally Handicapped, 1967).
4. Edward Zigler and Susan Hartner, "The socialization of the mentally retarded," in David A. Goslin, ed., *Handbook of Socialisation Theory and Research* (Chicago, Rand McNally, 1969).
5. Lewis Anthony Dexter, "A Social Structure Interpretation of the History of Concern about 'Mild' Retardation," paper read at the 91st

Annual Convention of the American Association on Mental Deficiency, Denver, Colorado, May, 1967.

6. Erving Goffmann, *Stigma: Notes on the Management of Spoiled Identity* (Englewood Cliffs, N.J., Prentice-Hall, 1963).

7. Robert B. Edgerton, *The Cloak of Competence: Stigma in the Lives of the Mentally Retarded* (Berkeley, University of California Press, 1967).

8. Jerome Nitzberg, "Casework with Mentally Retarded Adolescents and Young Adults and Their Families," paper presented at the University of Connecticut School of Social Work, Hartford, 1962.

9. Noel Timms, *Social Casework: Principles and Practice* (London, Routledge and Kegan Paul, 1964), p. 93.

10. T. A. Ratcliffe, "Relationship therapy and casework," *British Journal of Psychiatric Social Work*, V, No. 1 (1959).

11. Elizabeth McBroom, "Socialisation of parents," *Child Welfare*, XLVI, No. 3 (March, 1967); and Kermit T. Wiltse, "The hopeless family," *Social Work*, III, No. 4 (October, 1958).

12. Margaret Adams, "The burden of freedom: Some thoughts on the Mental Health Bill," *Case Conference*, 6, No. 5 (May, 1959).

13. Noel Timms, *Psychiatric Social Work in Great Britain* (London, Routledge and Kegan Paul, 1964).

14. Helen Harris Perlman, *Social Casework: A Problem-Solving Process* (Chicago, University of Chicago Press, 1957), Chap. 6.

15. Felix P. Biestek, S.J., *The Casework Relationship: Principle 2—Purposeful Expression of Feelings* (Chicago, Loyola University Press, 1957).

Chapter 9: SOME CONCEPTS OF GROUP WORK

1. William Schwartz, "The social worker in the group," in *New Perspectives on Services to Groups: Theory, Organization, Practice,* (New York, National Association of Social Workers, 1961).

2. *Ibid.*

3. Helen L. Beck, *The Closed Short-Term Group: A Treatment Adjunct for Parents of Mentally Retarded Children* (Washington, D.C., U.S. Children's Bureau, 1965); and Lawrence Goodman and Ruth Rothman, "The development of a group counseling program in a clinic for retarded children," *American Journal of Mental Deficiency*, 65, No. 6 (May, 1961).

4. S. Thomas Cummings and Dorothy Stock, "Brief group therapy of mothers of retarded children outside of the specialty clinic setting," *American Journal of Mental Deficiency*, 66, No. 5 (1962).

5. Salvatore Ambrosino, "A project in group education with parents of retarded children," *Casework Papers,* Family Service Association of America, 1960.

6. Joyce Smith and Leonard Tabizel, "Description of a group with parents of adult subnormals," *Case Conference,* 16, No. 10 (February, 1970).

7. Joseph T. Weingold and Rudolph P. Hormuth, "Group guidance of parents of mentally retarded children," *Journal of Clinical Psychology,* 9 (1953), 118–24.

8. Mary L. Yates and Ruth Lederer, "Small short-term group meetings with parents of children with mongolism," *American Journal of Mental Deficiency,* 65, No. 4 (January, 1961).

9. Bess Lander Bell and William Gordon Bell, "Parents in double jeopardy: The myth of community resources," in Norman Bernstein, ed., *Diminished People: The Problems and Care of the Mentally Retarded* (Boston, Little, Brown, 1970).

10. Stanley C. Mahoney, "Observations concerning counseling with parents of mentally retarded children," *American Journal of Mental Deficiency,* 63, No. 1 (July, 1958); James J. Gallagher, "Rejecting parents?" *Exceptional Children,* 22 (1956); and Dorothy Garst Murray, "Needs of parents of mentally retarded children," *American Journal of Mental Deficiency,* 63, No. 6 (May, 1959).

11. Arthur Mandelbaum, "Group processes with parents of retarded children," *Children,* 14 (1967), 227–33; and Robert M. Nadal, "A counseling program for parents of severely retarded preschool children," *Social Casework,* XLII, No. 2 (February, 1961).

12. Albert J. Solnit and Mary H. Stark, "Mourning and the birth of a defective child," *Psycho-analytical Study of the Child,* XVII (1961), 523–37.

13. Gisela Konopka, *Social Group Work: A Helping Process* (Englewood Cliffs, N.J., Prentice-Hall, 1963).

14. Beck, *The Closed Short-Term Group: A Treatment Adjunct for Parents of Mentally Retarded Children.*

15. Henry V. Cobb, "The attitude of the retarded person toward himself," in *Stress in Families of the Mentally Handicapped* (Brussels, International League of Societies for the Mentally Handicapped, 1967; reproduced in *Source Book on Mental Retardation for Schools of Social Work,* Vol. I, ed. by Meyer Schreiber and Stephanie Barnhardt).

16. Arthur Segal, "Some observations about mentally retarded adolescents," *Children,* 14, No. 6 (November–December, 1967).

17. Janet T. Ferguson, "The use of social group work to prepare residents for community placement," paper presented at Annual Meeting of

American Association of Mental Deficiency, Denver, Colo., May, 1967; and Joseph T. Parnicky and Leonard N. Brown, "Introducing institutionalised retardates in the community," *Social Work*, 9, No. 1 (January, 1964).

18. Konopka, *Social Group Work: A Helping Process.*

19. Sandra Kahn, "Programming with the 13–17 year old retardate," in Meyer Schreiber, ed., *Social Group Work with the Mentally Retarded* (New York, Second Annual Institute of the Association for the Help of Retarded Children, 1962); and Leah Niederman, "Programming for the 8–12 year old retardate," in *ibid.*

20. H. Michal-Smith, Monroe G. Gottsegen, and Gloria Gottsegen, "A group therapy technique for mental retardates," *International Journal of Group Psychotherapy*, 5 (1955), 84–90.

21. Etta Shephard, "Programming with the 18–32 year old retardate," in Meyer Schreiber, ed., *Social Group Work with the Mentally Retarded.*

22. Alan Klein, "Program as a tool in social group work with the mentally retarded," in *ibid.*

23. Dorothy Dewing, "Use of occupational therapy in the socialization of severely retarded children," *American Journal of Mental Deficiency*, 57, No. 1 (July, 1952), 43–49.

24. Meyer Schreiber, "Some basic concepts in social group work and recreation with the mentally retarded," *Rehabilitation Literature*, 26, No. 7 (1965), 194–203; *idem*, "Group work and leisure time needs of retarded youth," in *Group Work and Leisure Time Programs for Mentally Retarded Children and Adolescents* (U.S. Department of Health, Education and Welfare, Social and Rehabilitation Service, Children's Bureau, 1968); and Meyer Schreiber and Sidney Gershenson, "Mentally retarded teenagers in a social group," *Children*, 10, No. 3 (May–June, 1963).

25. Earl C. Butterfield, "The role of environmental factors in the treatment of institutionalized mental retardates," in Alfred Baumeister, *Mental Retardation: Appraisal, Education and Rehabilitation* (Chicago, Aldine Publishing Company, 1967); Erving Goffman, *Asylums: Essays on the Social Situation of Mental Patients and Other Inmates* (New York, Anchor Books, Doubleday, 1961); and Pauline Morris, *Put Away: A Sociological Study of Institutions for the Mentally Retarded* (London, Routledge and Kegan Paul, 1969).

26. Milton Cotzin, "Group psychotherapy with mentally defective boys," *American Journal of Mental Deficiency*, LIII, No. 2 (October, 1948); Louise A. Fisher and Isaac N. Wolfson, "Group therapy of mental defectives," *American Journal of Mental Deficiency*, 57, No. 2 (October, 1953); and Charles B. Rotman and Steven Goldburgh, "Group

counselling of mentally retarded adolescents," *Mental Retardation,* 5, No. 3 (June, 1967).

27. Sheldon Gelman, "Admission groups for mentally retarded girls," *Hospital and Community Psychiatry,* 20, No. 1 (January, 1969).

28. Arthur Woloshin, Guido Tardi, and Arnold Tobin, "De-institutionalization of mentally retarded men through use of a half-way house," *Mental Retardation,* 4, No. 3 (June, 1966).

29. Muriel W. Pumphrey, Mortimer Goodman, and Norman Flax, "The capability of a traditional group work agency to include individuals with impaired adaptive behavior in its usual services," paper presented at Annual Forum of the National Conference on Social Welfare, New York, May, 1969.

30. David R. Preininger, "Reaction of normal children to retardates in integrated groups," *Social Work,* 13, No. 2 (April, 1968).

31. Arthur Brodkin, "Programs for the mentally retarded," in *Group Work and Leisure Time Programs for Mentally Retarded Children and Adolescents* (U.S. Department of Health, Education, and Welfare, Social and Rehabilitation Service, Children's Bureau, 1968).

Chapter 10: COMMUNITY ORGANIZATION IN THE FIELD OF MENTAL RETARDATION

1. Jack Rothman, "Three models of community organization practice," in *Social Work Practice* (New York, Columbia University Press, 1968).

2. Rodger L. Hurley, *Poverty and Mental Retardation: A Causal Relationship* (State of New Jersey, Department of Institutions and Agencies, Division of Mental Retardation, Planning and Implementation Project, April, 1968).

3. Arnold Gurin and Robert Perlman, *Community Organization and Social Planning* (New York, Wiley, *in press*).

4. Roland L. Warren, *The Community in America* (Chicago, Rand McNally, 1963).

5. Gurin and Perlman, *Community Organization and Social Planning,* Chaps. IV and V.

6. Gunnar Dybwad, "Community organization for the mentally retarded" in *Community Organization,* National Conference on Social Welfare (New York, Columbia University Press, 1959); and "The mentally handicapped child under five," talk given to the Oxford and District Society for the Mentally Handicapped; reproduced by Pergamon Group of Companies, 1968.

7. Margaret E. Adams, "Social services for the mentally retarded in

Great Britain," *Social Work*, 9, No. 1 (January, 1964); and Howard R. Kelman, "Individualizing the social integration of the mentally retarded child," *American Journal of Mental Deficiency*, 60, No. 4 (April, 1956).

8. Margaret E. Adams and Ralph W. Colvin, "The deprivation hypothesis: Its application to mentally retarded children and their needs," *Child Welfare* XLVIII, No. 3 (March, 1969); and Whitney M. Young, "The retarded victims of deprivation," *PCMR Message* (January, 1968), pp. 1–8.

9. Hilda Knobloch, "Neuropsychiatric sequelae to prematurity," *Journal of the American Medical Association*, 161 (1956), 581–85: Abraham Lilienfeld, Benjamin Pasamanick, and Martha Rogers, "Relationship between pregnancy experience and the development of certain neuropsychiatric disorders in childhood," *American Journal of Public Health*, 45, No. 5 (May, 1955); Martha E. Rogers, A. M. Lilienfeld, and Benjamin Pasamanick, "Prenatal and paranatal factors in the development of childhood behavior disorders," The Johns Hopkins University School of Hygiene and Public Health, 1956.

10. Florence Haselkorn, ed., "Mothers-At-Risk," *Perspectives in Social Work*, 1, No. 1 (New York, Adelphi School of Social Work, 1966); and Miriam F. Mednick, "Prevention of mental retardation: Social work in maternal and infant care programs," *Child Welfare*, XLVIII, No. 11 (November, 1969).

11. Margaret E. Adams, "Developing child welfare services for the mentally retarded," *Mental Retardation*, 6, No. 5 (October, 1968); and *idem*, "Foster care for retarded children: How does child welfare meet this challenge?" *Child Welfare*, XLIX, No. 5 (May, 1970).

12. Pearl S. Whitman and Sonya Oppenheimer, "Locating and treating the mentally retarded," *Social Work*, 11, No. 3 (April, 1966).

13. A. D. B. Clarke, *Some Recent Advances in the Study of Mental Subnormality* (London, National Association for Mental Health, 1966), pp. 19–21.

14. Robert Segal, *Mental Retardation and Social Action* (Springfield, Ill., Charles C. Thomas, 1970).

15. R. C. Scheerenberger, *A Study of Generic Services for the Mentally Retarded and Their Families* (Springfield, Ill., Department of Mental Health, 1969); and Malin Van Antwerp, "An interdisciplinary approach to functional mental retardation," *Mental Retardation*, 8, No. 1 (February, 1970).

16. *Decade of Decision*, An evaluation report prepared by the National Association for Retarded Children Inc. for the 1960 White House Conference on Children and Youth (1959); A. H. Katz, *Parents of the Handicapped* (Springfield, Ill., Charles C. Thomas, 1961); and

Louis H. Orzack, John T. Cassell, Benoit Charland, Harry Halliday, and Jeffrey Salloway, *The Pursuit of Change* (Kennedy Center—Monograph No. 7, Parents and Friends of Mentally Retarded Children of Bridgeport, Inc., 1970).

17. Charlotte Green Schwartz, "Strategies and tactics of mothers of mentally retarded children for dealing with the medical care system," in Norman Bernstein, ed., *Diminished People: The Problems and Care of the Mentally Retarded* (Boston, Little, Brown, 1970).

18. David Kevin, "Group counseling of mothers in an AFDC program," *Children*, 14, No. 2 (March–April, 1967); and Louise P. Shoemaker, "Social group work in the ADC program," *Social Work*, 8, No. 1 (January, 1963).

19. Charles F. Grosser, "Community development programs serving the urban poor," *Social Work*, 10, No. 3 (July, 1965).

20. George Albee, "Needed—a revolution in caring for the retarded," *Transaction*, 5, No. 3 (February, 1968), 37–42.

21. Stanley C. Mahoney, "Special community programs for the mildly mentally retarded: Open doors or one-way turnstiles?" paper presented at the 89th Annual Convention of the American Association on Mental Deficiency (Miami, Fla., June, 1965); *idem*, "Special community programs for the mildly retarded: acceptance or rejection?" *Mental Retardation*, 5, No. 3 (October, 1965), 30–31; and *idem*, Safeguarding the retarded from isolating effects of special programs," in Meyer Schreiber and Stephanie Barnhardt, eds., *Source Book on Mental Retardation for Schools of Social Work* (New York, Selected Academic Readings, 1967).

22. Mervyn Susser, *Community Psychiatry: Epidemiologic and Social Themes* (New York, Random House, 1968), Chap. 13.

23. Scheerenberger, *A Study of Generic Services for the Mentally Retarded and Their Families.*

24. Robert B. Edgerton, *The Cloak of Competence: Stigma in the Lives of the Mentally Retarded* (Berkeley, University of California Press, 1967).

BIBLIOGRAPHY

Apthekar, Herbert H. *The Dynamics of Casework and Counselling.* Boston: Houghton Mifflin, 1955.

Baumeister, Alfred, ed. *Mental Retardation: Appraisal, Education, Rehabilitation.* Chicago: Aldine Publishing Company, 1967.

Beck, Helen L. *Social Services to the Mentally Retarded.* Springfield, Ill.: Charles C. Thomas, 1968.

Begab, Michael J. *The Mentally Retarded Child: A Guide to Services of Social Agencies.* U.S. Department of Health, Education, and Welfare, Welfare Administration, Children's Bureau, 1963.

Bernstein, Norman, ed. *Diminished People: The Problems and Care of the Mentally Retarded.* Boston: Little, Brown, 1970.

Bernstein, Saul. *Explorations in Group Work.* Boston: Boston University School of Social Work, 1965.

Biestek, Felix, S.J. *The Casework Relationship.* Chicago: Loyola University Press, 1957.

Casework Services for Parents of Handicapped Children. (Ten papers) New York: Family Service Association of America, 1965.

Clarke, Ann M., and A. D. B. Clarke. *Mental Deficiency: The Changing Outlook.* rev. ed. New York: The Free Press, 1965.

Davies, Stanley Powell. *The Mentally Retarded in Society.* New York: Columbia University Press, 1959.

Dexter, Lewis Anthony. *The Tyranny of Schooling: An Inquiry into the Problem of Stupidity.* New York: Basic Books, 1964.

Dittman, Laura L., ed. *Early Child Care: The New Perspectives.* New York: Atherton Press, 1968.

Dybwad, Gunnar. *Challenges in Mental Retardation.* New York: Columbia University Press, 1964.

Edgerton, Robert B. *The Cloak of Competence: Stigma in the Lives of the Mentally Retarded.* Berkeley: University of California Press, 1967.

Farber, Bernard. *Mental Retardation: Its Social Context and Social Consequences.* Boston: Houghton Mifflin, 1968.

Friedlander, Walter A. *Introduction to Social Welfare.* 3rd ed. Englewood Cliffs, N.J.: Prentice-Hall, 1968.

Goffman, Erving. *Asylums: Essays on the Social Situation of Mental Patients and Other Inmates.* New York: Anchor Books, Doubleday, 1961.

Goffman, Erving. *Stigma: Notes on the Management of Spoiled Identity.* Englewood Cliffs, N.J.: Prentice-Hall, 1963.

Gurin, Arnold, and Robert Perlman. *Community Organization and Social Planning.* New York: Wiley, in press.

Hamilton, Gordon. *Theory and Practice of Social Case Work.* 2nd ed. revised. New York: Columbia University Press, 1951.

Haselkorn, Florence, ed. *"Mothers-At-Risk," Perspectives of Social Work,* Vol. 1, No. 1. New York: Adelphi School of Social Work, 1966.

Hilliard, L. T., and Brian H. Kirman, *Mental Deficiency.* 2nd ed. London: J. A. Churchill Ltd., 1965 (Little, Brown in U.S.).

Hollis, Florence. *Casework: A Psychosocial Therapy.* New York: Random House, 1964.

Holmes, Lewis B., Hugo W. Moser, Thorlakur S. Halldorsson, Cornelia Mack, Shyam S. Pant, and Benjamin Matzilevich. *Mental Retardation: An Atlas of Diseases with Associated Physical Abnormalities.* New York, Macmillan, in press.

Kanner, Leo. *A History of the Care and Study of the Mentally Retarded.* Springfield, Ill.: Charles C. Thomas, 1964.

Kasius, Cora, ed. *Social Casework in the Fifties. Selected Articles, 1951–60.* New York: Family Service Association of America, 1962, pp. 350–53.

Klasmer, Leonard, and Leonard P. Ullman. *Research in Behavior Modification: New Developments and Implications.* New York: Holt, Rinehart and Winston, 1967.

Konopka, Gisela. *Social Group Work: A Helping Process.* Englewood Cliffs, N.J.: Prentice-Hall, 1963.

Mental Retardation: A Handbook for the Primary Physician. Report of the American Medical Association Conference on Mental Retardation. Chicago, April 9–11, 1964.

New Perspectives on Services to Groups: Theory, Organization, Practice. New York: National Association of Social Workers, 1961.

Parad, Howard, ed. *Ego-Psychology and Dynamic Casework.* New York: Family Service Association of America, 1958.

Perlman, Helen Harris. *Social Casework: A Problem-Solving Process.* Chicago: University of Chicago Press, 1957.

Phillips, Helen. *Essentials of Social Group Work.* New York: Association Press, 1957.

A Proposed Program for National Action to Combat Mental Retardation.

President's Panel on Mental Retardation. U.S. Government Printing Office, 1962.

Richmond, Mary. *Social Diagnosis.* New York: Russell Sage Foundation, 1917; reprinted Free Press, 1965.

Robinson, Halbert B., and Nancy M. Robinson. *The Mentally Retarded Child: A Psychological Approach.* New York: McGraw-Hill, 1965.

Ross, Alan O. *The Exceptional Child in the Family.* New York: Grune and Stratton, 1964.

Sarason, Seymour B., and John Doris. *Psychological Problems in Mental Deficiency* (with chapters by Frances Kaplan and M. Michael Klaber). New York: Harper & Row, 1969.

Schreiber, Meyer, ed. *Social Work and Mental Retardation.* New York: John Day, 1970.

Schreiber, Meyer, and Stephanie Barnhardt, eds. *Source Book on Mental Retardation for Schools of Social Work. Vols. 1 and 2.* New York: Selected Academic Readings, A Division of Associated Educational Services Corporation, 1967.

Stevens, Harvey and Rick Heber, eds. *Mental Retardation: A Review of Research.* Chicago: University of Chicago Press, 1964.

Susser, Mervyn. *Community Psychiatry: Epidemiologic and Social Themes.* New York: Random House, 1968, Chaps. 11–13.

Tredgold, R. F., and K. Soddy. *Tredgold's Textbook of Mental Deficiency (Subnormality).* 10th ed. Baltimore: Williams and Wilkins, 1963.

Wolfensberger, Wolf, and Richard A. Kurtz, eds., *Management of the Family of the Mentally Retarded.* Chicago: Follett Educational Corporation, 1968.

Yando, Regina. "Psychological assessment," in N. Talbot, L. Eisenberg, and J. Kagan, eds., *Behavioral Science in Pediatric Practice.* Philadelphia, Saunders, in press.

Zigler, Edward, and Susan Hartner. "The socialization of the mentally retarded," in David A. Goslin, ed., *Handbook of Socialization Theory and Research.* Chicago: Rand McNally, 1969.

INDEX

DATE DUE

APR 11 79			
OCT 13 79			
DEC 7 79			
APR 0 3 1980			
APR 9 1981			
DEC 1 8 1981			
OCT 2 1 1982			
NOV 1 1 1982			
DEC 2 1982			
DEC 9 1982			
DEC 1 3 1982			
OCT 2 6 1991			